Cruising the Eastern Caribbean

A Passenger's Guide to the Ports of Call

4th Edition

Cruising the Eastern Caribbean

A Passenger's Guide to the Ports of Call

4th Edition

Laura & Diane Rapp

HUNTER

HUNTER PUBLISHING, INC,
130 Campus Drive, Edison, NJ 08818
732-225-1900; 800-255-0343; fax 732-417-1744
www.hunterpublishing.com

Ulysses Travel Publications
4176 Saint-Denis, Montréal, Québec
Canada H2W 2M5
514-843-9882, ext. 2232; fax 514-843-9448

Windsor Books
The Boundary, Wheatley Road, Garsington
Oxford, OX44 9EJ England
01865-361122; fax 01865-361133

ISBN 1-58843-407-9

Printed in the United States

This and other Hunter travel guides are also available as e-books in a variety of digital formats through our online partners, including Netlibrary.com, Amazon.com and BarnesandNoble.com.

1 2 3 4

Acknowledgments

We would like to thank our publisher, Michael Hunter, for his continuing support of our project. Special acknowledgment is also given to the individual island tourism offices both in the United States and throughout the Caribbean. Thank you for the wonderful information, assistance and invaluable help.

About the Authors

Laura Rapp grew up in Santa Barbara, California. Upon graduating from Florida International University with a degree in Hospitality Management, Laura began work in the cruise industry, moving through the ranks to her most recent position as a Shore Excursion Manager. Making sure passengers enjoy tours in ports throughout the Caribbean, Mediterranean and Alaska has provided Laura with special insight that she shares with readers in this book.

Diane Rapp collaborated with her daughter, Laura, in writing this book. She has cruised throughout the Caribbean, and especially enjoyed writing the history, culture and unique shopping sections on each island. Diane is currently traveling the United States with her husband writing travel articles and a mystery novel.

We Love to Get Mail

Hunter Publishing makes every effort to ensure that its travel guides are the most current sources of information available. We encourage you to share your opinion and experiences. If you'd like to recommend something to be included in the next update of this guide, tell us! Feel free to include price updates and suggestions that you feel will improve this book for future readers. Please address all mail to *Cruising the Caribbean*, c/o Hunter Publishing, 130 Campus Drive, Edison, NJ 08818, or e-mail us at comments@hunterpublishing.com.

Contents

Maps

Introduction

What to Expect From Your Cruise

Throughout my experience working as a purser and shore excursions manager, I have dealt with a wide assortment of passenger problems which can be attributed to misleading information, or the lack of information, supplied by travel agents. Below, I have identified some important areas of cruising that potential passengers should investigate before making reservations.

Once you have made the decision to take a cruise, the next step is to locate a qualified travel agent to help you select the *type* of cruise that is right for you and your pocketbook. It is important to find an agent knowledgeable about the cruise industry, who has a good reputation for booking successful cruises.

One of the best places to find specialty travel agencies is the travel section of any major city newspaper or in the phone book. Friends or family members who have recently taken a cruise are even better sources. Speak with the agent in person, rather than only over the phone. A personal visit to the agent's office will also help you judge the professional quality of the establishment.

First, decide where you want to go. Next, select the appropriate cruise line. It is important to read the fine print in the back of the brochures, which offers information on things such as luggage insurance, cashing personal checks on board and liability limitations of the cruise line. You should evaluate your budget as well as your stateroom needs, including layout and amenities.

Staterooms

When choosing a stateroom from the ship's plans, remember that the rooms vary in many ways, even though they may appear the same on the plan. Cabins contain either two twin beds (that may or may not convert into one) or one standard queen- or king-sized bed. The age of the ship can also contribute to the comfort of the rooms, type of beds available and the overall condition of the cabins. Specialized cruise lines, such as Seabourn and Renaissance, tend to offer larger staterooms with queen-sized beds, but you have to be willing to pay for them. Newer ships have far fewer problems with their rooms, although older ships have a certain style that is lacking in the modern megaships. Fortunately, cruise lines have learned from their design mistakes over the years and standard cabins in the majority of newer ships have two twin beds that convert into one. The older ships, with a smaller percentage of cabins offering queen-sized beds or twin beds that convert, may visit more ports of call to encourage bookings.

Stateroom Layout

The cabin layout is different with every ship and individual cabin category. Once you have selected a cruise ship, you should study the cabin arrangements in the brochure. If you are concerned about specific needs, a good travel agent will make the necessary arrangements. You should consider the following in order to avoid disappointment:

- Some "veranda" categories or outside cabins may have obstructed views due to the ships lifeboat locations.
- Cabins below the main entertainment deck or lounges may be subject to sound from above.
- To avoid seasickness, choose a cabin midship, which will reduce the motion of the ocean.
- Passengers who suffer from claustrophobia should select a cabin with an outside window. Be sure to tell the travel agent to specify the medical problem when making the reservation.
- Honeymooners or anniversary couples should be aware that most cabins have twin beds that convert into one. As mentioned above, on many older ships the beds may not convert at all. Ask your travel agent to request a specific cabin number with beds that suit your needs.

If the cabin selection is important, have your travel agent request at least three specific cabin numbers when making the reservation and get confirmation of the cabin number. When your tickets arrive, check the cabin number you have been assigned. If it is unsatisfactory, have the travel agent call the cruise line and make the necessary adjustment. If your travel agent cannot secure the cabin reassignment, cancel the reservation! This may sound extreme but, in most cases, the cruise will be fully booked and cabin reassignment will not be an option.

Special Rates

If you are not particularly concerned with the category of the room, its size, or the type of beds, take full advantage of last-minute bookings that can save money. The downside is that upgrades are not guaranteed.

> NOTE: Travel agents are not employees of the cruise lines and cannot make promises regarding your trip. There are no guarantees in the cruise industry, and requests for all cabin specifics, such as beds and cabin layouts, are just that – requests.

You must decide what is the most important element of your vacation. If the concern is for a cabin type or bed configuration, select them with care. If lower prices or special deals are most important, be satisfied with the cabin assigned. Once you have made the cruise and cabin selection, the travel agent should submit all the specific requests to the cruise line in writing.

Life Aboard Ship

Absent-Minded Questions

What time is the midnight buffet?

All too often cruise passengers ask ship personnel some of the silliest questions. Fortunately, these passengers help to entertain the staff and provide material for ship comedians like Lewis Nixon, who uses these questions in his comedy act. The most often asked question directed to crew members is, "Do you actually live on the ship?" Yes, all of the crew members have to live on board to work and serve cruise passengers.

I have collected a few of the funniest questions so that new cruisers reading this book can avoid becoming the latest joke among crew staff members.

- Shore excursion personnel have reported cruisers asking, "If I go snorkeling, will I get wet?"

- Never ask a ship's engineer, "Does this ship run on generators?" Cruise ships have turbine steam engines (TSS) or large motor engines (MS).
- "Do these stairs go up or down?" No comment.
- A dining room waiter will die laughing if you ask, "What do you do with the ice carvings after they have melted?"
- If you cruise to the port of Nassau in the Bahamas, think of this lady's story. When a female passenger arrived in Nassau, she asked a crew member on the dock, "Where are all the missiles?" The crew member looked at her strangely and said, "What missiles?" The lady responded, "The missiles. I thought we were going to visit N.A.S.A."
- If you get the opportunity to meet the captain, refrain from asking him, "If you are here, who is driving the ship?" The captain is asked that question at least 20 times every cruise. The deck officers are the ones who steer the ship (not drive it), and the captain oversees the docking procedures when arriving or departing each port.
- Please refrain from asking the beauty salon, "How long does a 30-minute massage take?"
- The most amusing question was asked at sea, while the ship was moving, "What altitude do you think we're at?" Sea level might be a good guess!

Not all questions are ridiculous, so if you have one, don't hesitate to ask a crew staff member. They are there to assist you.

Nautical Terms

When you board the cruise ship, please refer to the vessel as a ship, not a boat. Ships carry boats. When exploring the ship, remember the nautical terms for the vessel.

LANDLUBBER	SAILOR
right side	starboard
left side	port
front	bow
rear	aft

Boat drills are mandatory for all passengers and a requirement of law, so be sure to attend promptly and give the ships' officers your full attention. This information may end up saving your life in the event of an emergency.

Authors' Note

During my time working aboard cruise ships, it has become apparent to me that the questions most frequently asked by passengers are not being answered by travel agents or ship lectures. Since cruise passengers are usually allotted between eight and 10 hours for sightseeing and exploring in each port, they need a guidebook specifically oriented to that time schedule. *Cruising the Caribbean* answers the most basic and commonly asked island questions and lists detailed activities to help travelers enjoy their Caribbean adventure.

To keep the size of this guidebook small enough to carry while exploring ashore, the islands featured in this edition were limited to the 10 most frequented by cruise ships in the Windward and Leeward chains, plus Puerto Rico. The chapters are presented in the same order as they appear on the Caribbean map from north to south, beginning with Puerto Rico and ending with Grenada.

Each island chapter supplies information on history, shopping, transportation, shore excursions, beaches and sports activities. The suggested taxi fares, tours, recommended beaches and shopping hints are designed to assist in planning before arrival. Please keep in mind that prices and taxi fares fluctuate from season to season. The rates given here should be used only as a guideline.

Chosen activities while on a cruise vary with each passenger. Remember that ship casinos (and, sometimes, bars) close when the vessel is in port. We have formatted this guidebook to correspond with the following activity categories:

- ⚓ **The Pier** (amenities available at the cruise ship pier area)
- ⚓ **In Town** (shopping, historical walking tour)
- ⚓ **Transportation, Excursions** (taxi and rental car information, self-guided tours, organized tours & activities, beaches, island activities, one-day itinerary)

The Caribbean Islands

The Land

The islands of the Caribbean were formed by massive upheavals caused by earthquakes and volcanoes. Some islands are coral-limestone mountains pushed up from the sea bottom, while others are mountains of volcanic ash with fertile soil and rain forests.

Coral islands, such as St. Thomas, Sint Maarten, Antigua and Barbados, are surrounded by reefs teeming with exotic tropical fish. They are generally less mountainous, and have a drier climate and less fertile soil than volcanic islands. Vegetation on coral islands is thick, low-growing, hardy and drought-resistant. On these islands, water can be scarce and may even be imported, water conservation is practiced, rainwater collected and used, and fewer crops are grown. Coral islands have naturally protected harbors and superb white sand beaches, attracting trade and tourism.

Luxuriant tropical vegetation and steep mountainous terrain are found only on those islands formed by volcanic eruption, such as Dominica, St. Lucia, St. Kitts and Nevis. Volcanic fumaroles are

Chenile tree.

nature's pipelines, transporting water and minerals from the depths of the earth to irrigate the craggy slopes of fertile soil. Mist continually clings to the tallest peaks, producing daily rain showers that range in force from a sprinkle to a deluge. The rain dissipates quickly and dries in the heat of the tropical sun, but it creates the dense rainforests, which make up the hothouses of the Caribbean.

Many varieties of plants were imported to the islands by settlers from all parts of the globe, who were anxious to re-create an atmosphere reminiscent of home. Plants grow so well in the rain forest that they become almost unrecognizable – taller, broader, greener and producing more fruit. Small garden variety ferns become giant trees, flowering bushes produce a profusion of blossoms and hothouse plants grow wild.

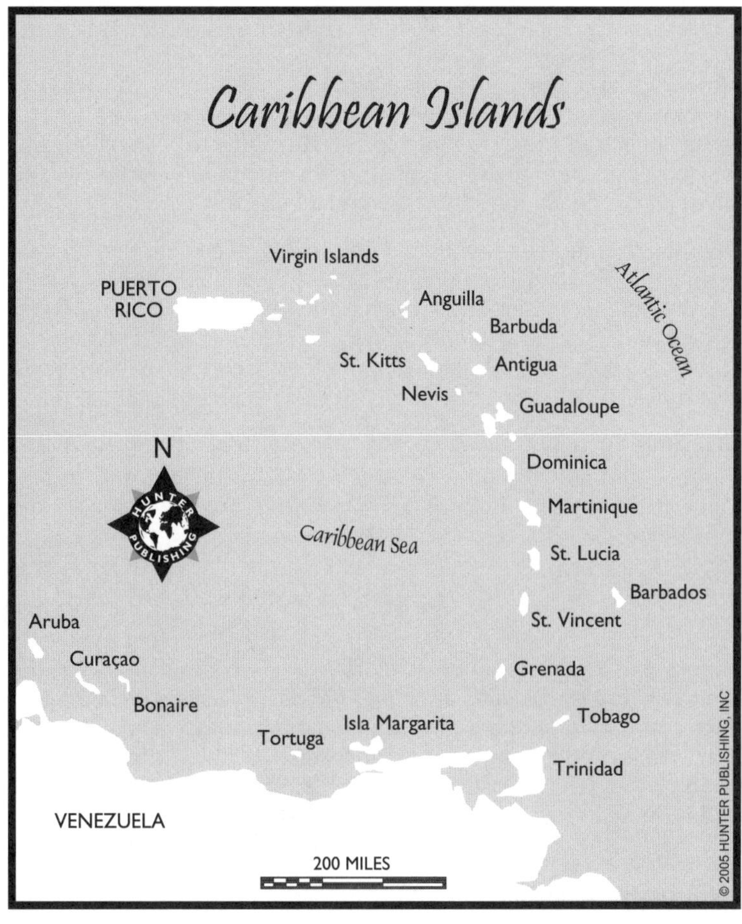

Be sure to plan a hike into the rain forest on at least one of the volcanic islands, arranging for a guide who knows the pathways and can point out interesting plants. To truly appreciate the rain forest, head for its deepest parts. Here you will discover a primeval atmosphere, you might hear the song of tree frogs, taste pure spring water and swim in a pool beneath a cascading waterfall.

> TIP: For any rain forest excursion, wear lightweight clothing that dries quickly, old tennis shoes or stable walking shoes, and bring a hat (rather than an umbrella) for the occasional rain shower. After all, if it doesn't rain in the rain forest, you've been cheated!

Poisonous Plants

Although snakes have been exterminated by the mighty mongoose, the islands are not entirely benign. Ask your guide to point out a manchineel tree and a stinging nettle, two plants to be avoided. You may never encounter these plants, but you should exercise caution when wandering through the tropical vegetation.

The **manchineel tree** produces a poisonous green fruit the size of a small apple. A bite of the fruit will certainly hospitalize and very likely kill its victim. The Carib Indians used the manchineel to poison war arrows and may be responsible for the tree's introduction to the islands. Even the sap or rain dripping off its leaves can cause painful blisters.

The **stinging nettle** plant is more harmful than its cousin in the United States and Europe. Touching the nettle's hairy leaves can create an irritating rash that will last for days and put a damper on any vacation.

Marine Life

Waters encircling volcanic and coral islands contain many of the same fish, but the ocean plant life differs vastly. Volcanic islands produce soft corals, sponges and sea fans that gently wave in the current, while underwater pinnacles formed by the volcanoes soar hundreds of feet from the sea floor. The terrain can be as exotic under the water as it is on land.

The waters around coral islands contain magnificent staghorn and brain corals that take thousands of years to grow. Diving around either type of island can be an exciting experience on trips led by an expert who knows the reefs.

TREAD LIGHTLY

Scuba divers and snorkelers should remember that corals, sponges and sea fans are easily damaged by a careless kick from a diver's fin or by touching them with bare, acidic skin. Most islands prohibit taking anything from the sea bottom, so divers and snorkelers are urged to be careful and leave the ocean floor as they found it for the pleasure of future divers.

Avoid touching bright orange fire corals or patches of orange or red growing on rocks and coral with your bare skin and do not pick up or touch the feathery fire worms. These harmless-looking creatures are provided with superb defensive mechanisms that can cause a painful rash or blisters, leaving the unwary diver in severe pain.

Beaches

Beaches on volcanic islands often consist of dark volcanic sand rather than the sparkling white sand associated with coral islands. Coral sand is amazingly cool to the touch as it consists of millions of particles of pulverized coral. The parrot fish, a multicolored fish named for the shape of its nose, which resembles a parrot's beak, is responsible for the sand. Each fish produces up to two tons of sand annually by eating tiny polyps – the living part of coral – and at the same time crunching pieces of indigestible hard coral skeleton. The residue left after digestion is white sand.

History

An announcer on a booze cruise in Grenada summed up Caribbean history in this way: "The Arawak Indians found Grenada, liked it and settled in, but the Carib Indians came and kicked them out. Then the Spanish came and kicked the Caribs out and the British came and kicked the Spanish out. When the Cubans came, they kicked everyone out, so the Americans came and kicked the Cubans out. Now we welcome the Americans to our beautiful little island." With some variations, his explanation applies to all the islands of the Caribbean.

Indians

Relics from the first inhabitants of the Caribbean suggest the ancient **Ciboney Indian tribes** moved up the island chain from South America as early as 3485 BC. Later, the **Arawak Indians**, an agricultural tribe from South America, arrived, striving to escape their enemies, the fierce Caribs. But the Carib Indians pursued the Arawaks and, when Columbus began exploring the islands on his second voyage in 1493, the Caribs were the dominant tribe on many of the islands.

European Invasion

The **Spanish** claimed all islands of the Caribbean, whether they had set foot on them or not. They concentrated their efforts in gathering gold and treasure from the New World, so those islands with little treasure attracted less attention. The Spanish quickly wiped out the remaining Arawaks, but when they used the same tactics on the Caribs, the Indians fought back and successfully repelled the Spanish on some islands.

By the 1600s other **European** countries were lured by the prospect of wealth here. They established settlements and claimed ownership of numerous Caribbean islands. During the next 200 years, Europeans played "settlement ping pong," with islands seemingly changing flags to appease passing warships. The French, Spanish and British were the major players, leaving the Dutch, Danish and Germans to slip in wherever they could.

Sugar – White Gold of the Caribbean

Few settlers dreamed of making the islands their home; instead, they planned on staying long enough to become wealthy before returning to Europe. But sugar trade changed the settlement picture. Sugar became the "white gold" of the Caribbean and, to grow sugarcane profitably, large land areas needed to be cultivated. Cheap labor was supplied by slaves. Establishment of plantations made settlements in the islands more permanent. The European owners built grand homes in European styles, planted formal gardens and fashioned European-style communities. Slaves on the plantations occupied housing designed to be easily moved from place to place. Later, these wooden "chattel houses" became the only property slaves owned. (See *Chattel House Village*, Barbados, page 255.)

Sugar prosperity ended in the early 1800s, when northern sugar beet production was perfected and began to compete with island-grown sugarcane. Finally, the emancipation of slaves marked the death of the sugarcane industry as a whole. Most islands freed their slaves well before the United States and former slaves became the basis for the majority of the population. Today, individual islands celebrate Emancipation Day with festivals, often expanding into several days of Carnival, with jubilant dancing, parades and calypso music.

Young girl on beach, St. Thomas.
(Image courtesy USVI Division of Tourism.)

Tourism

Sugarcane is currently produced on just a few Caribbean islands, but it is an important ingredient in rum production, a thriving industry on many islands. While volcanic islands with rich soil and a good water supply may depend on agriculture for a majority of their national product, tourism is a hugely important industry in the Caribbean as a whole. Islands which are less developed recognize the need to attract tourists and are studying the preferred ways to utilize resources without destroying their land and culture.

Many islands have new cruise ports that have been built (or are in the planning stages) to provide special cruise docking facilities. Island ports of call are offering more duty-free items from year to year and are improving tourist attractions. Restored sugar mills have been incorporated into hotels and restaurant buildings, while ruins of windmill towers dot the landscape, creating an atmosphere of romance and nostalgia. Rain forests are protected by conservationist governments, while guided tours into the primeval atmosphere stimulate the sense of adventure and excitement for city dwellers on vacation. Artificial reefs are created by intentionally sinking old ships and laws have been enacted to protect fragile coral and other marine life, while encouraging scuba diving and snorkeling enthusiasts.

As the cruise industry expands, introducing new ships and more options for the tourist, new island adventures and attractions emerge. Repeat cruisers may see an island they have already visited in a different way, and islands which were previously inaccessible may emerge as exceptional new tropical destinations.

Language

A close relationship exists between England, Canada, America and the Caribbean islands. The official language on most islands is English and, even where it is not, many islanders learn English as a second language to accommodate tourists. American passengers have no difficulty bargaining or asking directions in English.

> TIP: When visiting French islands, such as Martinique or Guadeloupe, you may wish to use a pocket language guide to assist with basic communication.

Creole, also called Patois, is a West Indian slang spoken in the Caribbean. The dialect changes from island to island – and sometimes from village to village on the same island – but the basic slang is understood all over the Caribbean. Patois blends French, English, Dutch, African and West Indian words, all spoken in a lilting, musical manner unique to the islands.

Holidays

The Windward and Leeward islands are made up of separate countries that celebrate unique holidays, including Independence Day, Emancipation Day and special days or weeks set aside for Carnival. Standard international holidays, such as New Year's Day, Christmas and Boxing Day (the day after Christmas) are also cause for celebration.

If cruise ships arrive in port during a holiday, a few stores will remain open for shopping. Even if stores close on a holiday, the beaches are open and taxi drivers are available to transport you around the island for sightseeing or exploring. If shopping or visiting a particular museum on an island is important to you, check the island's special holidays before booking a cruise. In each island chapter, we give you an idea of whether merchants are likely to be closed on a particular holiday and provide a list of basic holidays, but we do not list specific dates, as these may change from year to year. If a holiday falls on a weekend, banks, museums and government offices may close on either Monday or Friday.

What You'll Find in Each Chapter

Web Addresses

The Internet has become an integral part of society and the Caribbean is no exception. In this edition we took a look at websites established by island tourist boards, and describe the information we uncovered. E-mail addresses and websites are listed with the recommended businesses and tour operators in each chapter. You should take time to surf the Web and look for excursions that suit your needs. Prices and conditions change, and we recommend that you contact tour operators for current prices before your arrival.

The Pier

Each island has a pier to accommodate commercial vessels, or has specially designed terminals for cruise ships. Some have narrow wooden piers stretching out from the land to meet ships, while others have cement docking areas next to town where ships can pull alongside, allowing easy disembarkation. Occasionally, ships anchor in the harbor and run passengers ashore by small motorized boats, called tenders.

Piers offer a variety of amenities that may include shops, telephones, island information centers and taxi stations. Each island chapter outlines the facilities at the pier, with tips on the walking distance to town and special amenities found in the port area.

Pier Phones

All cruise ship ports offer phones for local and US calls. **Calling Stations** are offices where you can make long-distance calls from private booths, but these are available only in the larger ports. Fees can be paid in cash, by traveler's checks, or charged to a credit card.

AT&T has a long distance service (called USA Direct) for their card holders. This service is available on clearly marked telephones, or by dialing a special number from regular pay phones. Specifics are given in the *Pier Phones* section in each island chapter. Some islands also have a phone card system where the caller can purchase a phone card in the local currency in $10, $20 or $40 denominations. These colorful cards are available at the cruise terminals and make a good souvenir. Phone card machines are clearly identified and instructions for placing a call are printed directly on the telephone.

> ➡ TIP: The cost to place a call to the US is between $2 and $5 (this is to connect only, no talk time), so purchase a card with sufficient credit.

Calls to the US become more expensive as you travel farther south and are very expensive in the French islands. The location of phones for cruise passengers and the types of phone systems available are covered in the island chapters.

Many wireless phone companies offer service in the Caribbean islands. Before leaving on your cruise, check with your provider to temporarily add the Caribbean to your service. The extra cost may be a fraction of the long-distance or ship-to-shore charges you would otherwise accumulate.Phone calls from the French islands, Barbados and Sint Maarten are the most expensive.

In Town

Money Matters

Many stores, restaurants and taxi drivers accept and return change in US currency. However, some islands will give you change only in their own currency. It's best to carry small denominations of US dollars to avoid ending up with a pocketful of foreign coins. You can change foreign bills to US dollars at banks and international airports, but coins are not accepted. It is advantageous to use credit cards for most expenses to avoid exchange issues. In addition, card companies offer the best exchange rates.

To avoid carrying cash on vacation, read the fine print in your cruise ship brochure concerning the policies for cashing traveler's checks, personal checks or obtaining cash advances on credit cards. Most ships have limited cash resources, but banks in the larger ports of call can usually accommodate passengers. In an emergency, casinos often have credit card machines where you can secure a cash advance. Remember to set aside sufficient cash to tip shipboard personnel at the end of the trip.

Individual island chapters that follow contain currency information, approximate exchange rates, the location of banks and their banking hours. Antigua, Barbados, St. Kitts, Nevis, Dominica and Grenada all accept Eastern Caribbean (EC) currency, so any change received in EC on one island can be used on the next island.

> NOTE: Effective in January, 2002, the French West Indies – St. Martin, Guadeloupe, Martinique and St. Barts (not covered in this book) – will use the Euro dollar. See individual island chapters for more specific details.

Valuables

Cruise ships often have safety deposit boxes where you can store valuables, credit cards, traveler's checks and extra cash. Although cabin stewards and other ships personnel value their jobs and can generally be trusted to protect personal items left in a stateroom, we recommend you store cameras, jewelry and cash out of sight if leaving them in your cabin. Avoid leaving jewelry in an ash tray, under trash on a counter or in the bathroom. Busy cabin stewards dump trash and tidy rooms very quickly and may not notice a stray piece of jewelry in an odd location.

To avoid attracting the attention of thieves while exploring on land, don't wear excessive jewelry or carry expensive cameras. Carry small bills to pay for taxis and take only one credit card and a few traveler's checks on an excursion. Taking precautions eliminates risks and ensures the peace of mind necessary to enjoy a vacation.

Postage

St. Thomas and Puerto Rico are the only islands that are part of the US and use the US postal system. There, you can mail postcards or letters with US postage. Elsewhere, you need to purchase island stamps. As a convenience, stamps are often available at the purser's office or information desk on cruise ships. If you want to purchase your own stamps, we give the location of post offices and the price of postcard stamps in each chapter.

> NOTE: Stamp collectors should not miss the Philatelic Bureaus on islands such as Dominica, St. Kitts and Grenada.

Historical Walking Tours, Museums & Sites

On the islands of Puerto Rico, St. Thomas and Grenada, historical walking tours are outlined and accompanied by maps. Other island chapters provide information about significant buildings, forts and museums worth seeing, although some may require a taxi for transportation to the site.

Shopping

The allure of buying jewelry, china and myriad foreign goods at half the cost of home has caused many husbands to spend their vacations lugging shopping bags through store after store behind wide-eyed wives waiving credit cards at every clerk. An exaggeration, perhaps, but the phenomenon of **duty-free shopping** has created an entirely new industry in the islands.

What does duty-free really mean? Simply stated, import taxes (duty) normally added to the price on foreign goods are waived. Some islands waive the duty only for tourists and require identification when purchasing goods; you need to carry your ship's boarding pass, passport or driver's license while shopping. Specific information regarding the best duty-free shopping area and how to ensure a duty-free price is given in each chapter.

The amount of savings from duty-free shopping depends on the amount of duty charged at home. Do any of us know how much that is? Smart shoppers will do some research before the cruise and jot down prices of specific items they wish to buy. Another place to compare prices is at shops in the embarkation port of Puerto Rico, where many ships leave and return. Puerto Rico is an American port, but offers duty-free items. Knowing you will return to Puerto Rico at the end of your cruise, you can bargain for the best price on an item during your trip.

Good buys still exist, but don't assume everything is a bargain. Ask where the merchandise was manufactured. If the item was made in the United States, then it is cheaper at home. If it was manufactured in Europe or Japan, there may be a great savings over US prices. The very best bargains may be on goods actually produced on the island, so stores offering such products are listed in each chapter.

Here are some suggestions to prepare you for a successful shopping adventure:

- Make a list of specific items you want to buy and establish a maximum price range. Having a price limit makes bargaining easier.
- Visit shops at home and write down prices of name-brand merchandise you expect to find in the Caribbean. This may be the most valuable time you spend before your trip and will give you confidence when bargaining.
- Check the price per gram of gold before you leave home and compare it with island prices. Island jewelers may also be able to give great tips on looking for quality gemstones. Unset stones purchased in the Caribbean are not added to your US duty allotment and your local jeweler can mount them in a setting when you return home.
- When entering a duty-free store (which may sell watches, T-shirts, jewelry, souvenirs or liquor), look for items on your list. Narrow your focus and you will not feel overwhelmed by the abundance of merchandise.
- On the larger islands, visit major stores like Colombian Emeralds and Little Switzerland first to get a sense of their quality and prices. These stores have a set discount with no bargaining, so you will know the top price range when entering other shops. Smaller stores often carry the older styles in name-brand watches, crystal or ceramics, while the major stores carry the newest models available. (See *Major Duty-Free Stores*, page 20.)
- Buy film, batteries, bug repellent, sunscreen, medications and hair products at home, where they are much less expensive.

Shops Featured In Each Chapter

Shopping can be tedious if the same merchandise is offered from island-to-island. To make you aware of unique purchases, our *Shopping* sections focus on establishments that carry island-made products or unusual items. The jewelry stores we list have specially designed pieces and often repair and make their own jewelry on the premises. All shops listed in this book are accessible by walking or taking a short taxi ride from the pier. Exceptional shopping opportunities farther out on the island are described in the *Excursions* section for passengers using a taxi or rental car to explore.

Don't assume that shopping is good only on Puerto Rico, St. Thomas and Sint Maarten. Smaller islands offer quite reasonable prices and the shopping may also prove to be more pleasant. The following is a list of best buys for specific islands.

Best Buys

Gold	St. Thomas, Sint Maarten
Watches	St. Thomas, Sint Maarten
Electronics, cameras	St. Thomas, Sint Maarten
Tablecloths, linens	St. Kitts, St. Thomas, Sint Maarten
Silver & coral jewelry	St. Kitts and Antigua
Batik clothing	St. Kitts and St. Lucia
Coconut soap products	Dominica
Imported perfume/cosmetics	Martinique, Guadeloupe & French St. Martin
Island-made perfume	Grenada and St. Lucia
Spices	Grenada
Handicrafts	Barbados and Dominica
Crystal, china	St. Thomas, Sint Maarten, Barbados
Handmade clothing	Sint Maarten, St. Lucia, St. Kitts
Straw mats, baskets	Dominica
Jams, jellies	Dominica, Antigua, Grenada
Passion fruit products	Dominica

In addition, every island has its own brand of **rum**, which is sold at very tempting prices. Do some tasting first!

Buying souvenirs from locals often supports a family. T-shirts and carved coconuts are among the many souvenirs available on every island from local vendors. On Antigua, ladies string beaded necklaces and offer them to tourists at negotiable prices, often a great bargain. On Grenada, spice baskets are assembled by locals and sold on the streets and at tourist attractions. The baskets make excellent gifts at very reasonable prices.

In each chapter, unique shops are starred (☆). These shops offer products not sold elsewhere, have a high quality of artistry, or an atmosphere that must be experienced. It was a pleasure to discover these gems, so be sure not to miss them.

Unique Stores

- **The Butterfly People** in Old San Juan, Puerto Rico (see page 42).
- **Eudovics**, a master wood-sculptor in St. Lucia (page 238).
- **Guavaberry Tasting House & Shop**, selling a folk liqueur made for hundreds of years only on Sint Maarten (page 102).
- **The Goldsmitty**, an artist in fine gold jewelry, Antigua (page 130).
- **Pelican Village**, a craft village in Barbados (page 261).
- **Caribelle Batik**, factories of Sea Island cotton batik on St. Kitts (page 157) and St. Lucia (page 238).
- **Bernard K. Passman Galleries**, with black coral and gold sculptures on St. Thomas (page 75).

Bargaining Tips

Bargaining is a purchasing ritual in the islands, whether you're shopping for gold chains or a palm-frond hat. Shopkeepers selling products such as watches, gold jewelry and local crafts expect to bargain and usually price their items high, allowing room to negotiate. However, many stores set the price with no intention of bargaining.

To begin a bargaining session, ask the merchant if he gives discounts to cruise ship passengers; if he agrees to an initial discount, then begin to bargain. Passengers unwilling to play the bargaining game should ask the merchant for his lowest price and be prepared to go to the next store if the price is not acceptable. The same item may be offered at a better price down the street.

When shopping for gold chains and bracelets, ask the salesperson to weigh the item, compute the cost per gram and then negotiate to the store's lowest price. Write the quotation down on a store business card, then repeat the process in several other shops until you find the best price.

Prices are often quoted in both island and US currency. If only one price is given, ask which it is before bargaining. Shops will usually accept traveler's checks and credit cards, but you'll get a better deal with cash. Jewelry stores in particular may quote one price for credit cards and another for cash sales. Keep in mind that credit card companies often offer a better exchange rate, so the difference in price may be offset. Depending on the value of the item, it is often better to pay with credit cards or traveler's checks, saving your cash for taxis and tips. In either case, be sure to get a receipt for Customs.

Guaranteed Stores

Ask the cruise director or purser for a list of Guaranteed Stores before shopping. These businesses have a special arrangement with the cruise line to guarantee merchandise against defects through the duration of the cruise. If the item breaks or the passenger discovers a defect in the product during the remainder of the cruise, it can be returned to the store via the cruise director. Once the cruise director has returned the item, the passenger will receive a replacement item or a full refund. The arrangement between the cruise director and the store may differ slightly from ship to ship, but passengers receive extra protection when buying merchandise at one of these establishments.

Major Duty-Free Stores

The following chain stores are found in the major port areas and have virtually the same prices from port to port.

Diamonds International has stores on St. Thomas and St. Martin. It's sister-store, **Tanzanite International**, on the same islands, is a great place to find the radiant blue-purple gemstone first discovered in East Africa in 1967.

Colombian Emeralds has stores on St. Thomas, Sint Maarten and St. Lucia. In ancient times, the emerald was believed to impart mystical insight to its wearer and the green color was a symbol of immortality. Today, emeralds can be more expensive than fine diamonds. More than 90% of the world's emeralds come from Colombia. From collector quality to the finest investment quality, Colombian Emeralds brings stones direct from the mines and cutters to the buyer. All merchandise is guaranteed and Colombian Emeralds has a service office in Miami. Other gemstones, jewelry and the newest styles in designer watches are also offered.

Outlet Stores

Manufacturers and designers with a name to sell are earning greater profits by opening stores in outlet malls across America. With duty-free status, the Caribbean has always been a favorite of outlet stores and the name-brand outlets can offer bargains that might astound their name-dropping customers.

Polo/Ralph Lauren offers a broad selection of casual clothing and accessories from the famous designer. Stores are found in Sint Maarten and Puerto Rico.

Customs Regulations

Duty-free merchandise is only free of duty imposed by the country where the goods are purchased. Foreign-made electronics, jewelry, alcohol, cigarettes, linens and perfumes may be subject to a US duty when returning home.

Before leaving on a cruise, educate yourself on duty regulations and take care to keep sales slips and record all purchases on your declaration to Customs if they exceed duty restrictions.

Regulations can change at any time. We suggest you order a pamphlet entitled *Know Before You Go*, which provides specific information and the latest restrictions. Contact US Customs Service, PO Box 7407, Washington, DC 20229 for the pamphlet or view it on-line at www.customs.ustreas.gov, then click on the "Know Before You Go" section to access the on-line information.

- If you have been out of the country in a 30-day period before leaving on your cruise, you are limited to a $200 duty-free exemption on purchases. You also cannot combine family purchases for a larger allotment.
- Foreign-made items (cameras, watches, etc.) are dutiable any time you reenter the US with the item, unless you have proof of prior purchase. Carry your bills of sale, insurance policy, appraisal or register items in person with a Customs office prior to your departure.
- If you have not been out of the country during the 30-day period prior to cruising, you are allowed $800 in foreign purchases for personal use or gifts, one liter of alcohol (for family members at least 21 years old), 100 cigars and 200 cigarettes (one carton) per person during any 30-day period. Purchases over the limit may be subject to a 10% duty tax upon clearing US Customs. Cuban cigars are prohibited unless you are returning di-

rectly from Cuba or it is included on your ship's itinerary. At any rate, Cuban purchases are limited to $100 of total merchandise. Gifts not exceeding a value of $100 per day may be sent from foreign ports to friends and relatives in the US. You may ship $200 of gifts from the U.S. Virgin Islands, St. Thomas, St. John or St. Croix.

- Family members traveling together can combine their duty allotments (except for liquor allowances if children are under 21 years of age).
- Items purchased from Caribbean Basin countries have a duty allotment of $600 per person (the maximum for other foreign countries is $800). When visiting these countries and other foreign countries be sure that your combined purchases are not more than $800, with $600 maximum spent in Aruba, Antigua, Bahamas, Barbuda, Belize, British Virgin Islands, Barbados, Costa Rica, Dominica, Dominican Republic, El Salvador, Grenada, Guatemala, Guyana Honduras, Jamaica, Montserrat, Netherlands Antilles, Nicaragua, Panama, St. Lucia, St. Kitts, Nevis, St. Vincent & the Grenadines, and Trinidad & Tobago.
- When visiting the US Virgin Islands, the duty-free allotment is increased to $1,200 per person, plus one extra bottle of liquor (if it is made in the US Virgin Islands) and an extra 800 cigarettes (five cartons) only when purchased in the US Virgin Islands. Passengers who buy merchandise in the US Virgin Islands as well as beneficiary countries (see chart) and other foreign ports must deduct the amount purchased in the other ports, not exceeding $600 (including onboard purchases) from the total $1,200 allowed from the US Virgin Islands.
- Be absolutely sure to list all items you purchased on your declaration form – any undeclared items may be confiscated. The duty paid on the first $1,000 of goods purchased over the limit from the U.S. Virgin Islands is taxed at a flat rate of 1.5%. The tax is 3% on the first $1,000 purchased over the limit on other islands and onboard ship. You can pay the duty in U.S. currency, by personal check (with a valid ID) and, in some locations, by major credit card. Foreign currency is not accepted.
- Goods mailed for personal use can be imported duty-free if the total value is no more than $200. (This exemption does not apply to perfume containing alcohol val-

ued at more than $5 retail, alcoholic beverages or to tobacco products.)

- Items made in the US Virgin Islands, including locally made jewelry, are considered duty-free when returning to the US.Items purchased in Puerto Rico are duty-free and not added to other purchase allotments due to Puerto Rico's status as an American Commonwealth.

Specific Items & Their Status

- **Unset gemstones** are not generally considered part of the US Customs allotment upon re-entry to the United States. (Large purchases of stones may be considered commercial use and become taxable.)
- **Pets, plants, cuttings, seeds, unprocessed plant products** (including fruit and vegetables) and items made from **endangered species** – tortoise shell jewelry, ivory products (except antiques and certain skins), feathers, eggs and furs – are prohibited from being imported into the United States. State laws may further prohibit importation of products made from certain animals, so check your home state's regulations. Items made with dog or cat fur are prohibited, and a fine of $3,000 to $5,000 may be assessed.
- **Absinthe** or liquor with an excess of artemisia absinthium is prohibited and may be confiscated.
- **Gold coins, medals and bullion**, formerly prohibited, now may be brought into the US. However, such items from Cuba, Haiti, Iran, Iraq, Libya, Afghanistan, Serbia and Sudan are prohibited. Therefore, items must be properly marked by country of issuance.
- **Food products** (except bakery items and cured cheeses) are allowed only if sealed by the manufacturer. However, no products made with meat are allowed due to the danger of mad cow disease and other ailments.
- **Drugs** and drug paraphernalia are prohibited.
- **Firearms** and **ammunition** are restricted from entry into the U.S. without specific ATF approval in writing. Due to security concerns, cruise ships may restrict possession of firearms and ammunition without advance approval.

- No **counterfeit** Federal trademark copyright material may be brought into the U.S. Don't purchase bootleg copies of music, video, DVD, written material or fake designer clothing or perfume.

Customs Allowances

This chart shows the maximum US Customs allowance for items purchased on the islands covered in this book.

COUNTRY	MAXIMUM ALLOTMENT
Antigua & Barbuda	$600
Barbados	$600
Dominica	$600
Grenada	$600
Guadeloupe	$800
Martinique	$800
Puerto Rico (US)	No limit
St. Kitts & Nevis	$600
St. Lucia	$600
Sint Maarten	$800
St. Thomas	$1,200
On Board Ship	$600

US Customs Tips

Customs regulations might seem difficult to understand, but cruise passengers who do not purchase watches, jewelry, cigarettes or alcohol in large quantities usually do not exceed duty limitations. If you visit St. Thomas and other islands, an easy rule of thumb is to limit purchases from St. Thomas to $800 per person and $400 from all the other islands, combined with onboard purchases.

The Customs officials are very much aware of the retail value of items available for purchase. Do not think that you can get away with avoiding duty by wearing items you purchase, by having the shopkeeper write a receipt for less than the purchase amount or by failing to declare an item you purchase. The item could be subject to forfeit, or you may have to pay a penalty equal to the value of the item. It is much better to pay the duty!

When packing, do not place bottles of alcohol in your luggage in an attempt to hide it. Passenger luggage is handled quite roughly; the bottles can easily break and ruin your clothes.

To save time at Customs, pack the items you have purchased in a part of your luggage that is easy to examine, and have your Customs declaration form filled out before reaching the officials. If an official asks to open your luggage, do not hesitate; be honest and helpful to avoid costly Customs penalties.

Transportation

Taxis

Taxi drivers eagerly await ship passengers. The majority of vehicles used as taxis are minivans, but some independent taxi drivers use large passenger vans or standard four-door cars. Minivans are preferred for sightseeing and are more comfortable. Americans will have to cope with the strange feeling of driving on the left side of the road on many of the islands.

Taxis heading into town for shopping or out on the island for sightseeing and beachcombing may wait to fill their vans before departing. Allow time for this and have patience with the island way of doing things. Taxi drivers, as a whole, are not out to cheat the one-day visitor. When bargaining or asking for a taxi fare, don't approach the driver with a defensive attitude or assume he will try to gouge you. Most islands have established rates for trips around the island and drivers are required to follow their taxi association's rate guidelines. Be cautious, but not paranoid; most island drivers enjoy meeting new people and showing off their island.

Each island chapter gives specific taxi information, including current rates, tips for bargaining, and the time needed to reach island attractions. Taxi guidelines fluctuate from one island to the next, but you can usually negotiate lower rates with a group of four people or more. Minivans are capable of handling more than four, so the more people you can gather to share the ride, the better the deal for everyone.

If your group arranges a round-trip discounted rate with one driver, we recommended that you pay the entire amount at the end of the trip to ensure the same driver will come back for the return trip. Do not cheat by taking another driver back to the ship, which may cause problems with the taxi association or cruise port officials, and could be a legitimate cause for your arrest. Actions like this increase taxi rates and discourage drivers from wanting to help other visitors.

Local Buses

Local buses as a whole are not highly recommended for cruise passengers who need to get around quickly. They may be inexpensive, but you will probably not want to put up with the delays and crowded conditions that often are part of bus travel in the islands.

Rental Cars

Renting a car is an adventurous way to get out and explore the terrain. However, the road conditions leave a lot to be desired! Some roads have potholes large enough to swallow a small car and others are so steep and winding that even locals are extremely cautious when driving on them. Unless you are proficient at driving on both the left and right sides of the road and can remember which side to stay on when faced with a tight situation, driving in the islands can prove difficult. If you are not confident about driving on the left, try riding in a taxi first. A rental car can enhance your experience on some islands but cause only problems on others. Each chapter discusses the advantages and perils of renting a car.

Rental agencies usually require a credit card for a damage deposit and a valid driver's license. We strongly recommend that you get the optional collision insurance, too. You may need to purchase a temporary island license; rental agencies often provide assistance in satisfying this requirement. Each chapter supplies names and phone numbers for rental car agencies. Advance reservations save time when picking up the car.

Organized Tours & Activities

All tour prices are given in US dollars unless noted otherwise. Use these prices as a guideline, as rates vary from season to season.

Best Attractions on Each Island

- **Puerto Rico** – Río Camuy Cave Park (page 54), exploring Old San Juan (page 33).
- **St. Thomas** – Watersports, Coral World (page 80), shopping, sailing to St. John.
- **Sint Maarten** – Beaches, shopping, a trip to Anguilla.
- **Antigua** – Lord Nelson's Dockyard (page 133), resort beaches.

- **St. Kitts** – An island tour, day-trip to Nevis to tour plantation houses and sugar mills (page 160).
- **Guadeloupe** – Hiking to a waterfall, diving on Pigeon Island (page 210).
- **Dominica** – Waterfalls and rain forests, diving w/Dive Dominica (page 191).
- **Martinique** – Trip to St. Pierre (page 222, 224, 226) and Mont Pelée volcano (page 226).
- **St. Lucia** – Diving at Anse Chastenet (page 247), the drive-in volcano in Soufrière (page 242).
- **Barbados** – Beaches, Barbados Wildlife Monkey Reserve (page 266), *Atlantis* submarine (page 271).
- **Grenada** – Botanical Gardens (page 295), La Sagesse Resort (page 296).

Contact the ship's shore excursion office if you are interested in taking an island tour, snorkel trip or boat excursion. If you prefer to adventure on your own, read the three sections on excursions and activities – *Beaches, Island Activities* and *One-Day Itinerary* – before planning your activity.

Often, passengers new to cruising are reluctant to venture far afield without a tour group, for fear they will get lost or miss the ship. Rest assured, though, that many excursions can be coordinated to the boat's schedule. We have provided tables showing distances to specific locations, as well as recommended time allowances. These are designed to help you to explore safely and spend your time efficiently.

Beaches

Beaches are popular destinations for ship passengers, but there are important factors to consider before heading off to catch some rays. Most beaches in the Caribbean are open to the public, so you are welcome to explore them at will. Locals roam the beaches of many islands, offering to braid your hair or sell you everything from seashells to aloe vera plants for sunburn. If you are annoyed by their approach, a firm "no" usually sends them on their way.

Many resorts have beautiful beaches, changing facilities and beachside restaurants. If you are interested in a beach offering comfortable facilities within walking distance, choose a beachside resort. Remember you are at a resort; conduct yourself as if you were a hotel guest. Hotels will allow cruise passengers to use their facilities if they act appropriately and patronize the bar or restaurant.

Each chapter contains a beach chart illustrating the individual sports and facilities available at each beach as an easy, quick reference.

When spending time at any beach, avoid bringing cameras or other valuable personal belongings. Locker facilities are not usually available and valuables left on the beach encourage theft. To avoid problems, purchase a beach safe, a small waterproof cylinder that hangs around the neck to store cash and cabin keys. Another popular item is a disposable camera. Both of these are relatively inexpensive and found in stores across the US.

Bring bug repellent spray to the beach. Many of the islands have sand fleas or small biting bugs that can ruin a day outdoors. A small can of repellent can be quite expensive in the islands, so buy a brand of 100% DEET repellent before the cruise.

One last factor to consider is the intense Caribbean sun. Suntan lotion is much higher priced here than in the US. Buy a supply before your trip (choose one with higher SPF than you normally use).

Island Activities

All rates for island and ocean sports are quoted in US dollars unless otherwise noted. Use these prices as a guideline, as rates vary from season to season.

Ocean sports, such as windsurfing, water skiing, kayaking, diving and snorkeling, are among the most popular activities and can be found at public beaches around the islands. Golf, tennis and horseback riding are usually available on larger islands. The information supplied in the *Island Activities* and *Beaches* sections tells you everything you need to know concerning prices, availability and location.

Scuba diving is extremely popular on all the Caribbean islands. For this revision, we discovered new PADI and NAUI certified dive groups on each island and have included more dive operators. Competition has helped bring prices down to reasonable levels. There's also a list of useful dive websites.

Underwater safety and conservation of the fragile ecosystem is a high priority. It takes thousands of years to build coral that one careless kick might destroy. If you are not certified but are interested in diving, contact the ship's shore excursion office for details about lessons. St. Thomas, Dominica, St. Lucia and Antigua have quality dive operators who also offer introductory courses for first-time divers – perfect for cruise passengers who want to try the sport.

If you are interested in special activities like scuba diving or horseback riding, call ahead to reserve. Phone numbers are given throughout this book; you can contact the operators themselves, or have your travel agent do it for you. Tour operators try to work with last-minute requests from ship passengers, but reservations are highly recommended.

One-Day Itineraries

Drawing from our extensive experiences exploring the islands, we have created One-Day Itineraries that outline a full day's worth of things to do. The itinerary usually takes between six and seven hours to complete. You can follow the directions step by step, or use the section as a reference to design your own outing. If your port time is shorter, condense the itinerary by eliminating one or two parts.

Puerto Rico

The Enchantment Isle

Island Description

Puerto Rico went through a series of name changes before receiving its final title. The island was originally called **Borinquen** by the Taino Indians, meaning "Land of the Noble Lord." When Columbus landed on his second voyage to the New World in 1493, he renamed the island **San Juan Bautista** and the capital port **Puerto Rico** (rich port). At some point in the island's history, the island and the capital switched names. The Spanish, who were primarily interested in gold and treasure, quickly estab- lished what was to become the largest and oldest Spanish colonial settlement in the Caribbean chain. Although Puerto Rico's natural supply of gold quickly petered out, the colony thrived. Today, the island remains rich in Spanish history, tradition and culture.

One of Puerto Rico's sugar mill towers.

Puerto Rico's variety of vegetation, ranging from lush rain forests to fertile lowland meadows and white sand beaches, offers you an opportunity to escape the city's congestion and appreciate natural beauty.

More than 3½ million tourists visit Puerto Rico yearly, spurring the government and businesses to commit $350 million to the expansion of airports and seaports and $600 million to the construction and renovation of hotels. An additional $2 billion for development of new tourism projects includes a waterfront renewal project for cruise ship terminals and improvements in the city of Old San Juan. Although renovation can be an inconvenience, the new cruise ship terminals and improved tourist attractions in Old San Juan will make Puerto Rico a more enjoyable port for everyone.

San Juan, the metropolitan capital city, is located on Puerto Rico's northern coastline and has a population of over one million. Most visitors to the Caribbean pass through San Juan at some point during their journey, largely because San Juan offers one of the largest international airports and commercial harbors.

Cruise ships dock at the great walled city of Old San Juan, situated on a peninsula bordered by San Juan Bay and the Atlantic Ocean. Well-preserved historic sites, museums, churches, fortresses, colonial mansions and plazas are among the unique architectural treasures that led the United Nations to designate Old San Juan a World Heritage Site. Due to the size of Puerto Rico (about 3,500 square miles), the outer island takes time to explore properly. If this is your embarkation port, consider allowing an extra day before or after your cruise to enjoy sightseeing. (See *One-Day Itinerary* for suggested tours, page 54.)

Island People

The people of Puerto Rico are a blend of Taino Indian and African blacks, mixed with Spanish culture and American idealism. The result is a proud people with a laid-back attitude. Do not expect fast service, even in fast-food restaurants, as everything takes a bit longer; island time keeps its own clock.

The national symbol of Puerto Rico is the **coquí**, a tiny tree frog whose melodious chirp is often mistaken for a bird's song. This species of tree frog lives only on the island of Puerto Rico. When asked about the coquí, a taxi driver once told me that if it were ever taken away from the island it would surely die. He went on to say that the people of Puerto Rico are like the coquí: if they ever left their isle of enchantment, they too would perish.

Language

Spanish is the predominant language throughout the island, although most businesses have English-speaking personnel. If you plan to venture out of the towns, take a Spanish phrasebook along.

Holidays

Puerto Rico celebrates American holidays as well as holidays unique to the island. Post offices and banks normally close on the holiday itself or, if it falls on a weekend, the nearest Monday or Friday. Holidays and festivals occur throughout the year, so pick up a copy of *Que Pasa* at the tourist information center for a current calendar of events.

Annual Holidays & Events

For more details and precise dates, contact the island tourist board (see *Appendix*).

January . . . New Year's Day; Martin L. King, Jr.'s Birthday
February . . . President's Day
March . . . Emancipation Day
April . . . Good Friday; Easter; José De Diego's Birthday
May . . . Memorial Day
July . . . US Independence Day; Muñoz Riveras & José Celso Barbosa's Birthdays; Constitution Day
September . . . Labor Day
November . . . Veteran's Day; Thanksgiving; Discovery Day
December . . . Christmas Day

Useful Websites

The Tourism Office's official home page is **www.prtourism.com**. It includes maps, general information, an activity calendar and describes local attractions. Another good site, **www.puertorico-web.com**, offers detailed information about El Yunque rain forest and the Río Camuy Caves, as well as other areas around the island.

The most practical web page is **www.welcometopuertorico.com**, providing a wide range of island information, including driving directions, taxi charts and a people search or business search function.

Information available at **www.escape.topuertorico.com** includes rental car companies, hotel and restaurant information and phone numbers and web links for businesses.

The Pier

Cruise ships dock at one of the many piers along **Calle Marina** in Old San Juan. The terminals are air-conditioned and have phones, gift shops and Customs clearance. A luxurious new Wyndham hotel has opened just across from the cruise ship docks and may be a perfect place to stay before or after your cruise. You can enjoy the gourmet restaurant or book tours through the hotel's concierge desk. Arts and crafts are available at the "pink" Tourist Information on Calle Marina.

Pier Phones

The area code for calling Puerto Rico from the US is 787, and the local number for information is 411.

Every cruise ship terminal building has phones; local calls cost 10-25¢. If you want to arrange activities on other islands, make reservations or confirmation calls from Puerto Rico as rates here are far cheaper than on other islands.

In Town

The entire peninsula comprising Old San Juan is just eight blocks across, with the best shopping and historical sites close to the pier area. A free trolley car runs along Calle Marina with stops at the Tourist Information Plaza and the center of town. Look for a yellow "Parada" sign, designating stops on the streets of Old San Juan. Local vendors are always found in the park at the Tourist Information Plaza and a sampling of rum can be had inside the building.

Currency

Currency is the US dollar and most establishments accept credit cards and traveler's checks. For emergency cash, casinos often have an ATM and there is an established bank across the street from the Tourist Information Plaza. Check with the Wyndham Old San Juan Hotel across from the cruise ship dock to cash traveler's checks or use an ATM.

Postage

The post office is opposite the Tourist Information Plaza, a short walk to the left from the piers. (See "D" on Historical Walking Tour map, page 37.) Postal rates are the same as those in the US, but do not stock up on extra US stamps unless you plan to send mail from St. Thomas or here. All the other islands are foreign countries issuing their own postage and will not accept mail bearing US stamps.

Casinos

By law, all casinos must be located in a hotel and gambling is allowed from noon to 4 am. The Wyndham Old San Juan Hotel across the street from the cruise ship docks offers the nearest casino. You can also take a taxi to Isla Verde or Condado to enjoy casinos in the large resort hotels at the **San Juan International, Embassy Suites, Wyndham El San Juan, Ritz Carlton, Condado Plaza Hotel, Radisson Ambassador** and the **San Juan Marriott**.

The casinos offer live blackjack, craps, roulette, Caribbean stud poker, Pai Gow poker, and Let it Ride. They also have slot machines and video poker. Larger hotels offer entertainment and dancing. The minimum gambling age is 18.

Historical Walking Tour

Old San Juan contains the best examples of 16th- and 17th-century Spanish colonial architecture in the Caribbean. History buffs will marvel at the fascinating museums, forts and beautifully restored homes – all within walking distance of the port. The best way to explore the city is to walk through Old San Juan's winding cobblestone streets. The following walking tour guides you past historic buildings, museums and the more interesting shops (letters correspond to the city map on page 37). Depending on how long you linger at each stop, the tour should be completed in two to three hours.

Be aware that San Juan is hilly and some parts of this tour involve steep ascents on uneven pathways and cobblestone streets. Wear good walking shoes and a hat and carry some drinking water; the tropical sun can be hot here even in winter. There are plenty of taxis to run you back to the ship if you get too tired (fare, $6).

Start your tour at the cruise ship terminals on Calle Marina. With your back to the water, walk to the left until you reach the **Tourist Information Center (D)**, set in a pink building surrounded by a small park, usually filled with local craft vendors. Due to San Juan's refurbishing efforts, some exhibits may be closed or hard to find. Pick up the current copy of *Que Pasa* and ask locally if any museums are currently closed.

Follow the waterfront to the left past the Plaza de Arsanas, a bandstand area with open-air music events. Walk along the Paseo La Princesa, a tree-lined boulevard, past **La Princesa (E)**, a former 19th-century prison. The Puerto Rican Tourism headquarters is within the renovated La Princesa, as is a changing art exhibit open Monday-Saturday, 9 am to 4 pm at no charge.

The Paseo De La Princesa adjoins an impressive plaza containing the large bronze fountain entitled Raices. The **Raices Fountain (F)** depicts the island's mixed heritage and symbolizes friendship and a new future. The ensemble is meant to resemble a ship being steered out to sea, with frolicking dolphins leading the way into the 21st century. The magnificent fountain has San Juan Bay as a backdrop and was designed by architect Miguel Carlo to celebrate the New World's 500th birthday. It was finished in May of 1992.

Follow the Paseo De La Princesa to the right along the waterfront. La Fortaleza (the governor's mansion) can be seen above, supported by the massive **Muralla (G)**, city wall, composed of sandstone blocks up to 20 feet thick. Completed in the late 1700s, the wall surrounds the entire colonial city of Old San Juan, flanked by El Morro Fort at one end and San Cristobal Fort at the other.

The *paseo* ends at **San Juan Gate (H),** one of six massive doors that for centuries were closed at sundown to cut off access to the city. After passing through San Juan Gate, you will find a small park on the right. This is the waiting area for the guided tours to La Fortaleza (I), the governor's mansion.

La Fortaleza (I), built between 1530 and 1540, is the oldest governor's mansion in the western hemisphere. Still used today as the governor's residence, it is shown only by guided tour. Tour times do change, so check with the guards to confirm the current schedule. Free tours are normally conducted on the hour in English (on the

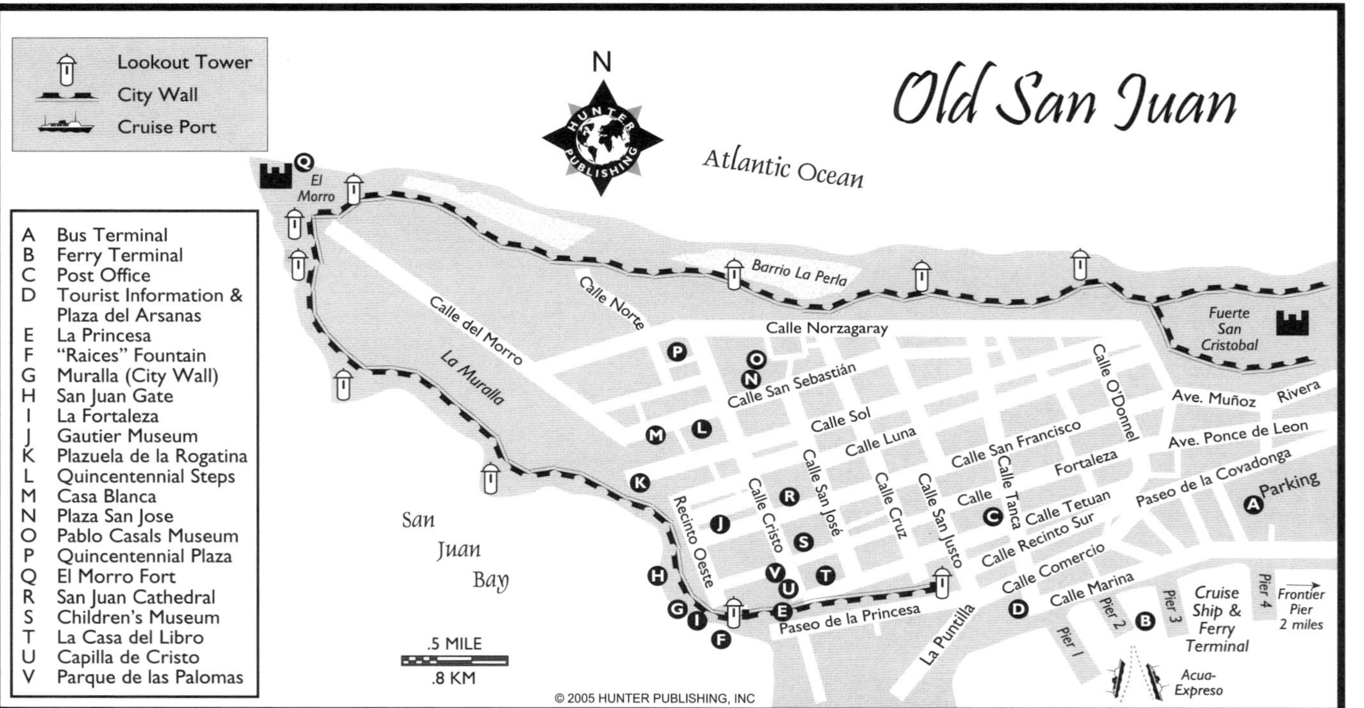
Old San Juan
Lookout Tower
City Wall
Cruise Port
N
HUNTER PUBLISHING
Atlantic Ocean
A Bus Terminal
B Ferry Terminal
C Post Office
D Tourist Information &
Plaza del Arsanas
E La Princesa
F "Raices" Fountain
G Muralla (City Wall)
H San Juan Gate
I La Fortaleza
J Gautier Museum
K Plazuela de la Rogatina
L Quincentennial Steps
M Casa Blanca
N Plaza San Jose
O Pablo Casals Museum
P Quincentennial Plaza
Q El Morro Fort
R San Juan Cathedral
S Children's Museum
T La Casa del Libro
U Capilla de Cristo
V Parque de las Palomas
El Morro
Barrio La Perla
Calle Norte
Calle del Morro
La Muralla
Calle Norzagaray
Fuerte San Cristobal
Calle San Sebastián
Calle O'Donnel
Ave. Muñoz
Rivera
Calle Sol
Calle Luna
Ave. Ponce de Leon
Calle San Francisco
Fortaleza
Paseo de la Covadonga
Parking
Calle San José
Calle Cristo
Calle Cruz
Calle San Justo
Calle
Calle Tanca
Calle Tetuan
Calle Recinto Sur
Recinto Oeste
Calle Comercio
Calle Marina
San Juan Bay
Paseo de la Princesa
La Puntilla
Pier 1
Pier 2
Pier 3
Pier 4
Cruise Ship & Ferry Terminal
Frontier Pier 2 miles
Acua-Expreso
.5 MILE
.8 KM
© 2005 HUNTER PUBLISHING, INC

half-hour in Spanish) on weekdays (except holidays), 9 am to 4 pm. If you prefer to continue on the walking tour for now, the route returns to this general area later. Reservations are necessary, ☎ (787) 721-7000, ext. 2211, 2288 or 2366.

Across the street from the San Juan Gate, visit the **Felisa Rincón de Gautier Museum (J)**, the home of San Juan's first female mayor, who held office for 22 years. The museum contains personal memorabilia, an impressive display of awards, keys to hundreds of cities worldwide and a collection of lace fans (upstairs). Open weekdays, except holidays, 9 am to 4 pm (no charge).

Climb the stairs next to the San Juan Gate to the top of the city wall. Follow the wall to the right, through **Plazuela de la Rogativa (K),** meaning "small plaza of the religious procession." The plaza is dedicated to a priest who led a procession of singing women with candles through the streets during the 1797 attack by British troops on El Morro Fort. Supposedly, the British saw the candle flames, mistook them for Spanish reinforcements, and retreated.

Just past the Plazuela de la Rogativa, look back across the wall for a good view of La Fortaleza. Cross the street and proceed on the spur (Calle Sol) that ascends to the gate in the massive wall ahead. This is the garden entrance to **Casa Blanca (M)**, the white house. Follow the pathway uphill, enjoying the cool shade and beautiful landscaping, until you reach the upper terrace and the entrance to Casa Blanca.

If the garden entrance is closed, turn right on Calle Sol to the **Quincentennial Steps (L)**, on your left. At the top of the steps turn left onto Calle San Sebastian and follow the street to the very end. Enter a gate labeled Casa Blanca, then follow the garden pathway leading to the house.

Although the governor never lived in the home, Casa Blanca was built as a reward for the island's first governor, Juan Ponce de Leon. His descendants lived here for more than 250 years after his death. Subsequent occupation by the military left the house in disrepair, until it was finally restored and furnished with period antiques to depict family life in 16th and 17th centuries.

Wander through the spacious rooms, cooled only by ocean breezes, and experience how the Spanish colonials lived. The top floor contains an exhibit of Taino Indian culture, labeled only in Spanish. Casa Blanca is open Tuesday-Sunday, 9 am to noon, and 1 pm to 4 pm. $2 for adults and $1 for children.

Leave from the upper level of Casa Blanca and walk straight ahead along Calle San Sebastian to Calle Cristo. To the left is the **Plaza San José (N)** with a statue of Ponce de Leon. Across the plaza you'll find the small **Pablo Casals Museum (O)**, which houses a charming exhibit of pictures and memorabilia, including the cello used by the world-famous musician Pablo Casals, who lived in Puerto Rico during the last 20 years of his life. Open Tuesday through Saturday, 9:30 am to 5:30 pm. Admission is $1 for adults and 50 cents for children.

From the Plaza San José, walk uphill toward Calle Norzagaray through the **Quincentennial Plaza (P)**. Completed in 1992, the $16 million project transformed a former parking lot into a fountained plaza to commemorate the 500th anniversary of Columbus' discovery of the New World. Two needle-shaped columns point at the north star (the explorer's guiding light) and a fountain with 100 streams represents the first 100 years of New World exploration.

The Quincentennial Plaza is the cornerstone of a $50 million restoration project of the historic **Ballaja sector** at Calle Del Morro. You may wish to consult *Que Pasa* to see if new exhibits have been opened in this area. Walk to the left along Calle Norzagaray and the route intersects with Calle Del Morro, the road leading to El Morro Fort.

Built by the Spanish in 1595, **El Morro Fort (Q)** contains mostly empty rooms (a free map is available at the entrance), so you'll need to put your imagination to work. The fort was built as an observation point as well as a defensive location, and offers dramatic views of San Juan Harbor, La Fortaleza, San Cristobal and the old city. An interesting feature on the upper level is an incongruous Victorian-style lighthouse inside the Spanish walls. It is the oldest lighthouse in Puerto Rico, built in 1848, and is still in working condition.

The great ramp (72 steps down a tunnel) goes down to the lower levels containing a dungeon, cannons, a sentry box, a vaulted tower, the garrison and a steep circular stairwell, leading back to the top. This route is not recommended for the elderly or very young. The small air-conditioned museum once served as storage and sleeping quarters. El Morro is operated by the US National Park Service and is open daily from 9 am to 5 pm, except on Christmas Day. Tours, orientation and a video presentation are offered for an admission charge of $2 for adults and $1 for children and seniors.

Return from El Morro by the main road. When you reach the intersection of Calle Norzagaray you'll see the large white building of the newly restored Escuela de Artes Plásticas, the **School of Fine Arts**. To the right is the former Asilo de Beneficencia, home for the poor, which currently houses the Institute of Puerto Rican Culture. Local crafts are offered for sale and several galleries feature changing exhibits open Wednesday through Saturday, 9 am to 4:30 pm. On the left is the Cuartel de Ballajá, once the barracks for Spanish troops and their families. The building will eventually house a permanent Museum of the Americas on its second floor.

Leave the area via Quincentennial Plaza to Calle Cristo and walk straight downhill. On the left (after passing several streets) is **San Juan Cathedral (R)**. Built in 1540, this is one of the oldest churches in the western hemisphere. The cathedral contains the marble tomb of Ponce de Leon, who was killed during his quest to find the fabled fountain of youth in Florida.

Walk to the left and toward the back of the cathedral to view the relic of San Pio, a Roman martyr encased under a painted wood replica within a glass coffin. Be sure to read the story about how San Pio came to rest in Puerto Rico. The building houses a museum with a changing exhibit of Latin American Folk Art. Open daily 8:30 am to 4:30 pm. Admission is free.

Walking down Calle Cristo is like stepping into another century. Some of the oldest and most historically important buildings can be seen on small streets radiating from the town center.

Take special notice of the blue cobblestones used to line the streets of Old San Juan. The stones were brought to Puerto Rico as ballast on Spanish ships and were replaced by gold and treasure on the return trip to Spain. The British and French used red brick ballast on other Caribbean islands to build their streets, making the blue cobblestones of Old San Juan unique.

The shopping area begins on Calle Cristo after passing Calle San Francisco. The time you spend here will depend on what catches your attention. (See *Shopping*, below.)

A new museum located at 150 Cristo Street is the island's first museum designed for children. The exhibits, featuring hands-on educational subjects, are fun for adults and kids. Open Tuesday through Sunday, admission is $3 for adults and $2.50 for children. Nearby is **La Casa del Libro (T),** a small museum containing a collection of rare books and manuscripts from Europe and the Americas that illustrate the history of fine printing. Open Tuesday to Saturday (except holidays), 11 am to 4:30 pm.

At the dead-end of Calle Cristo is the often-photographed **Capilla de Cristo (U),** Christ Chapel, dedicated to the Christ of Miracles. Legend says the chapel stands in honor of a youth whose life was spared in 1753 when his horse spontaneously stopped before it hurtled over the city wall, but historical records say the youth was actually killed and the chapel was built to protect against future tragedies. Open only on Tuesdays, 10 am to 3:30 pm.

Next to the chapel is the **Parque de las Palomas (V),** Pigeon Park, home to hundreds of pigeons ready to leave their mark on unsuspecting tourists! The walking tour ends here.

If you wish to return to the ship now, walk back on Calle Cristo to Calle Fortaleza and turn right. Continue to Calle San Justo, turn right and walk downhill to the Tourist Information Plaza. The pier area is left of the plaza along the waterfront. A free trolley car ride travels along Calle Fortaleza; look for a Parada sign.

If this walking tour has stimulated your appetite, have a bite to eat at one of the charming restaurants located in several of the side malls. Fast-food frenzies can be quenched at a number of places bordering Plaza de Armas (Calle San Francisco and Calle San José).

Shopping

Old San Juan

Although Old San Juan contains many jewelry stores, the prices are much better on St. Thomas and St. Martin. If Puerto Rico is your first stop, use these jewelry stores to check prices, but don't expect great bargains.

The best buys in Old San Juan are local crafts and rum. The Bacardi Rum distillery (see *Self-Guided Tours*) sells rum at a discount. (Remember, there is no Customs limit on Puerto Rican liquor when flying into the US.) Handmade lace, fabrics, musical instruments, hammocks, cigars and *Santos* figures (sculptures representing patron saints) are sold at the artisan markets at **La Casita** at Plaza Darsenas near Pier 1. Crafts are also available at **Convento de los Domincos** at 98 Calle Norzagaray, which houses the Institute of Puerto Rican Culture. The center sells baskets, masks, guitars, santos and Indian artifacts. The small shop at the **Museo de las Americas** sells authentic folk crafts.

The following stores in the areas around Calle Cristo and Calle Fortaleza are special.

Calle Cristo

Spanish colonial mansions were often designed with massive walls built right up to the street and an interior courtyard, allowing private enjoyment of the mild climate. Current owners have turned these old residences into shaded mini-malls, where you're encouraged to wander, absorb the ambience of Old San Juan and view ever-changing boutiques and shops. Prudent shoppers can find upscale merchandise at reasonable prices. Refreshments may be a priority after the heat of the day, and small cafés are sure to tempt you.

Spicy Caribbee, 154 Calle Cristo, has Caribbean handicrafts plus a good selection of Puerto Rican teas, spices, herbs and coffee.

☆ **Galeria Botello**, 208 Cristo, specializes in local and Latin American artists, with many unique pieces by its founder, Angel Botello. The gallery is housed inside a beautiful colonial mansion, nearly 200 years old. The roof is supported by giant beams and the floor is paved with the original antique bricks.

Also found on Calle Cristo are a **Ralph Lauren Factory Store, Coach Factory Store**, **Pusser's Factory Store** and **Tommy Hilfiger Company Store.**

Calle Fortaleza

☆ **The Butterfly People**, 152 Calle Fortaleza, upstairs; www.butterflypeople.com. This unique store will delight you with its incredible murals made entirely from shimmering butterflies protected by plexiglass. Classical music entices browsers to spend hours appreciating the exquisite creations. All displays are for sale, but photography is not permitted. The butterflies have been bred especially for the purpose of art. A charming café on the same level offers cool fruit drinks and light cuisine.

El Alcazar (just off Calle Fortaleza at 103 San José Street) is an antique store featuring a fine collection of old handmade Santos figures. True collectors appreciate the special Santos offered by this shop, regardless of the seemingly high prices.

☆ **Puerto Rican Arts & Crafts**, 204 Calle Fortaleza, could qualify as an art museum. It contains the best work by Puerto Rican artisans. Elegant Santos, delicate pottery, handmade dolls in island costume, masks, jewelry, tile scenes, hammocks and paintings are for sale. Open 9 am to 6 pm, Monday through Saturday, plus noon to 5 pm on Sundays from November to January.

The Haitian Gallery at 367 Calle Fortaleza carries Puerto Rican crafts, folksy gifts and inexpensive paintings from around the Caribbean.

Bareds, at the corner of Calle Fortaleza and Calle San Justo, is a chain with stores throughout Old San Juan. They carry Lalique, Lladro, Waterford, Swarovski crystal, Gucci watches and stylish fine jewelry, as well as other imported items like those found in the Little Switzerland stores on other Caribbean islands.

The **Hard Rock Café**, 253 Recinto Sur Street, one block north of the Tourist Information Center, is where to go for Hard Rock Café memorabilia. Walk downhill from Fortaleza Street on San Justo and turn left on Recinto Sur. Open daily, 11 am-2 am.

Transportation & Excursions

Taxis

Old San Juan has one of the largest port areas in the Caribbean and taxi stations are situated at each and every docking terminal. Under the new Tourism Taxi Program, taxis are painted white, bearing the new sun logo. There's no need for a taxi to explore Old San Juan, but if you want to see more of San Juan, the capital, a taxi is a must. Taxis are metered for trips around San Juan, with a $6 minimum fare. The price shown on the meter is for the whole taxi, regardless of the number of people. Prices for an island tour can be negotiated with the taxi driver. The majority of taxi drivers speak English and will be more than willing to bargain. All prices are given in US dollars.

Taxi Chart

Destination (from the cruise ship pier)	**Cost** (one to four people)
Airport	$16 (plus 50¢ per bag)
Condado Plaza	$10
Isla Verde	$16
Taxi charter	$20 (per hour)

Tipping taxi drivers is customary, approximately 10% of the fare. It is not necessary to arrange a pick-up time with a taxi driver if passengers are taking in the sights around San Juan. Taxis can be found at any large hotel, or flagged down on any busy street.

Local Buses

The **Metropolitan Bus Authority** in San Juan has bus stops (*Parada Metrobus*) marked by magenta, orange and white signs. The Covadonga Parking Lot, to the right (ocean behind you) of the cruise ship terminals, is the best place to catch a bus. A map of Old San Juan and the bus routes is available at the Tourist Information Plaza, left of the pier terminals on Calle Marina. Bus A7 (25¢) goes from Old San Juan, through Condado and Isla Verde, for passengers wishing to spend a day at the beach or at the blackjack tables.

As in most large cities, buses can be crowded and quite slow. On the positive side, a bus trip can be an interesting adventure and you may get to know some of the locals for only a quarter!

Rental Cars

Puerto Rico follows the American system of driving on the right.

> TIP: In San Juan, locals also follow the New York City system of driving fast with limited attention to rules of the road. Drive cautiously and always be alert!

Renting cars in the Old San Juan area can be difficult. Most agencies are based at the large hotels in the Condado area and the limited number of cars may be reserved for hotel guests. Contact one of the agencies listed below *prior to arrival* in San Juan. Requirements for renting a car include a valid driver's license and a credit card. The fees range from $50 to $100 per day, plus gasoline and insurance. You should definitely purchase collision insurance.

Driving in the city of San Juan can be very hectic, confusing and frustrating if you don't know the roads. The opposite is true once you head outside the city, but you must drive aggressively and use a detailed city map in order to get in and out of town. Most rental agencies supply an island map, but be prepared to get lost while attempting to leave San Juan. Traffic becomes busy between 4 pm and 6 pm, so if you need to be back on your ship before 5 pm, plan ahead!

Car Rental Agencies

The area code for Puerto Rico is 787, and is charged as a long-distance call from the United States.

AAA . . . . ☎ 791-1465/791-2609
Avis ☎ (800) 874-3556 (Puerto Rico); (800) 230-4898 (U.S.); www.avis.com
Budget . . . . ☎ in Condado, 791-3685, (800) 626-4516; www.budget.com
Hertz . . . . ☎ 791-0840 or (800) 654-3030/3131 www.hertz.com
National . . . . ☎ 791-1805/791-1810; (800) 227-7368 www.nationalcar.com
Thrifty... . . . . ☎ 253-2525 or (800) 367-2277

Self-Guided Tours

Take a **Historical Walking Tour of Old San Juan** (page 37). The close proximity of the cruise ship terminals to the streets of Old San Juan makes it an easy walk through Puerto Rico's historical past.

Bacardí Rum Factory

The Bacardí Rum factory, ☎ (787) 788-1500, is set across San Juan Bay and makes an interesting side trip for passengers with limited time. You can easily get there from Pier 2 on Calle Marina. The **ferry to Cataño** takes a 50¢ token, which can be purchased from the booth in the center of the station. Ferries leave every half-hour from the right side entrance to Station A. In Cataño, go outside the terminal and ask for the taxi van going to Bacardí. (There are usually several vans designated for the short trip to the rum factory.) The five-minute ride ($6) will whisk you to the Bacardí tent for a free rum drink while you wait for the guided tram tour.Deposit the token in the slot before the swinging doors and wait for the ferry. If you prefer to rent a car and drive, take Highway 22 West to the Cantaño exit, then take Road 165 about one mile. The plant is visible on the right.

The main Bacardí plant has an elevator, lounge area and Bacardí museum. The factory gives free 20 minute tours from 9:30 to 10:30 am and from 12 to 4 pm. The plant is open Monday through Saturday, except holidays.

Including the two ferry trips and the Bacardí plant tour, this day-trip should take one to two hours. Be sure to bring money for the rum products and souvenirs at the Bacardí gift shop. You can get better deals on Bacardí rum here than in any of the stores around Old San Juan or elsewhere in the Caribbean.

Batty Beginnings

The Bacardí trademark is the bat. When the family opened their first distillery in Cuba and found bats living in the tin roof rafters, they chose this as a symbol for the new company. At that time, the bat was known to symbolize good luck, intelligence and family union. Now the trademark is being phased out because management believes people today see the bat as a negative symbol, associated with Dracula. The canopy structure where you started touring the plant was built to resemble a bat.

Organized Tours & Activities

Sunshine Tours is a very reliable company with great excursions. Reach them at ☎ (787) 791-4500, toll-free (888) 786-3636, www.-puerto-rico-sunshinetours.com, or e-mail Rich Morales at richsun-shinepr1@hotmail.com. We recommend the following tours:

- **Half-day El Yunque Rain Forest** tour, $43 per person. After a 45-minute drive, you arrive at El Yunque. Out of the van, the driver leads your group to the Palo Colorado Trail, stopping at La Coca waterfall and the Yokahú Tower en route. Twenty minutes is allowed for an easy walk along the trail. Keep an eye out for giant Sierra tree ferns, matrix ferns, termite nests, exotic plants and bromeliads attached to tree trunks. As you listen for the birdlike trill of the coquí tree frog, watch for lizards and discover the nesting boxes of Amazon parrots. Expect a short, intense downpour of rain that stops abruptly – this is a rain forest, after all! No climbing is ever allowed due to algae and moss on the rock's surface.

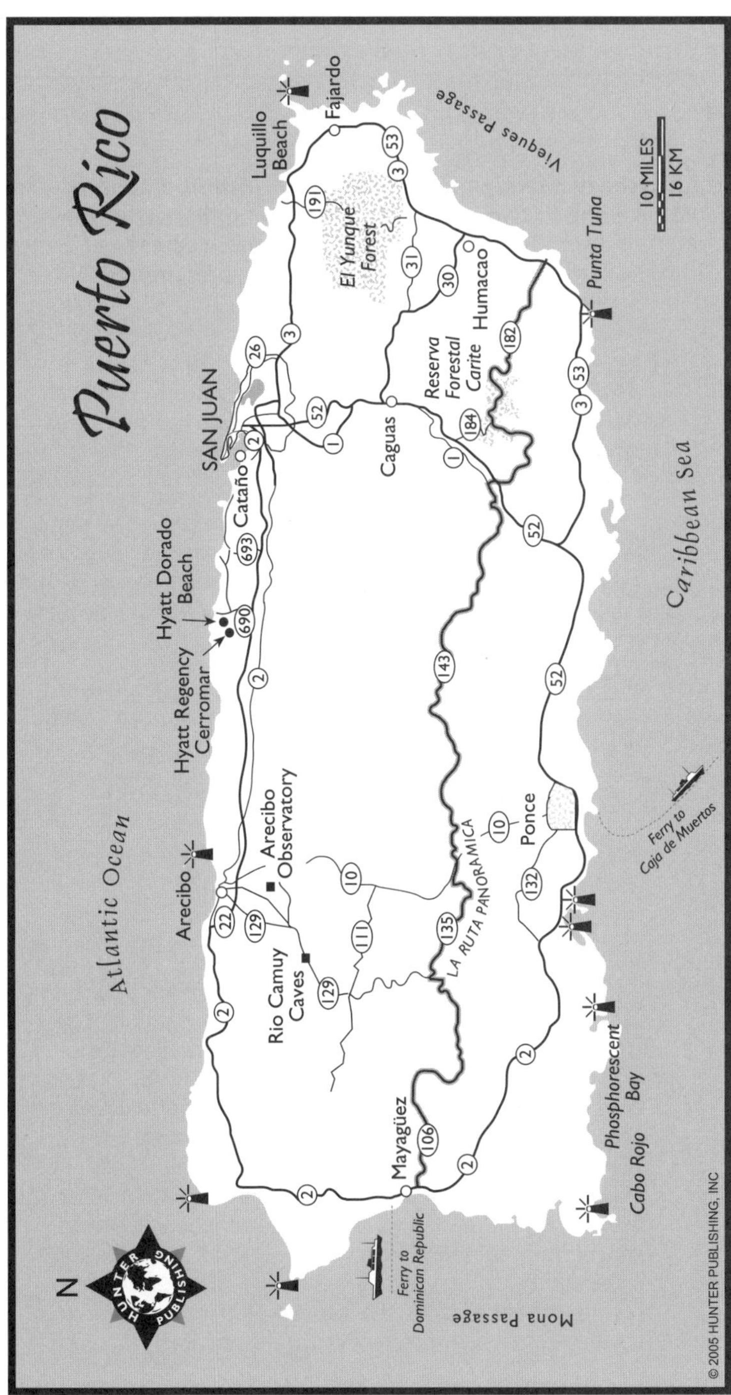
Puerto Rico
Atlantic Ocean
Caribbean Sea
Vieques Passage
Mona Passage
N
HUNTER PUBLISHING
SAN JUAN
Cataño
Hyatt Dorado Beach
Hyatt Regency Cerromar
Arecibo
Arecibo Observatory
Rio Camuy Caves
Mayagüez
Ferry to Dominican Republic
Cabo Rojo
Phosphorescent Bay
Ponce
Ferry to Caja de Muertos
LA RUTA PANORAMICA
Caguas
Reserva Forestal Carite
Humacao
Punta Tuna
El Yunque Forest
Luquillo Beach
Fajardo
10 MILES
16 KM
© 2005 HUNTER PUBLISHING, INC

- **Rain Forest and Luquillo Beach**, $58 per person. Extend the rain forest tour described above with two hours of swimming and sunning at nearby Luquillo Beach. Bring a towel and bathing suit.

- **Rio de Camuy Caves Park and Arecibo Observatory Shuttle**, $70 plus entrance fees of $13.50 (see *One-Day Itinerary*). A shuttle bus delivers you to the park entrance. From there, a park guide leads groups into the depths of a million-year-old cave. After your cave exploration, the shuttle takes everyone on to the Arecibo Observatory, the largest radar/radio telescope on earth. Scientists from all over the world use a 305-meter diameter dish to listen to sounds of the universe. The entire trip should take about seven hours.

Sunshine also offers a tour of Old San Juan and the Bacardí Rum distillery for $40 per person, an all-day snorkeling trip for $70 per person, horseback riding for $75 per person, and a special night kayak tour to the bioluminescent bay for $70 per person. Tours include transportation from San Juan, but do not include entrance fees or tips to the guide.

Puerto Rico Tours offers private customized tours for two to four people. If you prefer small tour groups or a customized schedule, contact Jorge Lopez, ☎ (787) 306-1540, letgeodo@coqui.net or visit www.puertorico-tours.com. The following tours are offered.

- Tour of **Old San Juan** includes a visit to San Jose Church, Casa Blanca, San Juan Cathedral and La Fortaleza. Jorge shares his knowledge of the history of Old San Juan, a special city. The final stop is at the Bacardí Rum distillery, where the guests are invited to sample complimentary rum drinks and enjoy a view of Old San Juan. The tour takes about four hours (no strict time limit) and costs $55 per person, with a minimum of two guests. Note: Bacardí is closed on Sundays.

- Tour of **El Yunque Rain Forest and Luquillo Beach**. Leaving San Juan in the morning, the tour stops at El Portal visitor center built recently by the government at a cost of four million dollars. Visitors interact with interesting exhibits and view a 15-minute video in an air-conditioned theater. The tour stops at La Coca Falls and hikes up a well-maintained trail (35-40 minutes at a comfortable pace) to the Mount Britton observation tower and a beautiful view of the eastern coast of

Puerto Rico. After the rainforest, it heads to Luquillo Beach, where snacks, drinks and souvenirs are on sale. You return to San Juan with a final stop at the Waterfront Restaurant, which offer great views and a house specialty of fresh red snapper. The day ends at about 4:30 pm, but this is a private tour with no strict time limits. The cost is $75 per person with a minimum of two guests (gratuities are not included).

⚓ Full-day tours to **Rio Camuy Caves and Arecibo Observatory** can be arranged for about $65 per person with a four-person minimum in a comfortable seven-passenger GMC Safari air-conditioned van. An experienced tour guide shares a complete review of Puerto Rican history and culture as you travel. The cost does not include food, refreshments, admission fees ($13.50) or gratuities. Tour times are limited, so call ahead to make reservations.

Spread Eagle II: **Snorkel, Picnic & Sail.** This excursion is great for swimmers and non-swimmers alike, who can enjoy the clear waters of the smaller islands on the eastern end of Puerto Rico. Sailing on a licensed catamaran, you are whisked to white sand beaches and taken to view tropical fish and a living reef. The trip includes a sandwich buffet lunch, snacks, sodas, piña coladas and rum punch. Everyone receives a new snorkel to use and keep. The boat leaves from Fajardo at 10 am, but transportation is available from San Juan by calling the toll-free number and making advance reservations, ☎ (888) 523-4511. Call for current rate. You can also contact them via their website, www.snorkelpr.com, or by e-mail, snorkel@coqui.net.

Beaches

Puerto Rico has more than 272 miles of white sand beach, but the best areas are those farthest away from downtown San Juan. If you want to spend the whole day at an exotic beach, you would be well advised to wait for another island.

BEACH CHART	Facilities	Windsurfing	Snorkeling	Scuba Diving	Wave Runners	Swimming	Parasailing	Sailing	Water Skiing	Nude/Topless
Condado Area	☆	☆	☆	☆		☆		☆		
Isla Verde Area	☆	☆			☆	☆				
Luquillo Beach	☆		☆			☆				

Close to Old San Juan on Isla Verde is **Alambique Beach**. A few of the city's best hotels are set along this beach, but some do not allow cruise passengers to enter their properties. The Sands Hotel does welcome visitors to their beautiful property. It offers a large pool with a Happy Hour between 6 and 8 pm and a casino that opens at 4 pm. If you're here at night, take in the Las Vegas-style show (one-drink minimum). If you are disembarking in San Juan and have time to spend before your flight home, the bell captain at Sands will store your luggage while you enjoy the beach, pool or restaurant. The Sands Hotel does everything it can to make your visit enjoyable.

Get dropped off at the public entrance to Alambique Beach (to the left of the Sands Hotel). The Isla Verde hotels offer a variety of watersports, swimming and plenty of beach. A 25-minute taxi ride brings you to this long stretch of beach for $16.

A 15-20-minute taxi ride will cost $10 from the cruise ship terminals to the **Condado area**, which is lined with hotels, casinos and an inviting strip of beach. The major resort hotels offer a range of activities, including tennis, water sports, horseback riding and kayaking. Check the concierge desk at the Wyndham Old San Juan for activities and transportation to their beachfront hotel, the Wyndham El San Juan Resort. The beach here is similar to Miami Beach and is frequently crowded, but it's close to Old San Juan and convenient for cruise passengers.

Luquillo Beach is about one hour from Old San Juan and only 15 minutes from El Yunque National Forest. It boasts a "Sea Without Barriers" program with professional staff trained to assist visitors in wheelchairs so they can join their families for a dip in the ocean. This public beach recently finished a major government redevelopment program to provide lifeguards, ample parking and new changing and restrooms. Offshore reefs keep the waters calm. Food and souvenir stands are nearby in a parade of brightly-colored kiosks near the entrance to the beach. Combine a trip here with a rainforest experience in El Yunqe.

Island Activities

On Land

Golf

One of the most challenging golf courses in the Caribbean is the East Course at the **Hyatt Dorado Beach**, designed by Robert Trent Jones, with a par of 72. The hotel's West Course is a little shorter but also beautifully manicured and maintained. Greens fees and cart rental for a non-guest player are $175. The hotel is a 30-minute drive from Old San Juan off Route 22 to 693. A chartered taxi to the golf course and back should cost $40-$50 (chartered taxi rate is about $20 an hour). Arrange a price before leaving and try to split the cost with your golf partner. For reservations, ☎ (787) 796-8961.

Bahia Beach Plantation, a par-72 course designed by J. Burton Gold, has 75 acres of lakes and two miles of beach. The course features 13 water holes, including three beachfront holes that are considered to be among the most beautiful finishing holes in the world. Green fees and cart cost $80 for 18 holes, $55 for nine holes. The course is only 30 minutes from San Juan on route 187, Km. 4.2 in Rio Grande. For reservations, ☎ (787) 256-5600 or e-mail prgolfer@aol.com. Open daily 6:30 am to 7:30 pm.

Dorado Del Mar, designed by Chi Chi Rodriguez, is in Dorado, 30 minutes from San Juan. Fees are $85 on weekdays and $95 on weekends. ☎ (787) 796-3070; fax (787) 796-3060.

Tennis

The Carib Inn is the closest and easiest spot to knock a few balls around. Located near Condado, the inn has eight courts available for $10 per hour, plus $5 per hour for racket rentals. ☎ (787) 791-3535; fax (787) 791-0104.

The **Hyatt Dorado Beach** (☎ 787-796-8961) has seven tennis courts, and the **San Juan Marriott Resort & Casino** (☎ 787-722-7000) has two tennis courts and a health club. The **Condado Plaza**, ☎ (787)

721-1000, and the **Caribe Hilton,** ☎ (787) 721-0303, both offer tennis. The charge on most courts is $10 per hour.

San Juan's **Central Park**, located in the heart of the city, has 17 courts open to the public from 8 am to 10 pm. The fees are very reasonable. ☎ (787) 722-1646.

Horseback Riding

Many resort hotels offer horseback riding, but the best rides are out of town. Near Luquillo Beach rides into the El Yunque Rain Forest can be arranged through **Hacienda Carbali,** ☎ (787) 889-5820. Another exotic place to ride is west of San Juan (on Route 643 near the Hyatt resort). **Tropical Trail Rides** keep 25 paso fino horses, small local horses known for their spirited mincing gait. The stable offers a two-hour guided tour along the beach or into Alemendros Forest. Open daily from 9 am to 4 pm, they offer two rides per day. ☎ (787) 872-9256.

In The Ocean

Hotels along the Condado beaches provide concessions for renting water toys. Check with the concierge desk at the Wynham Old San Juan, across the street from the cruise ship docks, for transportation to their sister hotel in Condado or take a taxi ($16) for a day at the beach.

Kayaking

The latest water sport to hit Puerto Rico is kayaking, which is often combined with snorkeling. Contact the **Canoe and Kayak Federation,** ☎ (787) 755-4793 for recommendations on where to go, or book a tour through the concierge desk of any major resort hotel.

Caribe Kayak provides ocean, lagoon and river excursions in small tour groups, accommodating both beginners and advanced kayakers. They provide all the equipment (including snorkeling gear), lunch and beverages, and can pick you up in San Juan for an extra charge. Caribe Kayak also recommends a night tour from Las Croabas into the bioluminescent lagoon in the Cabezas de San Juan Nature Reserve, about 40 minutes from San Juan. Call ☎ (787) 889-7734 for prices and ask for Mark or Monica. Their website, www.pinacolada.net/caribekayak has pictures and a reservation form.

Blue Heron Kayak offers the most incredible kayak experience if you can manage to extend your stay after the cruise and visit the island of Vieques (take a $2 ferry for a one-hour trip from Fajardo or fly 10 minutes from Fajardo for $40 round-trip). The Bioluminescent Bay in Vieques claims to be the brightest in the world, with over 750,000 tiny dinoflagellates per gallon of water that light up when they are touched. Imagine a bay filled with glowing fairy dust! The experience is actually indescribable. Blue Heron Kayak offers an all-in-one kayak tour from 1 pm to 8:30 pm. Kayakers float through mangroves, snorkel in the ocean, and end with a bioluminescent tour of the Biobay at night. The tour includes dinner for $85 per person. A morning kayak tour from 10 am to 2:30 pm costs $65, including a picnic lunch. (Add a 15% Resource Tax to each tour price.) Visit www.elenas-vieques.com/mangrove.html to view pictures and get hotel recommendations. ☎ (787) 741-4574 or cell phone (787) 615-1625; kayakelena@hotmail.com.

Scuba Diving

The water near the coastline may be murky from runoff, making snorkeling or scuba diving poor. However, diving is excellent around the nearby islands of **Culebra** and **Vieques**. Many of the larger hotels have watersports centers that offer boat trips to both islands.

Sea Ventures Pro Dive Center offers a full day, two-tank dive trip daily for $95 per person to the Spanish Virgin Islands or snorkeling for $60. Their custom dive boat departs Puerto Del Rey Marina in Fajardo at 10 am and returns around 4 pm. The trip includes a buffet lunch, fresh fruits, snacks, unlimited refreshments and all dive or snorkeling gear. A two-tank morning dive and a two-tank afternoon dive are offered for $80 for diving, $60 for snorkeling, including all gear, snacks and beverages. Transportation is available from the San Juan area hotels for $20 per person, round-trip. ☎ (800) 739-3483; www.divepuertorico.com.

Caribe Aquatic Adventures at the San Juan Hotel offers a one-hour snorkel tour with basic equipment for $50 as well as a local reef dive with tanks and weights at 9:30 am, 11 am, 2:30 pm or 4 pm for $50. BC and regulator rental is available for $20. ☎ (787) 281-8858; fax (787) 723-6770.

Culebra Dive Shop offers a two-tank dive for $90, with all equipment, lunch and refreshments included. All-day snorkeling costs $45 and includes snorkeling gear, lunch and refreshments. Ferries are scheduled to Culebra several times a day from Fajardo. ☎ (787) 742-0566 or (787) 501-4656 (cell); fax (787) 742-1953.

One-Day Itineraries

San Juan is a unique port of call in the Caribbean because it is the beginning and end point of so many cruises. I have outlined two itineraries that might appeal to you.

Río Camuy Caves

If you arrive in Puerto Rico a day before your cruise, or plan to stay a day at the end of the cruise, consider taking a whole day to explore the outer areas of the island. A unique site is Río Camuy Cave Park, just 2½ hours west of San Juan. It is one of the largest cave systems and sinkholes in the Caribbean.

Río Camuy Cave Park is a 300-acre national park currently offering two attractions – **Clara Cave** and the **Tres Pueblos Sinkhole**. Both sites feature mammoth stalagmite and stalactite formations, with canyons and caverns reaching several hundred feet in diameter and depth. The park has plans to expand and develop its attractions to show the extensive cave systems below the ground. The Tres Pueblos Sinkhole offers views of the Camuy River, the third-largest underground river in the world. Plan to spend two hours exploring the park, one of Puerto Rico's most fascinating natural wonders. Don't forget a flash camera.

Entrance to the park is $10 for adults and $7 for children. The park is open Wednesday through Sunday, 8 am to 5 pm, but the last tour leaves the entrance at 3:45 pm. There's a snack bar and gift shop for food and souvenirs.

Guided Tours

Due to the difficulty in renting a car, driving the congested roads of San Juan and battling the detours from recent construction on the highways, we highly recommended that you take a guided tour with a local tour operator.

Tour operators begin their excursions quite early in order to visit the caves and Arecibo Observatory and get back to San Juan within six or seven hours. Contact them in advance to ensure a reservation.

Camuy Cave Tour Operators

Castillo Tours runs cave trips on Tuesday, Friday and Sunday. The fee of $70 per person, includes admission to the park. ☎ (787) 791-6195; www.castillotours.com.

Sunshine Tours has daily tours for $75 per person, plus entrance fees. Contact Richard Morales toll-free at ☎ (888) 786-3636; e-mail richsunshinepr1@hotmail.com; www.puerto-rico-sunshinetours.com.

Travel Services, Inc. offers private tours and VIP taxi services at $45 per hour. This is a first-class way to see the entire island. ☎ (787) 982-1200; fax (787) 982-1220; www.destinationpuertorico.com.

Puerto Rico Tours offers customized tours (about $65 per person with a four-person minimum) to suit your needs, including trips to the caves. If you want to avoid being herded along with a large group, visit the website (www.puertorico-tours.com) for ideas, then call George Lopez at ☎ (787) 306-1540 or e-mail him at letgeodo@coqui.net for a quote and reservation.

On Your Own

If you cannot arrange to take a guided tour or you want to travel independently, rent a car and follow the directions below (call the park to make reservations and receive updated directions, ☎ (787) 898-3100/756-5555):

Travel on the new expressway (22) toward Arecibo and take exit 78/Route 129 south to Km 18.9. Route 129 will take you directly to the main entrance at Rio Camuy (***Parque de las Cavernas del Rio Camuy*** in Spanish). The parking fee is $2 per person in the vehicle.

Arecibo Observatory

A trip to the caves would not be complete without a stop at the Arecibo Observatory, just 20 minutes from the cave park (and part of this one-day itinerary). A modern visitor center has been built to demonstrate how the colossal structure is used to study distant galaxies. This is a radio telescope that monitors emissions from quasars, pulsars and other cosmic sources. If the observatory is not included in your organized tour, ask the company to arrange a side-trip. The opportunity to visit one of the most fascinating man-made structures in the western hemisphere should not be missed. The observatory is open to visitors Wednesday through Friday, noon to 4 pm, and on Saturday and Sunday, 9 am to 4 pm. ☎ (787) 878-2612. The entry fee is $3.50 for adults and $1.50 for children and seniors with ID. Driving here on your own may be difficult. Country roads are not well maintained and hard-to-spot signs are in Spanish. Follow Route 129 back toward Arecibo and make a right onto Route 134. Another right onto Route 635 will lead you to Route 625, ending at the observatory. (See map on page 43 for directions.)

Allow 45 minutes at the world's largest radar/radio telescope. Hike to the viewing platform, a 600-ton suspended platform that hovers over a 20-acre dish set in a sinkhole 565 feet below. An educational center with an audio and visual presentation explains how scientists monitor radio emissions from distant galaxies, pulsars and mysterious quasars. Does the scene look familiar? Arecibo Observatory was featured in the James Bond movie *Goldeneye* and in *Contact*, starring Jodie Foster.

Extraterrestrial Research

Arecibo is also the home base for **SETI**, the Search for Extraterrestrial Intelligence. SETI has begun an intensive program of sending signals into outer space in an attempt to detect life.

El Yunque Rain Forest

If you can get a flight in and out of San Juan on the day your cruise ship arrives, you may only have four to six hours left to sightsee. I recommend taking a four-hour tour to **El Yunque National Forest** and **Luquillo Beach**.

You might prefer to spend two or three hours wandering along the historical streets of Old San Juan sightseeing or last-minute shopping. (Also see *Historical Walking Tour*, page 37.) San Juan offers a little something for everyone, no matter how much time you have. If the rain forest does not interest you but a day at Isla Verde beach does, take the walking tour first, then spend the rest of your time at the Sands Hotel enjoying the sand and sun.

An excursion to the El Yunque Rain Forest and Luquillo Beach is one of the most popular tour attractions. El Yunque rain forest is a 28,000-acre Caribbean National Forest and the only tropical rain forest in the US National Forest system. Luquillo Beach, only 15 minutes from El Yunque, offers miles of sand.

El Yunque has a lot to offer. The first stop at **Yokahú Tower** offers views of the nearby cities of Luquillo, Fajardo and, on a clear day, the isle of Culebra. Three possible hikes through the forest begin at the Palo Colorado Ranger Station, where you can pick up a map. Time for hiking is not usually scheduled on the organized tours, but if you're traveling on your own, make sure you take a trek through the rain forest. Also, be sure to stop at the new multi-million dollar El Portal interactive visitors center and watch the 15-minute video about the area.

The **Big Tree Trail** is an easy 45-minute hike to **La Mina Falls**, a refreshingly beautiful waterfall. The hike can also begin at the main Ranger Station just to the left off Route 191 at the beginning of the drive to El Yunque.

A one-hour walk along the **Mt. Britton Trail** takes you to the Mt. Britton Lookout Tower. It's a great hike if you have only a half-day to explore El Yunque. The route starts on the El Yunque Trail, then makes a left up to the tower.

If you're truly adventurous, consider making the effort to hike **El Yunque Trail** to the top of the mountain. It takes about two hours to complete, and is worth every minute. You can view the sites from El Yunque Lookout Tower and Los Picachos Lookout Tower, 15 minutes off the main trail to the right (20 minutes before El Yunque Tower). The hike to the top of the mountain provides the best views of the rain forest, flora and fauna, and the opportunity to be serenaded by the coquí, Puerto Rico's tiny tree frog.

Whether you choose to hike or not, be sure to allow time to drive through this unique rain forest.

Guided Tours

The following companies should be contacted ahead of time to ensure space availability. Most tours will spend up to an hour at each location.

You can also arrange a custom tour by calling the Rent a Ranger program in advance at ☎ (787) 887-2875. Admission to the park is $3 for adults and $1.50 for children and seniors. Closed during Christmas holidays.

El Yunque Tour Operators

Castillo Tours offers a bus excursion that stops at viewing points in the rainforest for $40 per person. ☎ (787) 791-6195; www.castillotours.com.

Puerto Rico Tours offers customized private trips with George Lopez. He has a combined tour of the rain forest and a stop at Luquillo Beach for $75 per person, with a minimum of two people. ☎ (787) 306-1540; letgeodo@coqui.net; www.puertorico-tours.com.

Sunshine Tours, ☎ (787) 791-4500, charges $43 per person for a 4½-hour tour, including a swim at Luquillo Beach. Visit them at www.puerto-rico-sunshinetours.com.

On Your Own

If you are renting a car, take Highway 26 toward Carolina (east) until you reach Road 3. Take Road 3 toward Fajardo for 20 minutes and make a right on Highway 191 to El Yunque National Forest. There are plenty of vendors with food for lunch at the beach. The park has restroom facilities and picnic tables, and is equipped for wheelchairs.

St. Thomas

The American Paradise

Island Description

During his second voyage in 1493, Columbus was so struck by the countless islands of exceptional beauty that he named them the Virgin Islands. The name derived from the legend of St. Ursula, the beautiful Christian daughter of a third-century King of Britain. Although pledged to lead a life of saintliness, a ruthless pagan prince demanded to marry Ursula. To save her father and his kingdom, Ursula agreed to the marriage on the condition that 11,000 of the most beautiful virgins in the two kingdoms be her companions for three years, at which time she would marry the prince. Ursula's plan was to lead an army of Amazon women who would pledge their allegiance to Rome and thereby gain support against the prince. Her army made the long journey to Rome, but the enraged prince ambushed the returning virgins with his own army and slaughtered them all in a great battle.

Bluebeard's Tower.

The early history of the US Virgin Islands was much the same as that of other Caribbean islands, embroiled in battles between Spanish, French and English until persistent Danish settlers took possession of St. Thomas and St. John. The Danes later purchased St. Croix from the French in 1733 and the group of islands remained under Danish military rule for 251 years.

Due to its splendid harbor near popular sailing routes, St. Thomas drew the unwanted attention of pirates, who plundered ships laden with golden treasure. Notorious privateers, such as Blackbeard and Captain Kidd, were real island inhabitants at various times. In an attempt to protect the harbor at Charlotte Amalie, a large chain was strung across its mouth and raised when needed to block the entry from attacking marauders. The chain supposedly kept Blackbeard out for a month before he breached the defense.

St. Thomas is a coral island, which means the waters and bays are surrounded by incredible coral reefs teeming with tropical fish. The white sand beaches are cool to the touch because the sand is composed of pulverized coral excreted by the abundant multicolored parrot fish. The turquoise blue water is a pleasant 70 to 85°, which makes watersports and scuba diving popular.

Today, tourists can visit the castles of Bluebeard and Blackbeard, each now part of hotel complexes. The castle's stone observation towers provide panoramic views of the island's capital, Charlotte Amalie, nestled against a shimmering harbor filled with white sails that will evoke fantasies of buccaneers and pirate treasure.

The United States, eager to establish a Caribbean foothold to secure protection for the Panama Canal, purchased the US Virgin Islands for $25 million in gold on March 31, 1917. The islanders assumed they would receive US citizenship immediately, but the US military continued to rule in the same manner as the Danes. When the military regime finally ended in 1936, the US Virgin Islanders were granted home rule and US citizenship.

About Nearby St. John

The Danish West India and Guinea Company took control of St. John in 1694 and the first plantation was established in Coral Bay. After 15 years, 101 plantation houses had been built to house 208 white settlers, who controlled 1,087 black slaves. The large number of slaves is not remarkable considering the history of the Caribbean as a whole.

A large number of slaves on St. John were originally from the African Amina tribe, who believed tilling the land was women's work and therefore humiliating. Slaves were forbidden at dances, feasts and plays, and a slave caught in town after curfew faced severe punishment. During the year of 1733, a hurricane, a drought and an invasion by insects worsened the situation by making food scarce. Plantation owners refused rations to the already half-starved slaves, who banded together in desperation to secure their freedom.

At dawn on Sunday, November 13, 1733, slaves entered Fort Berg at Coral Bay carrying bundles of wood as part of their usual routine. Once inside, the slaves whipped out cane knives hidden in the wood and killed all the soldiers except one, who hid under a bed. The victorious slaves fired a cannon as a prearranged signal to the other slaves on the island. The entire island fell into the hands of angry slaves who burnt the sugarcane fields and killed entire white families during their rampage.

Fearing a spread of the revolt, the British sent troops from Tortola and St. Kitts and the French sent two warships from Martinique to fight the slaves in the hills of St. John. The rebels lasted until mid-May when, realizing they were hopelessly outnumbered, they gathered for one last feast in a ravine near Annaberg. After the meal the slaves committed ritual suicide rather than return to a life they detested.

Trunk Bay, St. John.
(© Lynn Seldon, courtesy USVI Division of Tourism.)

Today, the island of St. John enjoys a peaceful small-town atmosphere, and more than 60% of the land is designated as a US national park. Tourism is being handled with a conservative approach by the locals, who are trying to retain their quiet community and to protect the natural beauty of the island, while still earning a living. The resorts are low key and the shopping areas are quaint, with little of the hustle and bustle found on St. Thomas. Repeat visitors to St. Thomas sometimes choose to enjoy the solitude of St. John during their time in port. (See *Self-Guided Tours*.)

Island People

The protected harbor at St. Thomas and its strategic location on the trade routes to the New World attracted a wide assortment of settlers. The social melting pot of the islands was similar to that of America, but the dominant contributors to island culture were African slaves imported to work the sugar plantations.

Islanders today are a gracious but cautious people who cherish their privacy. They may seem reserved, but their congenial nature reveals itself when visitors smile and are friendly. Their fun-loving disposition is most apparent during Carnival, with its calypso music, parades and the traditional symbol of Carnival, Mocko Jumbies. These dancing figures on 17-foot stilts are dressed in bright colors and covered in mirrors. The spirit is invisible, so when you look at a Mocko Jumbie, you see yourself in the mirrors, not the spirit. The roots of Carnival go back to African slaves arriving in the islands. Their dances, called *bamboulas*, were based on ritual worship of the gods of Dahomey. The ritual was channeled by Christian missionaries into Carnival, with parades, costumed bands, beauty pageants, music and dance.

As an unincorporated Territory of the United States, the US Virgin Islands sends a non-voting delegate to the US House of Representatives; its natives are US citizens, but they do not vote for the US President and Vice President. The ruling government is modeled after the US government, with three branches – Executive, Legislative and Judicial. The Governor is elected every four years, the 15 Senators are elected every two years and the taxes collected within the islands are kept for use by the local government.

Holidays

Locals love to celebrate and will close their shops on scheduled holidays. Some holidays are celebrated on the closest Friday or Monday. The shops in Havensight often try to stay open, but if shopping in St. Thomas is important to you, plan your cruise itinerary to avoid landing on a scheduled holiday.

The exact dates for any upcoming year can be found at www.gov.vi, under the Legal Holidays link.

Annual Holidays & Events

For more details and precise dates, contact the island tourist board (see *Appendix*).

January . . . . New Year's; Three Kings Day (for the three wise men who searched for the Christ child); Martin L. King, Jr. Birthday

February . . . . President's Day

March . . . . Transfer Day (transfer from Danish to US ownership); Holy Thursday (before Easter)

April . . . . Good Friday; Easter Sunday & Monday; Carnival, St. Thomas

May. . . . . Memorial Day

June. . . . . Organic Day (granting US Citizenship and home rule)

July . . . . Emancipation Day; US Independence Day; Carnival, St. John

September . . . . Labor Day

October. . . . . Columbus Day; Hurricane Thanksgiving Day (end of hurricane season)

November . . . . Veteran's Day; Thanksgiving Day

December . . . . Christmas Eve; Christmas Day; Boxing Day (26th); Old Year's Day

Useful Websites

The official US Virgin Island government site for tourism is **www.usvi.net**. It gives general information and links. On the home page, click on St. Thomas, then follow the menu.

Another helpful website is **www.st-thomas.com/week**, hosted by the *St. Thomas This Week* publication (available in a magazine format on shore). It provides detailed information about attractions, services, hotels and restaurants, including phone numbers and links to other websites. At **www.virginislandsmap.com** you can find great maps of each island, including detailed shopping maps of Charlotte Amalie, Havensight and Cruz Bay on St. John.

The Pier

The majority of cruise ships arriving in St. Thomas will dock at the West Indies Dock at **Havensight Pier**, a short taxi ride from Charlotte Amalie. Havensight can easily handle three to four ships at one time and the facilities have been designed for the comfort of cruise passengers. An entire shopping mall was built here so that cruisers can avoid the hassle of taxis and traffic. A directory is conveniently located at dockside and an information office is on the dockside end of Building One. Havensight Mall contains restaurants, a bank, a US postal van and a variety of shops. Some ships anchor offshore at Charlotte Amalie and offer tender service to take passengers ashore.

Pier Phones

The area code for St. Thomas is 340, a long-distance call from the US.

St. Thomas is a good place to make calls home by direct dialing to the mainland, using US long-distance cards or major credit cards. The service is excellent and the prices are more reasonable than on other islands. Telephones at Havensight are found in several spots: near docking area number 3; at the dockside end of Building Three; and on the street side of Building Four. If you are tendering into Charlotte Amalie, your nearest phones are next door to the Visitor's Bureau, left of Emancipation Park and along Main Street.

For information on using your cell phone in St. Thomas area, dial 6611. AT&T built a new state-of-the-art communication center across the street from Havensight, next to the Paradise Point Tramway. It offers 15 desk booths for calls, fax and copy services, videophone and TDD (hearing impaired) equipment. Look for the white building with the blue logo.

Havensight Pier Shopping Mall & Vicinity

As St. Thomas is given extra duty-free exemption by the US Customs (see page 24), many shoppers prefer to do the bulk of shopping here. Havensight is the largest and most modern shopping center in the islands. Generally, the mall shops remain open on holidays and many downtown stores such as Colombian Emeralds, Little Switzerland, Diamonds International, A.H. Riise, Cardow Jewelers, Bool- chands and H. Stern Jewelers have branches here. There are ATM machines, a pharmacy, photo developing, bookstore, music store, post office, dentist and doctors' offices, too. Note that you can ship gifts home from St. Thomas, but be sure that the shipping charge does not exceed the 5% duty you might pay. In the mall, stores of note are **Beverly's**, which offers handmade clothing, T-shirts, gold jewelry and chains by the inch, and **The Draughting Shaft**, which sells great cards, gift wrap and art.

The English Shop offers the largest selection of dinnerware in the Caribbean. It is one of St. Thomas' oldest and most reliable importers, and carries the finest designer names in china and figurines. This store also accepts direct factory orders on all of the listed suppliers at duty-free prices 30%-50% less than Stateside. ☎ (800) 524-2013, toll-free, to order.

Port of $ale is the newest and most colorful shopping destination on St. Thomas, featuring a variety of festive shops right on the cruise-ship dock at Havensight. A unique collection of outlet, discount, off-price and specialty Caribbean retailing, Port of $ale takes St. Thomas' reputation for value shopping to new heights.

Pusser's Closeout Store, across the street from Havensight Mall, features discontinued first quality Pusser's Co. Store merchandise at tremendous savings (see *A.H. Riise Mall*).

An outlet of **Bernard K. Passman** is now located at Havensight Mall. This internationally known sculptor offers fantastic black coral and gold jewelry, including reproductions of famous Passman original sculptures. (See *Specialty Stores*, page 75.)

Water World Outfitters has been described by *Skin Diver Magazine* as "the best stocked dive shop in the Caribbean." The shop is also the starting location for **Underwater Safaris** diving operation's scheduled boat diving excursions. (See *Diving*.)

You can schedule a trip on the nearby ***Atlantis* Submarine** (see *Organized Tours*). The sub's store contains high-quality fish sculptures (not easily found on other islands), ocean-oriented gifts, books and videos and *Atlantis* Submarine T-shirts.

The newest attraction on St. Thomas is the **Paradise Point Tramway**, across the street from the Havensight Mall Dock on Long Bay Road. Here, modern cable cars (similar to a ski lift) depart regularly on a spectacular seven-minute ride, landing 700 feet above sea level on a hill overlooking Havensight. The round-trip price is $15 for adults and $7.50 for children. Reservations are not necessary.

The tramway is probably the best place on St. Thomas to capture a photo of your cruise ship with the island as a backdrop, so don't forget your camera. At the top of the tram ride are tropical bird shows, interesting shops, a café and a bar offering tasty frozen concoctions. The highlights of the trip – other than incredible views – are the live parrots. Free bird shows are scheduled at 10:30 am and 1:30 pm. Between shows you can have pictures taken with the colorful performers. The various retail shops stock souvenirs, batik clothing, artwork, antique coin jewelry, replica firearms and plenty of painted wooden parrots!

Charlotte Amalie Pier Area

If your ship doesn't dock at Havensight, you'll come ashore by tender to the waterfront near the center of Charlotte Amalie. A short walk to the right (with the ocean to your right) leads to Emancipation Park and Vendor's Plaza. But this town has more to offer than shopping, and many of the historically important buildings in Charlotte Amalie have been well preserved or recently restored. (See *Historic Walking Tour*, below.)

In Town

Currency

The official currency of St. Thomas and St. John is the US dollar. A Barclays Bank is at the street-side end of Building Four in the Havensight Mall and other banks are found along Charlotte Amalie's waterfront. Vendors and shopkeepers take traveler's checks and credit cards, but you should carry small denominations of cash for taxi drivers.

Postage

The US Virgin Islands and Puerto Rico are the only islands in the Caribbean chain where Americans can use US postage stamps to mail items home. The postal regulations and rates are the same as those in the continental United States and all first-class mail travels by air. The main post office is near Emancipation Gardens, and there's also a US postal van at Havensight Mall.

Historical Walking Tour

It will take about an hour to walk through the historic streets of Charlotte Amalie, ending near the town's most popular shopping malls. The malls are shaded, cobblestone alleyways meandering between the major streets, where the charming shops will tempt even the most jaded shoppers. (Letters refer to city map on page 69.)

Start at **Vendor's Plaza (A)**, an area near Emancipation Gardens in which all the street vendors set up shop. If you're a seasoned visitor, you may recall the chaos once caused by street vendors, who put their tables in shop doorways, adding to the already congested walkways. Vendor's Plaza was a brilliant idea, which creates a pleasant open-air bazaar under colorful umbrellas. Take a few minutes to browse through the booths, check the merchandise and the prices. You will end your walking tour in this area, so you can buy then.

Enter the brick red building, **Fort Christian (C),** to the right of Vendor's Plaza. Its entrance is on the side, facing the water. Fort Christian was constructed in about 1672 and once housed St. Thomas' entire colony. Designated a national historic site, the fort has been restored to its original appearance when under Danish rule. Further restoration work is underway with new exhibits planned. There's no entrance fee. A gift shop near the entrance sells handmade items, reprints of old pictures and historical books, plus island souvenirs.

The fort's main level contains the old dungeons, which exhibit museum-quality antique furniture from Europe, as well as large wicker baskets once used by women to carry coal on their heads, old maps and individual histories. Be sure to see the pictures of Transfer Day, when the Danes sold the island to the US in 1917. Imagine how the islanders felt; they had been deserted by the government they knew and traded to a country with little comprehension of their culture or problems.

Climb the steps to the second story for a good view of the waterfront, Vendor's Plaza and downtown. Notice the lime-green building across the street to the left. The 118-year-old **Legislature Building (D)** was once the Danish police barracks, but today it is the meeting place of the US Virgin Islands 15-member Senate. The building is open weekdays, 8 am to 5 pm.

Turn left out of the fort and walk through **Emancipation Park (B)**, which was named to commemorate the freeing of the slaves back on July 3, 1848. The governor at the time, Peter Von Scholten, was influenced by his black mistress, Anne Elizabeth Heegaard, to abolish slavery before 1859 when the Danish government mandated the abandonment of slavery. No doubt the slave revolt on St. John (see *St. John,* page 61) also influenced his decision.

Emancipation Park is a good drop-off reference for taxi drivers and a popular place to meet friends. The park contains a concert pavilion, a bust of King Christian V and a replica of the American Liberty Bell.

The **Visitor's Bureau (E)** sits opposite Fort Christian in a cream-colored building on Tolbod Gade. Visitors are free to use the adjacent hospitality lounge with restrooms, a luggage/package checking service, telephones and up-to-date literature about the island.

Little Switzerland, to the right of the Visitor's Bureau on Tolbod Gade, occupies the former **Danish Customs House**.

Walking away from the waterfront on Tolbod Gade, notice the yellow building on your left, the **Emancipation Garden Station Post Office (F).** The property contains two murals – a waterfront scene and a fortress vista – painted in 1941 by Steven Dohanos, who was subsequently a *Saturday Evening Post* illustrator.

To the right, across Tolbod Gade and opposite the waterfront, is the **Grand Hotel (G)**, a Greek Revival-design structure finished in 1840. Notice the second-story pillared porticos overlooking the park. The structure was originally built with three stories, but it lost the third floor during a hurricane. Inside, you'll find the Old Danish Warehouse, where you can buy gifts, T-shirts, pink coral, larimar and shell jewelry at reasonable prices (you return to this area at the end of the walking tour). Larimar is a semiprecious stone that comes from coral limestone deposits. It is a very light-blue turquoise with white matrix swirls.

Cross the street, Norre Gade, and turn to the right. The yellow building on your left is currently called **Bethania Hall (H)**. The house was built in 1827 as a posh residence for Jacob Lind. It was subsequently used as a post office, a home for the elderly, a school and now it is the parish house for the church next door.

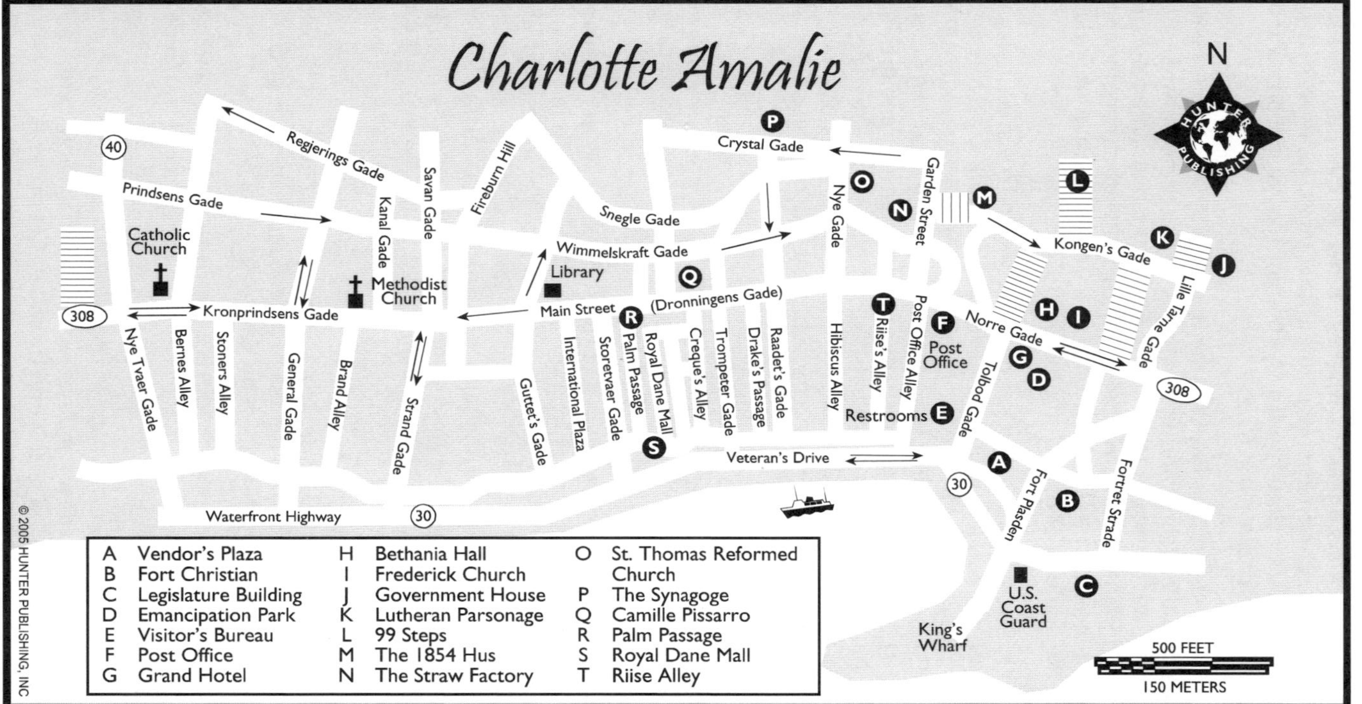
Charlotte Amalie
N
HUNTER PUBLISHING
40
Regjerings Gade
Prindsens Gade
Catholic Church
308
Kronprindsens Gade
Nye Tvaer Gade
Bernes Alley
Stoners Alley
General Gade
Brand Alley
Kanal Gade
Savan Gade
Methodist Church
Strand Gade
Fireburn Hill
Snegle Gade
Wimmelskraft Gade
Library
Main Street
(Dronningens Gade)
Guttet's Gade
International Plaza
Storetvaer Gade
Palm Passage
Royal Dane Mall
Creque's Alley
Trompeter Gade
Drake's Passage
Raadet's Gade
Hibiscus Alley
Crystal Gade
Nye Gade
Garden Street
Riise's Alley
Post Office Alley
Post Office
Restrooms
Veteran's Drive
Waterfront Highway
30
Norre Gade
Tolbod Gade
Kongen's Gade
Lille Tarne Gade
Fort Plasden
Fortret Strade
U.S. Coast Guard
King's Wharf
500 FEET
150 METERS
A Vendor's Plaza
B Fort Christian
C Legislature Building
D Emancipation Park
E Visitor's Bureau
F Post Office
G Grand Hotel
H Bethania Hall
I Frederick Church
J Government House
K Lutheran Parsonage
L 99 Steps
M The 1854 Hus
N The Straw Factory
O St. Thomas Reformed Church
P The Synagoge
Q Camille Pissarro
R Palm Passage
S Royal Dane Mall
T Riise Alley
© 2005 HUNTER PUBLISHING, INC

ST. THOMAS

The **Frederick Evangelical Lutheran Church (I)** is home to the second-oldest Lutheran congregation in the world, founded in 1666 when the first Danes arrived in St. Thomas. The original building on the site was dedicated in 1793.

During its history Charlotte Amalie has been besieged by catastrophes and the Frederick Church was hit by the same disasters. The building was gutted by a fire in 1826. It was rebuilt and destroyed again, this time by a hurricane in 1870. The steadfast congregation rebuilt the church as it stands today, in a Gothic Revival style, including the addition of gables and the bell tower.

Turn left (uphill) at the next narrow driveway and make your way to the top of the stairs to Kongens Gade (King's Street). Cross the street to the **Government House (J)**, with its red carpeted front steps. The first floor contains offices and three murals – one depicting Columbus' arrival, another the Danish transfer of the territory and the third a sugar plantation. The murals were painted by artist Pepino Mangravatti in the 1930s. The second floor has a ballroom with a balcony, while the third is reserved as the living quarters for the incumbent governor.

The neoclassic-style building was constructed between 1865 and 1867 to replace a building dating from 1819. Go inside the lobby to see the murals in the entry. A guided tour can be arranged by calling in advance, ☎ (787) 774-0001.

Leave the Government House and turn right, passing the **Lutheran Parsonage (K)** on your right. The Parsonage has been in use since 1725. Walk straight on Kongens Gade and pass the steep stairs, also on the right. Although named the **99 Steps (L),** there are actually 103. The next house on the right is **The 1854 Hus (M)**. Originally a residence, the building now contains a restaurant, offices and shops. Below The 1854 Hus is a pink building with steps leading down to Garden Street.

Across the street is a good place to buy a soda and take a shopping break at **The Straw Factory (N)**, a store selling straw hats, baskets, ornaments, carved wood items and other Caribbean-made gifts. You are just one block uphill from the Main Street Post Office.

Turn uphill (walking away from the water) on Garden Street and then left onto the first street, Crystal Gade. On the corner of Nye Gade is the **St. Thomas Reformed Church (O)**, built in 1846 with massive front columns in the Greek Revival architectural style.

Stay on Crystal Gade for another block and a half. On the right is the synagogue, **B'racha V'shalom Ug'milut Chasidim (P)** (meaning

Blessing, Peace and Loving Deeds). It's now called St. Thomas Synagogue. This building is an example of an early construction technique used on St. Thomas, where the bricks were made using molasses as a mixing agent. Inside, the floor is covered with sand as a reminder of the time Israelites spent in Egypt as slaves and were forced to worship in secret. They met in cellars and placed sand on the floor to muffle the sounds of their prayers. This is the third-oldest synagogue in the Western Hemisphere. The building was completed in 1833. The congregation was formed in 1796 and celebrated its bicentennial in 1996.

Walk back down Crystal Gade and turn right on the first street, Raadets Gade. Within two short blocks you'll return to Main Street. Turn right and walk a block and a half to the **Camille Pissarro Building (Q)**, on the uphill side of the street. This was the home and birthplace of Camille Pissarro (1831-1903), the father of French Impressionist painting. In the passageway leading to an inner courtyard is a description of the artist's early life in St. Thomas and his later fame in Paris.

St. Thomas Harbor.
(© Don Hebert, USVI Division of Tourism.)

Cross the street and turn left down **Palm Passage (R),** painted entirely in pink. This begins the shopping part of the walking tour. If you've done all your shopping and want to return to the ship, walk through Palm Passage to the waterfront and catch a taxi or take a tender boat back to the cruise ship.

Shopping

Charlotte Amalie

The alleyways and courtyards radiating from Main Street contain the most enticing and interesting shops in St. Thomas, but the majority of jewelry and watch stores are on **Main Street** (Dronnigens Gade). Barkers are paid to stand on Main Street and draw the attention of passing tourists to the stores they represent. These barkers are unique to St. Thomas and create their own type of carnival atmosphere, but if you do not wish to heed their call, simply walk on or give them a firm, "Not interested."

> TIP: You can stretch your duty-free allotment by buying items (including jewelry) that are actually made on St. Thomas and St. John and, therefore, entirely free of duty.

The Pampered Pirate on Main Street offers local pottery and condiments. The **Blue Carib Gems** in Bakery Square on Back Street is owned by Alan O'Hara, who cuts, polishes and creates his own jewelry settings. **Caribbean Safari**, located one block west on Back Street, carries West Indian crafts, hats, handbags, totes, dolls, masks and resort wear. **Down Island Traders** on the waterfront stocks Caribbean seasonings, hot sauces, jellies, coffee, herb tea, local pottery and jewelry.

The **Native Arts and Crafts Cooperative**, located next to the Visitors Bureau, markets all island-made goods, including ceramics, dolls, straw hats, wall hangings, honey and preserves.

The following describes some of the most intriguing shops and pleasant malls that sell locally made items:

Palm Passage

Palm Passage (R) is the most famous of St. Thomas' historic shopping malls. It is a lovely shaded courtyard painted pink and lined with exclusive designer-style shops. You may wish to linger here, but should not expect to bargain in the shops.

☆ **Pierre's** is this writer's favorite jewelry store on the island. Pierre's makes its own jewelry on the premises and carries only top-quality gemstones. Ask to see some of their original designs. You can also create custom designs with expert assistance from the staff and have them shipped home.

Janine's Designer Fashions offers top European names with savings of up to 24% on Louis Feraud of Paris, Valentino, Pierre Cardin, Y.S.L., Dior and other designers. European clothes are expensive, even with the discount, but those who know the labels will appreciate the savings.

Club Ryno Island Apparel and Accessories stocks casual, elegant, distinctive clothing by top designers for men and women, and a selection of fine cigars.

Enjoy lunch or a drink at the **Courtyard Café**. If you must buy a souvenir for a collector at the **Hard Rock Café** or the **Harley Davidson** store, turn right and walk a short distance to the entrance of International Plaza. If you do not wish to fight the crowd, simply turn left when exiting Palm Passage and enter the historic Royal Dane Mall.

Royal Dane Mall

The Royal Dane Mall (S) consists of three old-world passageways where you can meander and shop in shade and comfort. This mall is one of the oldest shopping areas on St. Thomas. Walking down the passageways is like stepping back in time.

Carson Co. Antiques offers museum-quality treasures from ancient civilizations. Items include charts of the China Sea, shards of Taino Indian pottery and unique Christmas ornaments.

SOS Antiques sells historical photographs, cannonballs, rare coins, vintage charts and authentic artifacts and antiques that are sure to intrigue.

Tropical Memories sells handmade Caribbean crafts and artwork. This store also carries nature's finest jewels, elegant illusions, manufactured gems and other jewelry.

Rio Cigars satisfies cigar and tobacco connoisseurs with an extensive selection of tobacco products. Avoid buying Cuban cigars (or be sure to smoke them before going through US Customs!).

Royal Dane Mall houses several boutiques. **Going Seanile** is a bouncy concept boutique carrying sought-after designer eyeglasses, swimwear, sportswear and sandals. **Just Add Water Too** sells seductive swimwear, and **Boutique Rendezvous** sells everything from linen suits to casual attire and accessories. **Java Wraps** offers island sportswear at its best; the designs are appealing and reasonably priced.

Gladys Café serves authentic Creole cuisine in a Danish colonial (but air conditioned) setting aglow with 18th-century architecture.

Riise Gift & Liquor Mall

After leaving the Royal Dane Mall, turn right on Main Street, walk three blocks and look for the Riise Mall (pronounced Rice) on the right. If you have only a short time for shopping and prefer to enjoy nature, play golf or take a specialized tour, this is the one mall we recommend you visit. Its historic setting, elegant shops and wide selection of merchandise in air-conditioned comfort is the best St. Thomas has to offer.

The Riise Mall began as a short walkway, but it has expanded to occupy a series of beautifully restored Danish warehouses stretching from Main Street to the waterfront. Make time to stroll through one of Charlotte Amalie's most picturesque passages with walls of aged stone and brick. **Tiffany, Gucci** and **Colombian Emeralds** can be found in this mall, along with the following shops that offer quality merchandise:

A.H. Riise Gifts has been in St. Thomas since 1838, making it the oldest duty-free gift and liquor store on the island. Riise carries almost everything: jewelry, liquor, perfume, cosmetics, crystal, art, watches, Icelandic woolens and furs (with satisfaction guaranteed).

Pusser's Company Store is renowned for its nautical shorts, tropical woven cotton shirts, floral print sarongs, linen and cotton blouses and tropical T-shirts for men and women. The clothing is custom-designed in the West Indies and produced to exact specifications. The store also carries nautical Swiss sport watches and chronographs, canvas totes and many unique gift items.

Davante, an unusual eye-wear collection, is a must-see. Choose from over 2,000 frames on display, from designers such as Cartier, Montblanc, Versace and more, all at duty-free prices. Prescriptions can be filled on all eyeglasses.

Down Island Traders carries specialty gifts made in the Caribbean and the Virgin Islands. The authentic Caribbean market features an array of spices, teas, coffees, seasonings, candies, jellies, jams, hot sauces and condiments. This lively, colorful store has reasonably-priced, quality gifts in fun, tropical packaging, local cookbooks, exclusively designed T-shirts, silk-screened bags, Haitian metal sculptures, handmade jewelry, Caribbean folk art and children's gifts.

Café Amici is located nearby on Main Street. This delightful alfresco restaurant may tempt you to stop for lunch or a cool beverage.

Specialty Stores

If you are looking for a particular item, try on of these unique shops:

Leather Goods can be found at **The Leather Shop**, on Main Street across from Riise Mall and at Havensight Mall. **Purses and Things**, in International Plaza, and **Coach Boutiques**, 34 Main Street, carry high fashion leather items.

Cameras & electronic equipment are available at **Boolchands**, on Main Street near Trompeter Gade and at the Havensight Mall.

☆ **Bernard K. Passman**, 38 Main Street, is an internationally known artist who has sculpted black coral and gold pieces for the White House, the British royal family and museums. The gallery contains reproductions of Passman's original sculptures as well as black coral and gold jewelry for sale. A visit to Passman's gallery is like visiting a fine art museum. Marvel at the skill, craftsmanship and creativity of this artist and take home a bit of black and gold.

Mr. Tablecloth, Inc., carries more than tablecloths and linens. Great prices are offered on lace and hand-appliqued dresses or aprons. On Main Street, near Raadets Gade.

Fabric in Motion, Storevataer Gade, carries Italian linens, batik fabrics, ribbons and silky cottons.

Larimar jewelry is unique to the Caribbean. It's quite beautiful, but not well known. Look for larimar in small jewelry stores, at Mountain Top Mall and The Old Danish Warehouse in the Grand Hotel at Post Office Square (#7 on the Historic Walking Tour) and at **Captain's Corner**, across from H. Stern on Main Street.

Tanzanite is available at **Tanzanite International**, located downtown on Main Street. This radiant blue-purple gemstone was discovered in East Africa in 1967. The store also carries a very impressive selection of unset diamonds in all sizes. (Unset stones are not added to the US Customs duty allotment.) The friendly staff provides the time and information it takes to make you a diamond expert!

Outside Charlotte Amalie

If you plan to explore either St. Thomas or St. John, you can shop duty-free at any of the following places.

☆ **Mountain Top Mall** is a destination mall with 28 shops to tempt you. It boasts the best location on St. Thomas to photograph the island of St. John and Magen's Bay. Enjoy a famous banana daiquiri at the restaurant/bar while snapping photos to amaze friends at home.

St. John

Many cruisers who have visited St. Thomas previously, or those who are jaded by crowded streets and barkers, choose to spend the day on St. John. A rural atmosphere still exists on St. John (pronounced Sin-JUN by locals) and their handmade sinjun baskets are highly prized. Pick up a free copy of *The St. John Guidebook* at the Tourist Information Center, a short walk along the water to the left of the cruise dock. It has an island map and articles that reveal the sinjun sense of humor.

The **Wharfside Village** sits at the water's edge to the right as you come off the ferry dock. This tropical mall is a collection of 30 fine shops, a food market, a bar and a restaurant. **Verace Design Jewelry** offers unique designer jewelry, including a collection of titanium jewelry. You can view pictures of their designer collections at www.verace.com.

Downtown Cruz Bay, just one block from the ferry dock, is a small town Caribbean-style, with chickens running away from mongooses and neighbors stopping their car in the middle of the street to chat or offer someone a ride. Almost everything in Cruz Bay is a short walk from the ferry dock. The key here is to take your time and enjoy the slow pace. Shops on St. John are usually owner-operated by artists who fell in love with the island and stayed. Since locally made items are not added to your duty allotment, shop freely and support the local community.

Pink Papaya features original artwork, household and gift items designed by Lisa Etre, plus quality merchandise by other local artists. Lisa's unique household artwork includes trays, teapots, lampshades, dishes, bath items and more – all decorated in island designs. Pink Papaya is in the Lemon Tree Mall, on the same street as Stitches II (make a right turn rather than a left at the corner).

Pusser's Company Store (see *A.H. Riise Mall*, above) is the place to purchase nautical sportswear, accessories, memorabilia and rum in fancy bottles. This store offers a better-than-average selection of T-shirts.

Mongoose Junction is a short walk from the ferry dock at Cruz Bay. The Danish-style stone building houses a collection of charming studio shops where artists work on site and display their wares. To visit Mongoose Junction before walking into town, turn left from the ferry along the waterfront. Follow the curve of the water (stop at the Tourist Information Center for a free copy of *The St. John Guidebook*) and keep to your left as you pass the post office. Within a few minutes you should reach the inviting arcade. (When finished shopping here, follow the road back and go straight past the post office to visit the shops described in the downtown Cruz Bay section.)

Mongoose Junction is the location of **Colombian Emeralds** and the **Island Galleria,** where great deals can be found on jewelry, watches, china, crystal and collectibles. Unique shops in Mongoose Junction include the following. **R & I Patton Goldsmithing** offers real treasure for sale as well as many unique designs. Gold and silver treasure coins are crafted into jewelry. **The Canvas Factory** contains rugged canvas luggage, bags, hats and island clothing handcrafted on the premises. **Batik Kitab** offers work by artist Juliana Aradi, who creates batiks that capture the colors of the islands on silk, cotton, linen and paper. **MAPes MONDe Ltd**. sells fine reproductions of historic Caribbean maps, etchings, quality prints and note cards. **Donald Schnell Ceramic Studio** displays original ceramic designs, pottery and gifts.

The Mighty Mongoose

Mongoose Junction was for the mighty mongoose, a weasel-like creature. The *St. John Handbook* features drawings of the mongoose with a comical sneer on his face. Mongooses (not mongeese) were imported from India to the Caribbean to combat the snake and rodent population. The idea was successful in reducing the number of snakes, but the nocturnal rats often escaped the attention of the day-feeding mongooses. Watch the brush for a fleeting glance of the lightning-fast mongoose.

Transportation & Excursions

Taxis

Ships docking at Havensight Mall draw a line of taxis. Drivers wait to fill their vehicles (usually large American-made vans) before heading out from the pier area. They'll take you anywhere you want to go – to town, beaches or on a sightseeing tour. Rates are set by the Taxi Commission and approved by the Virgin Islands Legislature. Call ☎ (340) 774-3130 for rates and to register complaints.

Ships arriving at Crown Bay will also find taxis awaiting their arrival. Fewer ships dock here, so the rates we give throughout this chapter assume a starting point of downtown Charlotte Amalie. A taxi from Crown Bay into town will run $4 per person. Prices are in US dollars.

Taxi Chart

Destination from downtown	**Cost** (two people)
Bluebeard's Castle	$6
Coki Beach/Coral World	$14
Havensight Mall/Cruise Dock	$8
Magen's Bay	$12
Mahogany Run Golf & Tennis Resort	$14
Mountain Top	$14
Yacht Haven Marina	$6
Red Hook	$16
Secret Harbour	$12
Sapphire Beach Club	$12

Taxis can be found almost everywhere on the island, at the most popular attractions and major hotels. If you can't find one, call the VI Dispatch at ☎ (340) 774-7457 and they will send a taxi to your location. You should arrange discounted round-trip fares at the beginning of the trip. A two-hour tour in a standard-sized sedan costs about $35 per couple, and a four-hour tour costs $70 per couple. The fare reduces proportionately if more people share a larger van or safari-style vehicle.

Most taxi drivers are great sightseeing guides. Take advantage of their knowledge and ask questions. The drivers love to tell you all they can about St. Thomas. Tipping drivers for a quick ride into town is not necessary; however, for island excursions, or for specially arranged pick-ups, a 10% tip is recommended.

Look for a dome light on taxis and the letters TP on a taxi license plate. Other taxis are not licensed and the taxi commission rates do not apply.

Local Buses

St. Thomas has the **Safari Bus Service**, open-air buses that provide public transportation. The regular routes are between downtown Charlotte Amalie and the Red Hook ferry dock, passing by Havensight Mall. The fare is $2, payable to the driver when leaving the bus. The buses are also used as sightseeing transportation, so if one does not stop when flagged down it may already be booked for a tour.

Rental Cars

Driving is on the left, and most rental cars are American made with the steering wheel on the left. This makes life more difficult for American drivers. The roads on St. Thomas are not hard to navigate, but they were designed for smaller vehicles, not the industrial-sized vans the taxi drivers use. If you're brave enough to attempt negotiating the sharp bends, remember to honk before entering a curve and be constantly aware of other cars!

The basic price for a four-wheel-drive jeep or small automatic is $50-$90 per day. The minimum age for renting a car is 25. A valid driver's license is required and a credit card is needed for a security deposit. Collision insurance is necessary to protect you in the event of accidents on the winding roads.

A long-distance call from the US can secure a rental car in advance, but most agencies will have vehicles available in busy St. Thomas.

Car Rental Agencies

The area code for St. Thomas is 340, a long-distance call from the US.

Avis . . . . ☎ (800) 228-0668 or 774-1468 www.avis.com

Budget (Havensight Mall) . . . . ☎ (800) 626-4516 or 776-5774, www.budgetstt.com

Hertz Rent A Car. . . . ☎ (800) 654-3131, www.hertz.com

Discount Car Rentals. . . . . ☎ (877) 478-2833 (offers free pick up and delivery) info@discountcar.vi

L&L Jeep Rental (St. John). . . . . ☎ 776-1120 www.bookajeep.com

Self-Guided Tours

Coral World

Coral World Underwater Observatory and Marine Park was destroyed several years ago by a major hurricane, but we are happy to announce the park is now completely rebuilt and improved. Coral World, just 15 minutes from Charlotte Amalie, is a five-acre park next to Coki Beach (an excellent place to snorkel or scuba dive).

One of the highlights of the park is the **Caribbean Reef Encounter**, an 80,000-gallon donut-shaped tank that allows 365° viewing from inside the circular room. The eight-foot-high glass walls are exposed to the sun, air and rain at the top to re-create a natural reef atmosphere, complete with exotic tropical fish, lobsters and stingrays. The park recently installed a wheelchair lift to enable handicapped tourists to experience the wonders of the Caribbean Reef Encounter. It transports wheelchair-bound travelers safely above the steps to the center of the exhibit. Walkways and ramps at the park allow wheelchair access to Palm Court, Shark Shallows and the Touch Pool exhibits, interactive areas with staff available to explain about the animals.

SEA TREKKING' & SNUBA

Sea Trekkin' and SNUBA are both offered at Coral World. SNUBA divers use a light harness, fins and mask with air hoses directly attached to the mask; the hose leads to an air tank that floats on the water's surface. Sea Trekkers use a dive helmet that's tethered to a raft at the surface for air. Even first-time divers safely experience the thrill of descending to a maximum of 20 feet underwater for a 30- or 40-minute dive session. Divers at Coral World are allowed to feed the fish that always show up for a handout. The cost of Sea Trekkin' is $68/adult and $59/child age 8-12, and can be scheduled at www.coralworld.com. SNUBA costs $59/adult and $57/child under 12. ☎ (340) 693-8063 or fill out an e-mail reservation at www.visnuba.com. Book well ahead for either of these popular attractions. Costs include an entrance pass ($18) to Coral World. SNUBA is also available on St. John when visiting the Virgin Islands National Park.

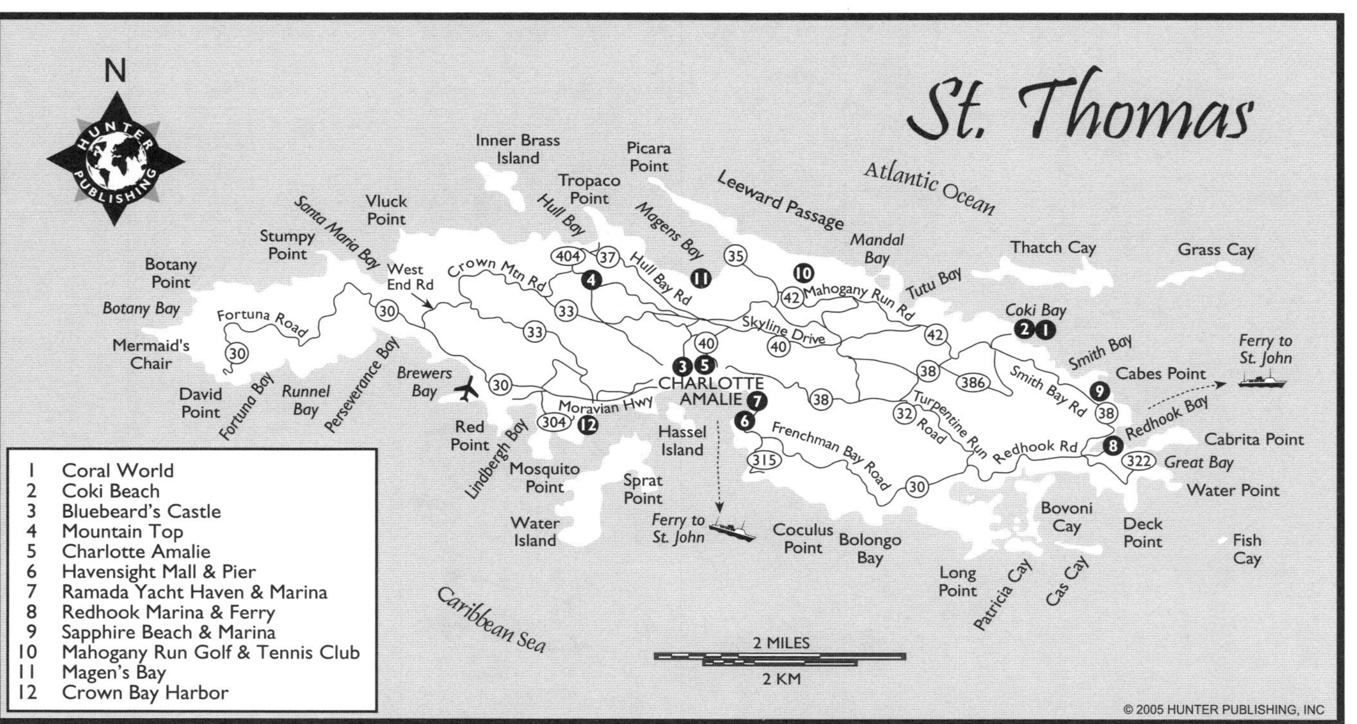
St. Thomas
N
HUNTER PUBLISHING
Atlantic Ocean
Caribbean Sea
Leeward Passage
Inner Brass Island
Picara Point
Tropaco Point
Hull Bay
Magens Bay
Mandal Bay
Tutu Bay
Thatch Cay
Grass Cay
Coki Bay
Smith Bay
Cabes Point
Redhook Bay
Ferry to St. John
Cabrita Point
Great Bay
Water Point
Fish Cay
Deck Point
Bovoni Cay
Cas Cay
Patricia Cay
Long Point
Bolongo Bay
Coculus Point
Hassel Island
Sprat Point
Mosquito Point
Water Island
Lindbergh Bay
Red Point
Brewers Bay
Perseverance Bay
Runnel Bay
Fortuna Bay
David Point
Mermaid's Chair
Botany Bay
Botany Point
Stumpy Point
Santa Maria Bay
Vluck Point
West End Rd
Fortuna Road
Crown Mtn Rd
Hull Bay Rd
Moravian Hwy
Skyline Drive
Mahogany Run Rd
Smith Bay Rd
Redhook Rd
Turpentine Run Road
Frenchman Bay Road
CHARLOTTE AMALIE
2 MILES
2 KM
© 2005 HUNTER PUBLISHING, INC
1 Coral World
2 Coki Beach
3 Bluebeard's Castle
4 Mountain Top
5 Charlotte Amalie
6 Havensight Mall & Pier
7 Ramada Yacht Haven & Marina
8 Redhook Marina & Ferry
9 Sapphire Beach & Marina
10 Mahogany Run Golf & Tennis Club
11 Magen's Bay
12 Crown Bay Harbor

The unique **Underwater Observatory** on the edge of the park extends 20 feet below the sea, affording live ocean views. Several times a day, a scuba diver feeds the marine creatures in their natural environment while you watch.

To learn more about the park visit the Coral World website at www.coralworldvi.com. The park is open daily from 9 am to 5 pm and entrance fees are $18 for adults and $9 for children (three-12 years old). A family pass (covering two adults and up to four children) is available for $52. If you plan to spend time at **Coki Beach**, rent a locker for $3 per day (with a refundable security deposit). Snorkel equipment and underwater cameras are offered for rent at the Coki Dive shop, and taxis are always available for rides back to town or to other island attractions.

Sea trekkin is a great experience for non-divers.
(© Steve Simonson, courtesy Coral World.)

Day-Trip to St. John

The island of St. John is worth exploring for its beaches, private coves and US national park. Only a short ferry ride from St. Thomas, this unspoiled wonderland has excellent snorkeling reefs and white sandy beaches. **Cruz Bay**, the ferry docking town, has a seaside shopping area specializing in island crafts and unique Caribbean items. Mongoose Junction and Wharfside Village are two areas offering unusual shops (see *Shopping*, page 76).

On St. John, stop at the Visitor's Center, open from 8 am to 4:30 pm, for information about the **Virgin Islands National Park** (www.virgin.islands.national-park.com). The park encompasses more than two-thirds of the island and provides a variety of walks and tours for everyone. Inquire about the daily tours, which we've listed below.

- The **Annaberg Plantation** has cultural demonstrations three times a week between 9 am and noon. A taxi ride takes 15 minutes to cross the island and runs $12.50 per person.
- A historic island tour is conducted three times per week by a park ranger for $14 per person.
- A glass-bottom boat trip led by a park ranger runs three mornings a week. It takes about 1½ hours and costs $20 for adults, $10 for children.

If you prefer to spend the whole day at one of St. John's beaches and snorkeling reefs, consider the following suggestions.

The **Friends of the US Virgin Islands National Park** offers seminars and snorkeling tours on a regular schedule. Visit their website at www.friendsvinp.org and contact them directly (by e-mail only) to schedule an event during your visit.

Trunk Bay (entrance fee, $4 per person), is the island's most popular beach with good reason. The wide sandy shore is surrounded by green-blue waters, with an underwater snorkeling trail designed by the National Park Service. There's food,

St. John offers many bays for exploration.
(© Lynn Seldon, courtesy USVI Tourism Dept.)

bathrooms and showers. You can rent snorkeling equipment on the beach for $15 per set. A 15-minute taxi ride out here will cost approximately $8 for two people or $3.50 each for three or more people traveling tog- ether in a group.

Once a week a park ranger leads a 1½-hour tour of the snorkeling trail at Trunk Bay. This is a vigorous swim, and is not recommended for beginners or people with medical problems. Bring your own snorkeling gear, a towel and a T-shirt. The tour is free, although you will still pay the entrance fee of $4. ☎ (340) 776-6201 for schedule information.

Snorkeling tours via motorboat leave from the Cruz Bay Visitor's Center at 9:30 am, Tuesday through Saturday, aboard m/v ***Sadie Sea***. Be sure to bring your own snorkel gear, towel, food and drinks. The Wednesday tour ($50 per person) is a six-hour jaunt that circumnavigates St. John, with three snorkeling stops. Shorter tours on Tuesday, Thursday, Friday and Saturday last 2½ hours and cost $35 per person. Call ☎ (340) 776-6922 to make reservations, and be sure to catch the 9 am ferry from Charlotte Amalie to St. John ($14 roundtrip; see St. John under *Self-Guided Tours*) to allow sufficient time.

SNUBA is also available to visitors at the Virgin Islands National Park from the same company that operates the Coral World's SNUBA. Visitors are not allowed to feed the fish on this trip, but the coral formations are more beautiful. Both experiences are unique. SNUBA activities take place on a nice reef on the West End between Jumbie Beach and Trunk Bay Beach, not on the labeled snorkel trail. Orientation and a guided SNUBA trip take 1½ hours. Allow additional time to snorkel on the park trail. For SNUBA reservations, ☎ (340) 693-8063, visit the website, www.visnuba.com, or e-mail info@visnuba.com. The cost to SNUBA on St. John is $57 per person (children must be a minimum of eight years old).

Cinnamon Bay beach sits next to a campground with facilities that include a restaurant, grocery store, watersports center (you can rent equipment here) and restrooms with showers. The rocks and coral just offshore make this an excellent environment for snorkeling when the waters are calm. A hiking trail to an old plantation and a nature trail are just a short walk from the sand. A taxi ride here will take no more than 15 minutes, costing $8 for two or $3.50 each for three or more people in your group.

Caneel Bay/Honeymoon Beach are five minutes from Cruz Bay and offer one of the nicest places to spend the entire day. Caneel Bay, one of the world's premiere resorts, permits use of the beach off the main lobby, while the other six beaches along the property are reserved for hotel guests. A walk through the beautiful grounds will entice you to come back and stay for a week. Honeymoon Beach is an easy walk to the left of Caneel Bay and it offers undisturbed coral reefs – great for snorkeling. Charter boats from St. Thomas anchor off the beach, so the waters can be crowded for an hour or two, but not the entire day. Both beach areas are worth visiting. Watersports equipment is available for rent from the Caneel Bay Resort. A taxi ride costs $8 for two people. Caneel has its own water transport from Charlotte Amalie. ☎ (340) 776-6111 for pricing and schedule.

The ferry to St. John leaves the waterfront in Charlotte Amalie every two hours from 9 am to 3 pm, then one ferry leaves at 4 pm and the last ferry of the day leaves at 5:30 pm. The returning ferries leave Cruz Bay every two hours from 7:15 am until 1:15 pm, then one ferry leaves at 2:15 pm and the last ferry leaves at 3:45 pm. The 45-minute trip costs $7 one-way for adults or children. The ferry leaves from Red Hook every hour from 8 am until midnight and the return ferries from Cruz Bay leave every hour from 6 am until 10 pm. The 20-minute trip costs $3 one-way for adults and $1 for children under 12. Call ☎ (340) 776-6282 for more information. A 20-minute taxi ride to Red Hook from downtown Charlotte Amalie or Havensight costs $16 per couple, and you should allow for extra time during morning rush hour.

Two car ferries operate between Red Hook and Cruz Bay for $40 round-trip. Call **Boyson** at ☎ (340) 776-6294 or **Republic** at ☎ (340) 779-4000.

A private water-taxi service can be booked by calling ☎ (340) 775-6501.

ST. THOMAS

Island Tours by Taxi

Two tours are available around the island through the local **V.I. taxi association**. As you leave the ship, just ask one of the many willing taxi drivers if they will conduct an island tour. Most will agree, but they may wait to fill their van with other sightseers.

- **#1** is a two-hour trip to Mountain Top Shopping Mall, Drake's Seat, Blackbeard's Castle and Bluebeard's Castle. The cost for two people is $30, or $12 per person with three or more passengers.
- **#2** is similar to #1, but it lasts three hours and covers more of the island. The cost for two people is $40, or $20 per person with three or more passengers.

Blackbeard's Hill

Blackbeard's Hill is a residential district with two small restaurants and a hotel complex surrounding Blackbeard's Castle, a stone tower built in 1679. The tower, named Skytborg, was reputedly used as a lookout by Captain Edward Teach, the British pirate Blackbeard, from 1716 until he was killed in 1718. The tower was originally built by a man naned Charles Bogaert, and was apparently a source of annoyance to Governor Iverson because it was higher than the fort. Today, the tower has been incorporated into a hotel/pool area with breathtaking views. **The Mark**, next door, is a Danish-style residence of ballast brick and local stone with ornate ironwork trim built in the late 1700s and listed on the National Register of Historic Homes. A taxi to the castle from downtown Charlotte Amalie or Havensight Pier will run $4 per person. To save a few dollars, try hiking up the famous 99 Steps to reach Blackbeard's Castle from town, but remember that the Caribbean heat and humidity can make it a struggle.

Organized Tours & Activities

Submarine Adventures

***Atlantis* Submarine** offers a unique experience in the Caribbean. The submarine dives to a depth of 150 feet, where you spend an hour viewing colorful coral and the abundant sea life in this air-conditioned submarine. A 20-minute ferry ride takes you to the sub at the Buck Island National Wildlife Preserve dive site. After you board the sub and dive, you'll be able to watch a scuba diver feed hundreds of fish right in front of your window.

Reservations for the *Atlantis* Submarine can be at ☎ (800) 253-0493. The *Atlantis* Submarine office is in Building Six of the Havensight Mall (look for the sign in front). If your cruise ship does not offer a scheduled submarine tour, check in the office for space availability . The cost for the dive beneath the sea is $84 for adults, $42 for children; children must be a minimum of 36" high. There are seven dives scheduled daily between 9 am and 3 pm and you should arrive 15 minutes before the hour for a special orientation.

Atlantis also has a submarine tour in Barbados. If you're scheduled to visit both islands, take the submarine dive in Barbados, which is more dramatic and includes a visit to a shipwreck.

Atlantis Submarines has expanded its tour business and now offers high-speed jet rides aboard the ***Screamin' Eagle*** for $39/adults and $35/children (a height minimum of 48 inches is required due to restraint size). The company also schedules various trips to St. John, nature hikes and eco-tours with snorkeling. Most of their tours are sold through the shore excursion office of your cruise ship. Visit www.atlantisadventures.com and click on "St. Thomas" for more information and to reserve submarine/jet boat trips on your own.

Day Sails

Several yachts offer private day sails. To take a peek preview of the three yachts listed below, go to www.st-thomas.com, click on "Attractions," then on the boat name under "Day Sails" heading. Each trip includes a gourmet lunch, snorkeling, floats and open bar (bloody Mary's and rum punch) in the price. All can be booked through st-thomas.com.

- ***Fantasy*** requires a four-person minimum. The full-day trip ($120/adults, $110/children under age 12) sails from the American Yacht Harbor in Red Hook at 9:30 am and returns at 4 pm. The half-day trip ($90 per person) lasts three hours and includes one snorkel stop on St. John. ☎ (340) 775-5652, www.daysailfantasy.com.
- ***Nightwind*** offers a full day's sail at $110 for adults and $85 for children under 12. The yacht normally carries 10-12 passengers, but is rated to carry 18 passengers. *Nightwind* leaves at 9 am and returns at 4 pm to Sapphire Marina near Red Hook. ☎ (340) 775-4110, 775-0377; info@beachtops.com; www.sailyachtnightwind.com.

New Horizons, a 64-foot sailboat, offers daily trips around St. Thomas and St. John from 9:30 am to 4 pm. The cost is $110 for adults, $55 for children under age 12, including an alfresco lunch, snorkel gear and instruction. Their sunset cruise is $55 for adults, $27.50 children, and the dinner cruise is $85 for adults and $42.50 for children. New Horizons is located at Sapphire Beach. Children under age two ride free on all their cruises. To see pictures of this beautiful yacht, visit www.newhorizons.daysails.com, ☎ (800) 808-7604, (340) 775-1171 for reservations, or e-mail newhorizons@st-thomas.com. Mention viewing the website to get a 10% discount.

Beaches

BEACH CHART	Facilities	Windsurfing	Snorkeling	Scuba Diving	Wave Runners	Swimming	Parasailing	Sailing	Water Skiing	Nude/Topless
Magen's Bay	☆	☆		☆		☆				
Sapphire Beach	☆	☆	☆	☆		☆	☆	☆		
Coki Beach	☆		☆	☆		☆		☆		
Secret Harbour	☆		☆	☆		☆	☆			

Magen's Bay, named for a lady who lived at the tip of this crescent peninsula, has been called one of the most beautiful beaches in the world by *National Geographic* magazine, and you might be inclined to agree. The heart-shaped mile-long beach is perfect for sailing, swimming and sunbathing. There's plenty of room for large families, as well as picnic tables for lunches. Facilities include lockers ($3/day), bathrooms, a snack bar, boutiques and a beachside bar. A taxi ride takes approximately 20 minutes from downtown and will cost just $6.50 per couple. Entry to the beach park is 50¢ per adult, 25¢ for children and $1 for vehicles.

To the right side of the beach are sailboats, including some catamarans, that can be rented for $30 an hour, paddle cats and Sunfish ($20 an hour) and sailboards ($15 an hour). A deposit equivalent to an hour's rental is required. Magen's Bay is one of the most popular beaches on the island, so try to arrive early and secure your spot for the day.

Sapphire Beach Resort & Marina is the place to come for watersports, diving and sailing excursions. If you're a sports enthusiast, jump in a cab for the 15-minute ride ($12 per couple) to the beach of your dreams. Located at the east end of the island, the beach has views of St. John and the British Virgin Islands. The resort offers restroom facilities, a volleyball court and a restaurant serving lunch, beachside. Visitors are limited in their use of the hotel and the pool is reserved for hotel guests only.

Coki Beach, at the northeast end of the island, has some of the best reef snorkeling on St. Thomas (see *Island Activities,* below). Coki Beach Dive Club offers dives for beginners with no experience, but who want to enjoy the pleasures of the open water. There are changing areas (no showers) and a concession stand for snacks and refreshments. Coki Beach is only a 15-minute taxi ride ($14 per couple) from downtown.

Secret Harbour Beach Resort and Villas is the island's newest water resort. It's near Red Hook, a 15-minute ride from the dock ($12 per couple). Situated on a calm lagoon, the resort offers beach activities, four tennis courts, a freshwater pool with Jacuzzi, a café for breakfast, lunch and dinner at seaside, a beach bar, a gift shop and Aqua Action PADI Dive Center (see *Diving*).

Island Activities

On Land

Golf

Golfers of any skill level will fall in love with the **Mahogany Run Golf & Tennis Resort**. Situated on the northern coastline, this beautiful course rises and drops like a roller coaster. The ultimate challenge holes – #13, #14 and #15 – are called the Devils Triangle, and if you manage to play them without a penalty stroke you'll be rewarded a Devils Triangle Certificate. Rates vary through the seasons, but are about $100 for 18 holes (including cart rental); nine-holes run $65. Clubs can be rented for $30 (18 holes) or $15 (nine holes). Call to reserve your tee time, ☎ (800) 253-7103, (340) 777-6006, or fax your requests to (340) 777-6280. Take a look before you leave home at www.mahoganyrungolf.com, and be sure to ask about special packages for cruise ship passengers at a price that includes transportation. Although the golf course normally reserves tee times no earlier than 48 hours in advance, they offer cruise ship passengers the opportunity to reserve a tee time if they call the Friday before their ship's departure date.

Tennis

Mahogany Run Golf & Tennis Resort (☎ 800) 253-7103 has two courts that cost $10 an hour. Play a round of golf and a set of tennis at one of the most naturally beautiful settings on the island. In addition, **Sapphire Beach Resort** has four courts available through the Guest Service Desk for $10 per hour. Call ahead to arrange times and court space. ☎ (340) 775-6100.

Marriott Frenchman's Reef has two courts at $10 per hour. ☎ (340) 776-8500, ext. 6818, for reservations. **Renaissance Grand Beach Resort** has six courts at $8 per hour. ☎ (340) 775-1510, ext. 7800.

On St. John, **Caneel Bay Plantation,** ☎ (340) 776-6111, ext. 234, has 11 courts and charges $10 per person per day for use of all outdoor facilities. **The Westin Hotel,** ☎ (340) 693-8000, has six courts and charges $15 per hour.

In The Ocean

Windsurfing

Locals say that the best place for windsurfing is **Vessup Bay**, across from Red Hook. There are consistent winds, quiet waters and some big waves on **Pillsbury Sound**. Check with **West Indies Windsurfing** in Vessup Bay at ☎ (340) 775-6530 for board rentals. Expect to pay between $25 and $40 per hour, depending on gear, with discounts for half-day rentals.

Parasailing

Caribbean Parasailing offers rides from most hotels along the Charlotte Amalie waterfront, at Sapphire Beach and Secret Harbour near Red Hook, and the cruise ship dock, costing from $50-$65 per ride. Get a discount by reserving with Caribbean Parasail directly at ☎ (340) 775-9360 or (608) 848-8781. Mention the website (www.viwatersports.com) to get the discount, or place your reservation online.

On St. John, the **Westin Hotel** offers parasailing at prices similar to their competitor's standard fees.

Parasailing is also available at **Coki Beach** near Coral World.

Sailing/Power Boats

Secret Harbour Beach Resort and Villas, the newest water resort in St. Thomas, is near Red Hook and offers all manner of ocean-related activities. There's scuba diving (see Aqua Action under *Diving*), sea kayaks, paddleboat rentals ($10 per half-hour; $15 per hour), ocean vu (a motorized board with steering for $20/half-hour and $30/hour), and snorkel gear and float rental ($7.50/half-day and $10/full day). ☎ (888) 775-6285 (toll-free), (340) 775-6285 (local); www.aadivers.com; e-mail AquaAction@islands.com.

Scuba Diving

Diving is the best watersport on St. Thomas. The crystal-clear waters allow you to see a hundred feet, and the warm water is a real pleasure. If you've never seen staghorn coral, brain coral, angelfish, stingrays, green turtles or colorful parrotfish, take the opportunity to immerse yourself in the undersea world of the Virgin Islands here on St. Thomas. Many reasonably priced dive operators are eager to serve, and the following are all PADI and/or NAUI approved operations.

Coki Beach Dive Club offers the lowest prices for diving. They run a snorkel Guided Certified Reef Tour for $30 and a one-tank dive for $40, plus $20 for the second dive for certified divers. For visitors with no experience, they offer a Resort Course & Reef Tour for $60, plus $40 for second dive optional. All dives include equipment and tank rentals are available for $10 for certified divers with their own equipment. A new program, which takes kids to a maximum depth of six feet, is open to children over eight. Two children are assigned per instructor (special arrangements can be made for a parent to dive along) at the cost of $40 per child, including all equipment. Coki Beach is only a short swim from a coral reef loaded with fish hungry for attention. ☎ (340) 775-4220 or (800) 474-2654; www.cokidive.com. Coki takes walk-ins, but they offer free one-way transportation leaving at 8:30 am from the cruise ship dock, so it saves $14 per couple if you call ahead. Underwater camera rentals and a full dive shop are available for your convenience.

Chris Sawyer Diving Center offers daily underwater excursions. A one-tank dive costs $60 and a two-tank dive is $85. The two-tank dive leaves at 9:30 am, and the one-tank dive leaves at 2 pm and returns by 4 pm, in time for cruise ship sailing. Call toll-free ☎ (877) 929-3483 or e-mail sawyerdive@islands.vi.

St. Thomas Diving Club also runs daily dive trips. A two-tank dive costs $70, with an additional $15 for BC and regulator rental. A 10% service charge is added to all diving fees. They will hold your place with a 24-hour advance reservation at ☎ (877) 538-8734 or by e-mail Bill2381@viaccess.net. The dive center is located in the Bolongo Bay Beach Club.

Aqua Action, at the Secret Harbour Beach Resort near Red Hook, offers a one-tank boat dive (leaving at 1:30pm) for $50, and a two-tank boat dive (leaving at 8:30 am) for $70. Prices include use of equipment. To get here by taxi costs $12 per couple. ☎ (888) 775-6285 (toll-free), (340) 775-6285; www.aadivers.com; e-mail aquaaction@islands.vi.

Underwater Safaris, at Water World Outfitters in the Havensight Mall, offers daily snorkeling and diving tours. If you don't have dive experience, take the Introductory Scuba Safari for $69, in which expert instructors will guide you through the fundamentals of scuba diving. Certified divers can opt in on a one-tank dive for $59 or a two-tank dive for $89. Dive trips run from 8:30 am to noon and 1 pm to 5 pm. All safaris include full scuba equipment and snorkeling gear. Call ahead to arrange dive trips, ☎ (340) 775-3737; fax (340) 775-8738; uws@diveusvi.com; www.diveusvi.com.

One-Day Itinerary

Our suggested day-trip takes you to the two most popular attractions on St. Thomas, one of the most beautiful beaches in the world and allows time for duty-free shopping. Due to the congested roads and traffic, taxis are preferable. Schedule six to seven hours to follow the itinerary.

The sites, driving time from one location to the next and the taxi fares listed below are per person for each segment. It is not necessary to arrange for one taxi for the entire trip, but if you prefer one driver the fare should be approximately $35 per person. If you pay for each leg separately, it will cost a little more. Do not have the driver wait, but specify a time for him to come back. The following estimated taxi rates are point-to-point based on distance.

Coral World (15 mins.). . . $14 (plus entry $18 per person)
Bluebeard's Castle $10
Mountain Top $7
Charlotte Amalie $14

What to Bring

Bring or wear your bathing suit for time at the beach and snorkeling. If you have snorkel equipment, take it along; otherwise, the equipment costs $15 per set to rent at Coral World. A towel and waterproof sunscreen are also necessities. There are locker facilities at Coral World, so you should be comfortable bringing a camera to capture the fantastic views. Underwater cameras are available for rent at the dive shop on Coki Beach.

Refer to the island map for numbers corresponding with the suggested sites described.

An Island Tour

Begin your journey at 9 am with a taxi ride to **Coral World** (also see *Self-Guided Tours, Coral World*, page 80). Don't miss the Caribbean Reef Encounter and the Underwater Observatory. In our opinion, these are the best marine-life exhibits in the Caribbean. Allow two hours for exploring the park.

Change into your bathing suit and store your valuables in a locker ($3 charge). Upon leaving the park, arrange for a re-entry pass and head to the beach. **Coki Beach** is just steps away from Coral World and is the perfect place to spend time soaking up the sun, snorkeling the nearby reef, trying SNUBA and Sea Trekkin' (see page 80) or scuba diving. You can rent snorkel equipment at the Coki Beach Dive Club. Their beach shop offers fins, mask and vest for $15. It also runs guided snorkeling tours, including all equipment, for $25, and a full schedule of scuba diving for kids, beginners and certified divers (see *Ocean Sports/Diving*, page 91). Allow for two or three hours for swimming, snorkeling or relaxing on a beautiful white sand beach.

Call a taxi and head out to **Mountain Top Shopping Mall**, a shopping plaza featuring island craft stores. Here, a balcony overlooks the north side of the island with excellent views of Magen's Bay, the island of St. John and the British Virgin Islands. Order one of their famous banana daiquiris at the bar here, spend an hour shopping and taking pictures, then take a taxi back to downtown Charlotte Amalie.

It should be approximately 3:30 pm as you return, so the traffic into downtown Charlotte Amalie may be heavy. But within 20 minutes you will be in the most popular duty-free shopping port in the entire Caribbean. Ask the taxi driver to drop you off at Emancipation Gardens at the far left side of town (facing the waterfront). Walk up to Main Street to begin your shopping spree (see page 72). You'll find merchants are more eager to bargain when the crowds have diminished in the afternoon. Depending upon your ship's departure time, you may wish to spend a few hours wandering through the historic malls and arcades radiating off Main Street or take the Historical Walking Tour (page 67).

Sint Maarten/ Saint Martin

The Dutch/French Island

Island Description

The Carib Indians called the island Soualiga, the land of salt, which was an appropriate title. Although ship's records of the second voyage of Columbus indicate that he did not pass close enough to actually see the island, it was renamed by Columbus to honor Saint Marten of Tours. The Dutch spell the name Sint Maarten and the French spell it Saint Martin.

Although the Spanish claimed the island, they were too involved with more lucrative discoveries in the New World to establish a settlement. In the 1620s the island attracted the attention of the Dutch, who needed salt for their herring industry and for meat preservation. They settled and began to harvest the abundant salt ponds. The strategic location attracted other European countries striving to establish a foothold in the New World. A series of skirmishes between the Spanish, French, English and Dutch caused the island to change hands 16 times.

The 1648 Treaty of Concordia was the foundation for the current dual occupancy of the small island. The treaty split the island between the French and the Dutch and established unrestricted access to both sides for both parties. Legend says that a Frenchman and a Dutchman decided the territory by a walking contest. Each man departed from his respective capital city in the morning and the amount of the land walked by evening determined how much territory would belong to each country. In reality, the French claimed the largest portion of the island due to the intimidating presence of the French navy in the vicinity. The majority of inviting beaches are found on the French side, while the Dutch side contains the largest salt ponds, gambling facilities and most of the renowned duty-free shopping areas.

The 37-square-mile island is geologically part of the **Anguilla Bank**, a limestone coral reef in the outer arc of the Eastern Caribbean Islands. The island was formed 35 million years ago when geological movement pushed the reef above sea level. The irregular coastline, with its lush green hills, clear emerald waters and white sand beaches, creates the perfect setting for a tropical paradise that claims 300 sunny days per year.

Island People

The peaceful coexistence of two diverse cultures for over 300 years, with roots tying them to many different countries of the world, has produced a cosmopolitan society with a reputation for warm hospitality. The Dutch salt trade made way for other lucrative commerce as the Caribbean began to produce rum, sugar, bananas and other crops. Aware that Sint Maarten's small size, lack of fresh water and poor coral soil would make crop plantations unprofitable, the industrious Dutch abolished all import and export taxes in 1939 and became the hub of trade in the Caribbean. A truly duty-free port, where even the locals buy goods at duty-free prices, Sint Maarten attracts tourists and buyers from other Caribbean islands as well as foreign countries.

Carnival dancer.
(Image courtesy St. Martin Tourist Board.)

As the salt industry dwindled, tourism has become the island's main source of income and merchants here offer quality merchandise and friendly service. The Dutch coined the phrase "The Friendly Island" to describe their gregarious people and hospitable nature. The motto appears on their license plates and promotional literature and is noticeable in the attitude of the Dutch people.

In general, the French have a reputation for brusque behavior toward tourists and each other. On French St. Martin, merchants and tour operators have encouraged locals to improve their attitude toward visitors. If treated with genuine respect, the French will respond with a warm smile and helpful demeanor.

Holidays

The island celebrates most holidays, and the majority of the shops remain open Sundays and holidays when cruise ships are in port.

Annual Holidays

For more details and precise dates, contact the island tourist board (see *Appendix*).

January . . . . New Year's Day

April . . . . Good Friday; Easter Monday; Queen's Birthday (Dutch)

May . . . . Labor Day; Ascension Thursday (French); Whit Monday or Pentecost

November . . . . Sint Maarten Day

December . . Kingdom Day (Dutch); Christmas; Boxing Day

Useful Websites

The official government website for Dutch Sint Maarten **www.st-maarten.com**. It has good information about the island's history, geography and culture, as well as a lengthy list of links to businesses by category. Another general site, **www.stmartinst-maarten.com**, has maps, descriptions of attractions and more links to local businesses, including car rentals agencies. More business links are available at **www.sxmtravelguide.com**.

The best on-line resource we found for French St. Martin is **www.frenchcaribbean.com**. This site has good activities information – it lists names, phone numbers and prices of tours. You'll also find information here about other French islands.

The Pier

Large cruise ships sailing into Sint Maarten dock on the Dutch side of the island at Philipsburg, the capital. Smaller cruise lines that can maneuver their ships into the harbor of Marigot may choose to dock on the French side. Throughout this chapter, Philipsburg will be used as a starting point for excursions and activities.

Cruise ships docking at A.C. Wathey Pier, located at Point Blanche, are one mile southwest of Philipsburg. Ships may also anchor in the mouth of the harbor, tendering passengers to Little Pier (directly downtown) or to Bobby's Marina (just east of Philipsburg). Tendering (transportation of ship passengers by the use of smaller boats) can take time, so make the trips count and be aware of the extra time needed to return to your ship.

The **A.C. Wathey Pier** has expanded to accommodate up to four cruise ships along a concrete causeway. The new dock was officially opened in January of 2001, but ships began docking in December of 2000. The new facilities provide telephones, tourist information and a parking area for taxis and tour buses. The dock is an easy one-mile walk (20 minutes) to downtown Philipsburg. A new and safer (less traffic) walkway along the bay is in the works. if you arrive by tender into Little Pier, a short wooden structure, browse the covered walkway where locals display souvenirs. A short walk along the pier leads you directly to Front Street, the heart of Philipsburg's commercial center. Bobby's Marina – the other tendering drop-off point – has a general store and a few restaurants. Philipsburg is an easy 10-minute stroll along Front Street, just to the left of the marina.

Pier Phones

Whether you dock at A.C. Wathey Pier or tender into Little Pier or Bobby's Marina, there are few public phones available. The **AT&T USA Direct** number from Sint Maarten is ☎ (800) 872-2881, which will put you in touch with an AT&T operator in the States. The AT&T Direct number from the French side is 0800 99 0011. You can then use an AT&T credit card, or call collect. Public phones are available at Bobby's Marina and there are also two phones on either side of Little Pier. Calling from a major hotel by using a calling card may be more comfortable, but remember that a call from St. Maarten to the US is an overseas call with prices to match.

When phoning the Dutch side of Sint Maarten from the US, dial (011) 599, plus the seven-digit number. When calling the French side, dial

(590) 590, plus the six-digit phone number. Calls from the US to the islands are international and charged as such.

Calls made from the island are very expensive. If you own a wireless phone, contact your provider before leaving the US and arrange to use your own phone from this island. The additional cost will be lower than ship-to-shore or regular long-distance fees.

Arts & Crafts On The Pier

Local merchants sell handmade crafts and island T-shirts in downtown Philipsburg and on the pier at Point Blanche. After a day of shopping in both Philipsburg and Marigot, think of these crafts as last-minute souvenirs. Bargain with the various merchants, but understand the items are only souvenirs, not valuable commodities.

In Town

Passengers docking at A.C. Wathey Pier can travel to downtown Philipsburg by taxi ($3 per person), or by walking one mile (20 minutes). If you choose to walk, be cautious of speeding taxis. Remain on the road leading away from the pier with your left shoulder to the ocean, until the road gradually turns left onto Front Street. In another few minutes, you will be in the center of downtown Philipsburg.

Currency

The currency used by the Dutch is the **Netherlands Antilles guilder**, which has an exchange rate of 1.82 guilders to US $1. All merchants, restaurants and taxis accept US currency, traveler's checks and credit cards on both sides of the island. The N.A. guilder is strictly used by the Dutch locals and visitors are often given change in US currency. Banks are open 8 am to 1 pm, Monday through Thursday, and on Fridays from 4 pm to 5 pm for money exchange only. There are several banks on Back Street and in the general area near the government buildings. Start at Front Street and Little Pier and walk away from the ocean down one of the side streets toward the government buildings. Emergency cash is also available from casinos along Front Street.

On the French side of the island, the **euro** is the official currency. One US dollar is worth about 1.25 euros. Banks in Marigot are located on Rue de la République, a short walk from the marina parking lot.

Postage

Stamps in St. Maarten are more expensive than US stamps and, whether you use French or Dutch stamps, the letters can be mailed only on-island. Keep in mind that you have left the States and the US Postal Service. US stamps are not accepted here.

The Dutch post office is near the government buildings on the corner of Camille Richardson Road and St. Jansteeg. It keeps irregular hours. Stamps for postcards cost about 80¢. The post office accepts US currency, but gives change in guilders. Stamp collectors should ask at the regular window to see collectible stamps available for purchase.

The French post office is on Rue de Général de Gaulle in Marigot and sells postcard stamps for 85¢. Collectors may be disappointed, as there are no special island issues.

Casinos

While the casino on the cruise ship is closed, St. Maarten offers six casinos connected with the larger Dutch hotels and two casinos on Front Street, conveniently located near the shops and restaurants. Truly adventurous visitors should learn to play Caribbean Poker, a game native to the islands.

Museums & Historical Sites

Due to its relatively peaceful history, St. Maarten is not replete with interesting historical sites. **Fort St. Louis**, perched on a hill at 1,500 feet overlooking Marigot, is the most exciting ruin on the island. It was built in 1776 to protect the French population from British attacks. To reach the fort, take a cab to the Sous-Préfecture parking lot (visible from town and easy to find) and climb a few flights of stairs to the ruins. Although the fort has not been restored, photographers are drawn by the superb panoramic views of Baie de la Potence, Anguilla and Marigot harbor and town.

The **Philipsburg Historical Museum**, 119 Front Street, was built in the West Indian gingerbread style in 1888. Indian artifacts, pictures, china and antiques are exhibited in one room, while an adjacent room offers reproductions of maps and old pictures for sale. The museum is part of the **Museum Arcade**, consisting of specialty shops designed to reflect the West Indian culture. The museum is open 9 am to 4 pm, Monday through Friday, 9 am to noon on Saturday, and is closed on Sunday. Donation requested.

The **Marigot Museum** has moved to a new building on the road to Sandy Ground. Pre-Columbian dog figurines have recently been discovered here by archaeologists. Excavations that began in 1987 on the Hope Estate near the airport in Grand Case have uncovered evidence that dogs were an essential part of the Arawaks culture. Ceramic dog figurines have been carbon dated to as far back as 550 BC and early chronicles suggest the Arawaks believed dogs were a link between the living and the dead. Burial sites have been found containing human and dog skeletons side-by-side. The charming air-conditioned museum displays pre-Colombian treasures from the Hope Estate, a reproduction of a 1,500-year-old burial mound discovered in 1994, artifacts dating back as far as 1800 BC, and some beautifully adorned ceramics from around 550 BC. Open daily.

Shopping

Best Buys in Philipsburg

Downtown Philipsburg is a long strip of land between the ocean harbor and the Great Salt Pond. **Front Street** runs adjacent to the harbor and the majority of stores offering gold jewelry, gem stones, watches, linens, cameras and electronics are here. Gold jewelry is one of the best buys in the Caribbean and the low prices and extensive selection offered in Philipsburg cannot be matched. Many stores carry similar gold chains, jewelry and watches, so be sure to shop around.

Comparison shopping along Front Street and adjoining alleyways can take two to three hours, but be sure to explore the *steegijes*, pronounced STAKE-yas (Dutch for alleyways), to find the most unusual items. Although it is difficult to get lost, you might want to pick up a copy of *St. Maarten Events*, which has a fold-out map of shops and the island.

Old Street Mall

The most attractive shopping arcade in all of Philipsburg is Old Street Mall, which has been fully restored to offer an old-world atmosphere. Turn right on Front Street when leaving Little Pier and walk about two blocks until you see the mall entrance on the left. The stately entry gate with rows of colorful flags arching overhead is a tempting scene to capture on film. Shops of interest in Old Street Mall are:

Beach Stuff carries everything necessary when visiting the beach, as well as some local items. You can purchase everything from colorful jams in every size to reef sandals, T-shirts, sunglasses and exclusive swimwear seen in the *Sports Illustrated* swimsuit issue. They have an excellent collection of kid's clothing as well as an outlet in Marigot.

Tommy Hilfiger offers a wide selection of men's and boy's apparel that looks like classic American sportswear with a twist. The boutique features clothing and accessories, bags, belts, socks, caps and wallets. The quality is superior. Another outlet of this store can be found in Marigot on Boulevard de France.

Colombian Emeralds can be found in this delightful location, and also has two additional stores, one on Front Street and the other in Marigot on Rue de la République.

Dalila is part of a chain of stores that can be found on several islands. It carries a tremendous selection of authentic batik sarongs and other clothing from Indonesia, plus mobiles, jewelry and curios. Dalila has another branch at Marina Royale in Marigot.

The Scuba Shop has two locations – at Captain Oliver's Marina in the Oyster Pond Resort, and at Palapa Marina, Simpson Bay. The Scuba Shop sells name-brand equipment at duty-free prices. You may wish to upgrade your equipment or buy a whole new setup. Check prices at home before you come so you know when to bargain.

Special Shops On Front Street

☆ **Guavaberry Tasting House & Shop** offers liqueurs to suit all tastes and is just one block away from Old Street Mall and worth the short walk. The locals in St. Martin have been brewing guavaberry liqueur for hundreds of years. Enjoy visiting the 200-year-old West Indian house, built on the site of an ancient synagogue, while you sample wild lime, mango, amaretto, sambuca or the legendary guavaberry.

Greenwith Gallery, near Guavaberry on Front Street, carries the widest selection of well-known Caribbean artists' work – original pottery, fine art and unusual gifts and collectibles. Worth a visit.

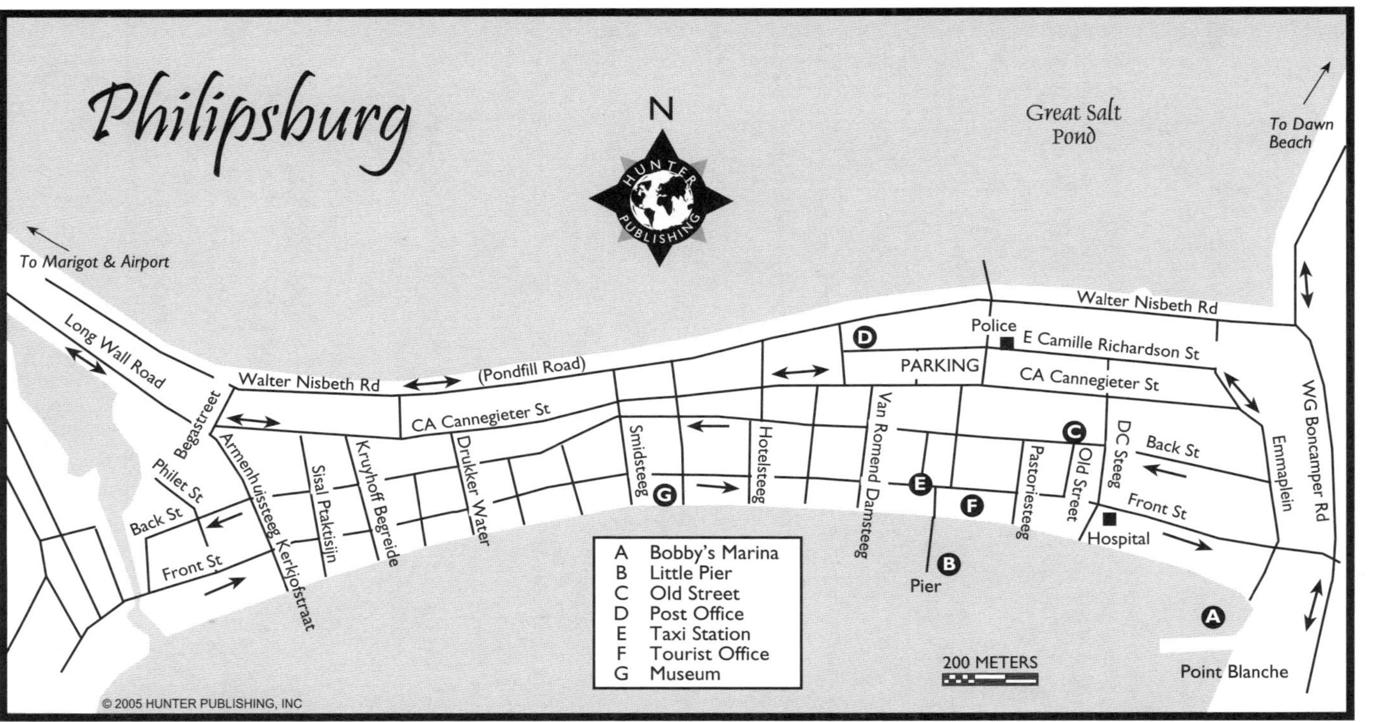
Philipsburg
N
HUNTER PUBLISHING
Great Salt Pond
To Dawn Beach
To Marigot & Airport
Long Wall Road
Walter Nisbeth Rd
(Pondfill Road)
Police
E Camille Richardson St
PARKING
CA Cannegieter St
WG Boncamper Rd
Emmaplein
Begastreet
Armenhuissteeg Kerkjofstraat
Philet St
Back St
Front St
Sisal Ptaktisijn
Kruyhoff Begreide
Drukker Water
Smidsteeg
Hotelsteeg
Van Romend Damsteeg
Pastoriesteeg
Old Street
DC Steeg
Hospital
Pier
Point Blanche
200 METERS
A Bobby's Marina
B Little Pier
C Old Street
D Post Office
E Taxi Station
F Tourist Office
G Museum
© 2005 HUNTER PUBLISHING, INC

Last Mango In Paradise sounds like a Jimmy Buffett song, and that's not far wrong. The singer has turned designer and this exclusive shop claims to offer the hottest selection of Caribbean soul T-shirts this side of Margaritaville. Set across the street from the Guavaberry Tasting House, Last Mango sells a wide selection of snorkel gear, sunglasses, Solar Tan-Thru swimwear, as well as Buffett-designed T-shirts.

The Shipwreck Shop, just a half-block west of Old Street Mall, offers a great selection of locally made items, curios, island art and T-shirts. The shop also sells books about St. Maarten, the islands and sea life. The store is nicely decorated with a variety of Caribbean handicrafts, including Caribelle batiks. (If you cannot visit St. Lucia or St. Kitts, this might be your best chance to buy Caribelle batiks.) Other outlets are open at various resorts.

The Dutch Delft Blue shop sells beautiful handcrafted blue-and-white Delft pieces, ranging from museum quality to inexpensive tiles and Christmas ornaments. On Front Street, near Shipwreck Shop.

H. Stern Jewelers has earned a reputation for trend-setting jewelry creations at substantial savings and purchases are backed by a one-year exchange guarantee. Watches by top name designers are also available. Stern is at 56 Front Street. (H. Stern also has a shop on St. Thomas.)

Little Switzerland is at 52 Front Street and also has a location along the Marigot waterfront at 6 Rue de la Liberté.

Polo Ralph Lauren has two locations, one on Front Street and the other in Marigot. Both outlet stores offer merchandise at lower prices than those in the US.

Boolchands carries a large assortment of designer fashions from Pierre Cardin, Givenchi, Mario Pucci and other top designers. They also carry a selection of embroidered tablecloths. Check out their bargain counter.

Rams offers electronics, cameras and accessories at its two stores (28 Front Street and 67 Front Street). You'll find good prices and honest service.

Tanzanite International, on Front Street, carries a large assortment of tanzanite, a radiant blue-purple gemstone that was discovered in East Africa in 1967. The store also sells diamonds and other precious gems.

Best Buys in Marigot

Marigot is truly a French town that happens to be on an island in the Caribbean. There are French-style boutiques, art galleries and bakeries. The best buys in Marigot are French perfumes, French fashions and local crafts along the waterfront. The stores primarily sell to locals, so the town has not attracted the same high-volume jewelry and electronics stores seen in Philipsburg. Near the harbor, where the tour buses drop off their crowds, **Colombian Emeralds, Polo Ralph Lauren, Little Switzerland** and **Beach Stuff** have opened stores.

The best shopping in Marigot is found in the **open-air market** next to the marina. Local craftsmen make sure their tables and booths are set up during peak tourist hours when the tour buses roll in. Handmade coral jewelry, fabric dolls, wood carvings, hand-painted shirts, batik, original art, reproduced art and curios are all available in the market stalls. Take some time to wander through the cheerful displays after filling up with French pastry. Shops in Marigot close for lunch, so the open-air market is the only shopping available between 1 and 3 pm.

Specialty Stores In Marigot

The **Gingerbread Art Gallery** specializes in the vibrant colors of Haitian art, which finds its inspiration in nature and the island tradition. The gallery is at 14 Marina Royale (next to Café de Paris).

Dalila has opened an outlet near the Marina Port La Royale. (See *Shopping in Philipsburg,* page 101.)

Transportation & Excursions

Taxis

There's an abundance of taxis at A.C. Wathey Pier. They can take you to town for shopping, on sightseeing tours (see *Self-Guided Tours*, page 110), or to one of many beaches on the island.

Ships tendering passengers into Little Pier and Bobby's Marina will find taxis on Front Street, directly in front of either pier area.

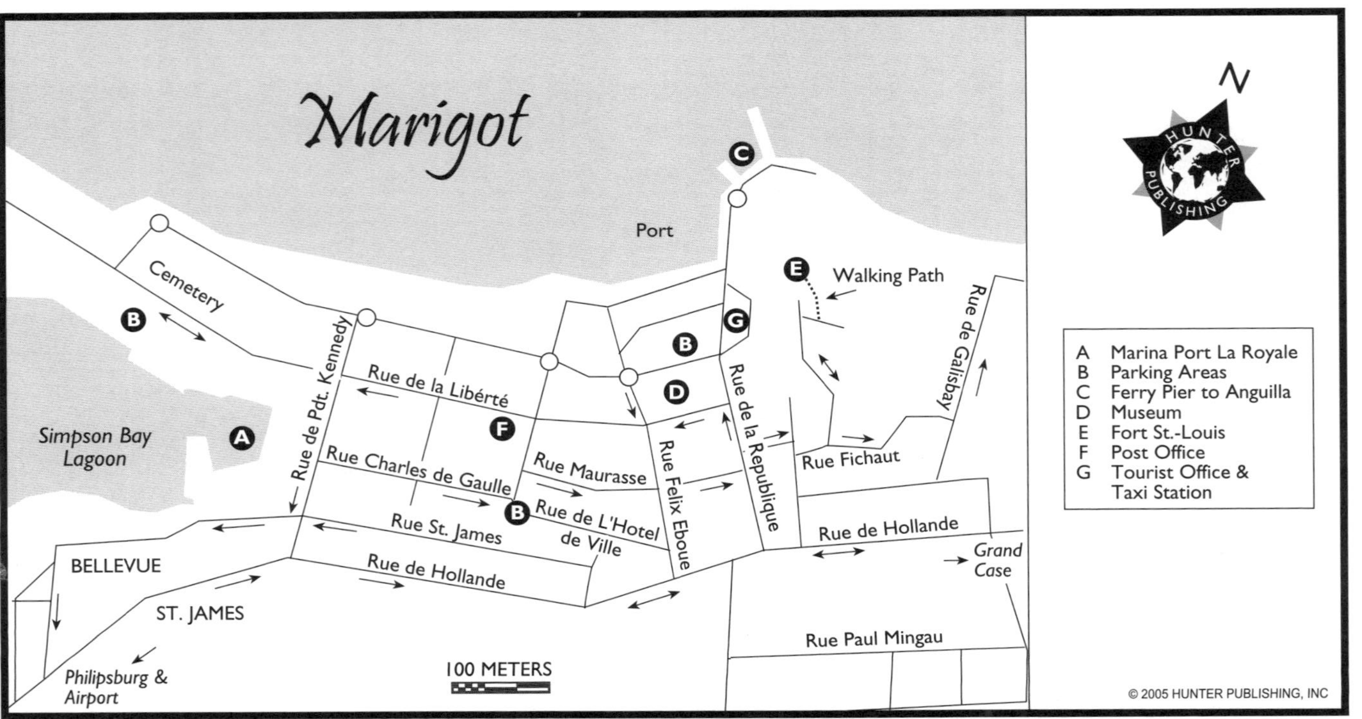

Marigot
N
HUNTER PUBLISHING
Port
Cemetery
Simpson Bay Lagoon
Walking Path
Rue de Galisbay
Rue de Pdt. Kennedy
Rue de la Libérté
Rue Charles de Gaulle
Rue Maurasse
Rue de L'Hotel de Ville
Rue St. James
Rue Felix Eboue
Rue de la Republique
Rue Fichaut
Rue de Hollande
Rue de Hollande
Grand Case
BELLEVUE
ST. JAMES
Rue Paul Mingau
Philipsburg & Airport
100 METERS
A Marina Port La Royale
B Parking Areas
C Ferry Pier to Anguilla
D Museum
E Fort St.-Louis
F Post Office
G Tourist Office & Taxi Station
© 2005 HUNTER PUBLISHING, INC

Taxis in St. Maarten are not metered but have a standard set of prices for trips to the major destinations. Prices fluctuate with the number of people and one-way or round-trip passages, so discuss the rate with the driver prior to getting in the taxi. Tipping drivers is not as customary as it is in the US, but if you take a taxi-guided tour, or have a driver pick you up at a particular location, it is generally appropriate to give a tip. Taxi drivers and locals are quite helpful and friendly without expecting money.

Taxi Chart

All prices are given in US dollars.

Destination	**Cost** (per couple)
from Philipsburg	
Baie Longue	$18
Baie Orientale/Baie l'Embouchure	$18
Bobby's Marina (walking distance)	$6
Dawn Beach/Oyster Pond	$15
Grand Case	$20
Juliana Airport	$15
Marigot	$15
Mullet Bay	$16
Pelican Resort	$10
Philipsburg (from A.C. Wathey Pier)	$6
Simpson Bay Lagoon/Kim Sha Beach	$15
Sightseeing tours,	2½ hours, $50
Shopping tours	$20 per hour (waiting time over first hour charged at $5 per 15 minutes)

Local Buses

Island residents use a local bus system for travel between Philipsburg and Marigot. The fare is only $2 per person, with various stops along the road. However, the same type of vehicles (minivans) are used for buses and for taxis. If you are unsure whether a minivan is a locals bus, simply ask the driver. Some drivers will wait to fill the bus before departing, but after a short delay passengers will be on their way to the French capital, for very little money.

To find a locals bus in Philipsburg, look for "Bushalt" signs only on Back Street, one block away from the water (and Front Street). In Marigot, the signs are written in French, so look for "Arrêt" signs for the buses to Philipsburg. The drivers will let you off anywhere you request, but when paying the fare be sure to have small change or dollar bills.

For a trip to Marigot, the local buses are the easiest and cheapest way to travel. The bus stops are easy to find and buses are frequent.

Rental Cars

Driving is on the right in St. Maarten and roads are well marked and in good condition. If you're interested in renting a car for the day, contact an agency prior to arrival. Most rental agencies have established their offices at the airport, so if you decide to rent a car after you arrive, you'll need to take a taxi out to Juliana Airport. If you call ahead, the rental agency may make arrangements to deliver the car near the pier area. Hertz has rental cars at the cruise ship dock, and has a website specifically for cruise ship passengers to make reservations, www.piercars.com.

The basic price for a full day's rental is $30-$45 for either automatic or stick-shift vehicles. Agencies require a current driver's license and a credit card for a rental deposit. If your ship docks at A.C. Wathey Pier, ask the rental agency if it's possible to drop off the car on the pier at the end of the day.

Car Rental Agencies

To call St. Maarten from the US, dial 011 (the international access code), then 599 (the country code), then dial 5 (the area code) and finally the local number.

Avis . . . . ☎ (800) 228-0669; www.avis.com

Budget . . . . . . ☎ (800) 786-2277; www.budget-sxm.com

Hertz (at dock) . . . ☎ (877) 769-1002; www.piercars.com

Paradise Cars . . . ☎ 553737; www.paradisecarrental.com

St. Louis Car Rental . . . . ☎ (590) 87-45-71 (French side) www.st-louis-car-rental.com

Thrifty . . . . ☎ (786) 866-2865

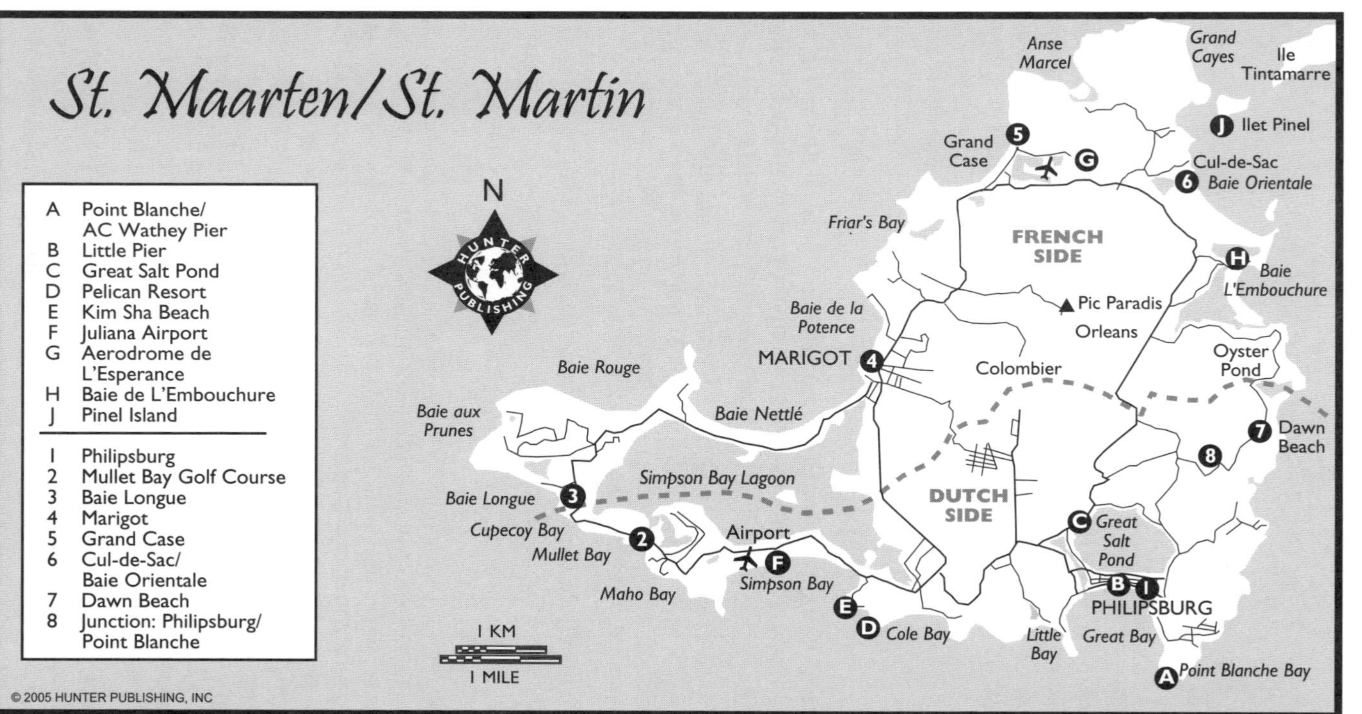
St. Maarten/St. Martin
A Point Blanche/ AC Wathey Pier
B Little Pier
C Great Salt Pond
D Pelican Resort
E Kim Sha Beach
F Juliana Airport
G Aerodrome de L'Esperance
H Baie de L'Embouchure
J Pinel Island
1 Philipsburg
2 Mullet Bay Golf Course
3 Baie Longue
4 Marigot
5 Grand Case
6 Cul-de-Sac/ Baie Orientale
7 Dawn Beach
8 Junction: Philipsburg/ Point Blanche
N
HUNTER PUBLISHING
1 KM
1 MILE
© 2005 HUNTER PUBLISHING, INC
Anse Marcel
Grand Cayes
Ile Tintamarre
Ilet Pinel
Grand Case
Cul-de-Sac
Baie Orientale
Friar's Bay
FRENCH SIDE
Baie L'Embouchure
Pic Paradis
Baie de la Potence
Orleans
MARIGOT
Baie Rouge
Colombier
Oyster Pond
Baie aux Prunes
Baie Nettlé
Dawn Beach
Simpson Bay Lagoon
Baie Longue
DUTCH SIDE
Cupecoy Bay
Great Salt Pond
Airport
Mullet Bay
Simpson Bay
Maho Bay
PHILIPSBURG
Cole Bay
Little Bay
Great Bay
Point Blanche Bay

ST. MARTIN

Self-Guided Tours

Marigot

Visit **Marigot**, the French capital, with unique culture, gourmet restaurants and charming boutiques. The restaurants are wonderful and the architecture is typically French. Jump on a local bus or take a taxi and within 20 minutes you will be exploring a little bit of France. Toward the end of the day, a taxi ride back to Philipsburg will take a least 30 minutes due to heavier traffic, so plan accordingly.

Island Tour by Taxi

The taxi association offers several standard island tours.

The Mountaintop Tour (3½ hours, $35 per person). This tour circles the island, stopping at various mountaintops for panoramic views. You have time to get out and photograph the scenery.

City-to-City Tour (2½-3 hours, $25 per person). This is the most popular taxi excursion. It stops for 45 minutes in the French capital, Marigot, and 15 minutes at Orient Bay Beach. You get to see the island and have time to buy souvenirs.

Private all-day tours run $250 for up to six people for the entire taxi.

Anguilla Day-Trip

If you've already explored St. Maarten, we highly recommend a trip to the beautiful British isle of **Anguilla**, which offers long stretches of beach and clear blue water. The coral reefs here are great for snorkeling or scuba diving (see *Island Activities, In the Ocean*, page 117). If you want to spend a day on Anguilla, you'll need to take a taxi or bus to Marigot, then a ferry to Blowing Point. Ferries leave from Marigot Harbor every half-hour, starting from 8 am until 5:30 pm. Returning ferries also leave every half-hour, starting at 7 am. The last one leaves at 5 pm. The ferry trip takes 20 minutes and the cost is $10 per person, one way. Visitors to Anguilla need to carry a picture ID, passport, or driver's license for departure from French St. Martin.

Once you arrive in Blowing Point, take a taxi to one of the island's spectacular beaches. **Shoal Bay** ($32 for two people, round-trip) is a two-mile white sand beach with plenty of privacy. **Shoal Beach** is popular for watersports and has a variety of restaurants where you can enjoy a light lunch. **Shoal Bay Scuba & Watersports**, ☎ (264) 497-4371, operates a full-service dive center here (see *Scuba Diving*).

A new **dolphin/stingray swim** is offered on Anguilla and Antigua. After orientation, you get into the water with stingrays for 15 minutes or dolphins for 30 minutes. (See *Dolphin Fantaseas*, page 116.)

Organized Tours & Activities

Serious Sailing

The **America's Cup 12-Metre Challenge** is becoming the most popular excursion on St. Martin. For $70 per person you can join one of three crews on a real sailboat race, but no prior sailing experience is needed. The *Canada II, The Stars and Stripes* and the *True North* have all participated in the world famous America's Cup Race. Although your trip is shorter, it is an actual race, so you'll experience the thrill that has hooked many. The fleet sails from Bobby's Marina (a short walk from the cruise ship dock). This event is popular, and we recommend that you book the excursion through your ship, or call ahead, ☎ (011) 599-544-3354, to reserve space.

Guided Wave Runner Tours

Kontiki Watersports (☎ 590-27-02-45, manuflogarcia2@wanadoo.fr) offers a guided **Wave Runner excursion** along the coast. The tour starts at Orient Bay and heads to Green Key island, stopping for snorkeling along the wild uninhabited Tintamarre Island. You then head to Creole rock and the waters around Grand Case village and Friar's Bay. After a stop for a complimentary drink at a local beach bar, you'll cruise back along the scenic coast with a stop at Pinel Island. The cost is $120 for one person and $145 for two on a double-seater.

Off-Shore Islands

Kontiki also offers a **taxi-boat service**. Choose your hours of departure and return and take a trip to Pinel ($15 per person) or Green Key Island ($10 per person), where you can spend your day swimming, snorkeling and enjoying the sun. Snorkel gear is available for rent, and the underwater life is abundant. ☎ (590) 590-87-46-89/590-27-02-45; manuflogarcia2@wanadoo.fr; www.sxm-game.com/wspen.html.

Mountain Biking

Frog Legs provides guided mountain bike tours, a great way to experience this small coral island (if you are fit enough to try). Tour #1 ($39 per person, three hours, 5% climb) is an easy trail around the Guichard Pound, with a stop at Friar's Bay Beach Café. Tour #2 ($39 per person, two hours, 30% climb) is tougher, but it's a beautiful trail on private land overlooking Simpson Bay lagoon. Tour #3 is moderate. It starts at the Marigot Museum for a history lesson, then travels by the seashore to Grand Case to an archeologic site at Hope Estate to view Arawak Indian ruins ($44 per person, four hours, 10% climb). For reservations, ☎ 590-87-05-11; frog.legs@wanadoo.fr.

Bike rentals are available at Simpson Bay for $22/day.

Beaches

One of the longest beaches on the island is at **Mullet Bay**. The beach is perfect for swimming, snorkeling or simply sunbathing. The Mullet Bay Resort that stood here was destroyed by a hurricane and has yet to re-open. However, the golf course remains open and the exceptional beach is less crowded. A taxi ride from downtown Philipsburg or A.C. Wathey Pier will take 20 minutes and cost $16 per couple.

BEACH CHART	Facilities	Windsurfing	Snorkeling	Scuba Diving	Wave Runners	Swimming	Parasailing	Sailing	Water Skiing	Nude/Topless
Mullet Bay						☆				
Baie Oriental	☆	☆	☆		☆	☆				☆
Baie l'Embouchure	☆	☆	☆			☆				
Kim Sha Beach	☆		☆	☆	☆	☆		☆	☆	
Dawn Beach	☆		☆			☆				

Baie Orientale/Orient Bay is the most popular clothing-optional beach on the French side of the island. A taxi will take 30 minutes from either downtown or the A.C. Wathey Pier. It is not necessary to arrange a pick-up with the driver because taxis are available at the beach. Average fare is $18 per couple.

You may choose to bare all on the beach, but Orient Bay is also a top spot for swimming and watersports. Sea kayaks ($7/hour, $30/day), float pads ($6/day), Sunfish sailboats ($20/hour), Lazer sailboats ($30/hour), Hobiewave 13' catamarans ($45/hour) and boogie boards ($12.50/day) are available for rent. If you are uncomfortable with the *au naturel* style, head for the stretch of sand on the left side of the shopping tents (these sell some of the best bathing suits on the island, as well as T-shirts). Unwritten rules of a nude beach are no photography and respect for one another's space. Orient Bay also has two restaurants and restrooms ($1). Round-trip water taxi rides to Pinell Island cost $20 and to Green Key Island cost $12.50.

A nude full-day cruise on the ***Tiko Tiko*** costs $95 per person, and leaves daily except Sundays at 9:30 am. The price includes lunch (steak, chicken or mahi mahi), wine and drinks. Contact **Dolphin Watersports** at ☎ (590) 590-872875 or (599) 557-8814, or visit www.cluiborient.com and click on "Dolphin Watersports."

☆ **Baie l'Embouchure**, down the road from Orient Bay, is situated in a private cove. If you're not interested in going to the nude beach, we recommend that you spend the day here. **Tropical Wave**, a windsurfing and snorkeling operation based here has created a spectacular snorkeling trail. Have lunch at the Beach Bistro (with restroom facilities).

Kim Sha Beach is across from Simpson Bay Lagoon and to the right of the Pelican Resort. Known more as a local's beach, Kim Sha is an ever-changing area that is close to Philipsburg and has activities for every member of the family. It offers watersports, a beach for sunbathing and a unique shopping area nearby. You can enjoy the beach, walk to the Pelican Resort for lunch or gambling in the casino, then browse through the shopping area across the street at Plaza de Lago.

A taxi ride here takes 20 minutes and goes over the mountain to reach Kim Sha Beach. If you're traveling in a group, try bargaining for a lower-priced round-trip rate, which usually runs $15 per couple. Westport Watersports (no phone given), located on the beach, offers the most powerful Jet Skis on the island.

Jet Skis can be rented at Simpson Bay Lagoon for $70/hour, and a guided tour costs $75/hour or $120 for two hours. A kayaks tour around the mangroves in Simpson Bay Lagoon takes five hours and costs $49 per person. Reserve Jet Skis or kayak tours at www.saint-martin-activities.com.

One of the best spots for rough ocean waves offshore and calm-water snorkeling near land is **Dawn Beach**. The pounding surf and frequent waves make swimming and surfing more enjoyable here than anywhere else on the island. A taxi can drop you off there ($15 per couple). It is only 15 minutes from Philipsburg, so you can spend a half-day shopping and enjoy the remaining time at the beach.

Island Activities

On Land

Golf

Mullet Bay Resort was destroyed by a hurricane. However, its golf course remains open to the public. This is one of the most challenging 18-hole golf courses in the Caribbean. Greens fees are $75-$93 (18 holes), depending on season. Club rentals are available for $26 (18 holes). Tee times are available Monday-Thursday from 7 am to 5 pm and reservations must be made a week in advance by calling ☎ (011-599) 5-52801 or 5-53069.

Horseback Riding

☆ **Bayside Riding Club** is just to the right of Orient Bay. Guides lead riders on natural dirt paths to a private beach, where you can gallop along a mile of sandy beach, then guide your horse for a swim through the water. The stable uses neoprene saddles, which are much more comfortable than regular leather saddles. Be sure to bring your bathing suit and a hat for sun protection. Beach rides are scheduled at 9 am and 2 pm and cost $40 for a one-hour ride, $60 for a two-hour ride, and $60/hour for private beach rides. For reservations, ☎ (011-590) 87-36-64 or, on the Dutch side, (599) 5-76822. Advance reservations are preferred, but they are willing to make arrangements to help cruise passengers. Visit the Bayside website at www.baysideridingclub.com, or e-mail them at baysideridingclub@yahoo.com.

Lucky Stables is in the Cape Bay area on the Dutch side. Cape Bay (originally a cattle plantation) is one of the few undeveloped areas on the Dutch side, and is accessible only by the horses of Lucky Stables. While riding, you may encounter mongoose, butterflies and tropical birds in the lush vegetation and rocky hills. You'll enjoy excellent views of nearby islands and the harbor. The stables are a 10-minute taxi ride (about $20 round-trip for two people) from the cruise ship dock. Rides are scheduled at 9 am, 11:30 am, 2 pm, 4:30 pm and 8 pm. A one-hour ride costs $25 per person; two-hour rides cost $50 and include a refreshing ocean swim with your horse and riding on Cape Bay beach. ☎ (599) 544-5255; www.luckystable.com.

Butterfly Farm

Butterfly Farm on Le Galion Beach Road, French St. Martin, offers guided tours of its butterfly operation. Visitors are shown the evolutionary cycle from microscopic eggs to exotic caterpillars, pupae and (early in the morning) the birth of a butterfly. After touring, visitors can browse the farm and gift shop at their leisure. The price ($12/adults, $6/children, under age three free) includes a pass for another visit during your stay, but cruise ship passengers are offered a $2 discount in lieu of the pass. The farm recommends wearing bright colors and perfume to encourage the butterflies to land on you. ☎ (599) 54-43562; www.butterflyfarm.com.

In The Ocean

Windsurfing

The best *wind* is found on **Orient Bay** and **Galion Beach** on the *wind*ward side of the island. These areas are noted for windsurfing, which is particularly good from November to April. The water can get too choppy, so ask about conditions before going out, and be aware of your own limitations and skill level.

Windy Reef Center on Galion Beach provides equipment and monitors to keep you safe (especially good for novices). Windsurfing board rental alone costs $20 per hour, $45 for three hours and $65 for five hours. Windsurfing board rental including a monitor costs double or more ($40/one hour, $125/five hours). Surfboard rentals will run you $10 per hour, $20 for three hours and $35 for five hours. Surfboard rentals, including a monitor, are $40 per hour and $125 for five hours. Kayak rentals are $10 per hour and $20 for three hours. ☎ (011) 590-87-08-37; www.sxm-game.com/surfen.html; e-mail: windyreef@powerantilles.com.

Pelican Resort (☎ 599-544-2640) on Simpson Bay Lagoon offers a variety of watersports rentals. **Westport Watersports** (no telephone) at Kim Sha Beach (Simpson Bay) and Little Bay Beach (near Phillipsburg) rent boards for about $25 per hour.

Dolphin Fantaseas Encounter is a new company that operates on Anguilla and Antigua. Animal behaviorists give detailed briefings and guidance for feeding and touching of stingrays and dolphins. Stingrays actually enjoy having their satin-like wings touched. You feed the rays their favorite foods for 15 minutes under the guidance of the staff. The dolphin encounter involves a 30 minutes of feeding and playtime. Bring your own swimsuits and towels; lifejackets, booties and masks are provided. Group size is limited to 10 people age five or older. During the dolphin encounter, the group is divided into two groups of five visitors. Visit the Dolphin Fantaseas website, www.dolphinfantases.com, to reserve space on your own for $140 per person without transportation or lunch included. (Taxi and ferry transportation costs run about $70 for two people, round trip.)

If you book this excursion on the St. Martin Activities website, www.saint-martin-activities.com, the trip includes lunch and snorkeling (but does not include the $5 departure tax on the ferry from Marigot). The cost is $185/adults, $160/children and $70 for people who want to watch but not swim. (This website cannot book Disney cruise passengers.) The excursion leaves on the 9 am ferry from Marigot and returns at 5 pm in time for ship sailing times.

Parasailing

Kontiki Watersports on Orient Beach offers parasailing along the two-mile beach. The cost is $50 for a single rider and $80 for double riders. ☎ (011) 590-87-46-89 or 590-27-02-45; manuflogarcia2@wanadoo.fr; www.sxm-game.com/wspen.html.

Parasailing at Simpson Bay is available through **Kim Sha**. Rides run 15-20 minutes and cost $50 for a 500-foot high ride and $60 for 600-foot ride.

Personal Watercraft

The **Pelican Resort** offers a variety of personal watercraft. Rates for WaveRunners are $40 for a half-hour (single rider), $45 for double riders. Next to the Pelican Resort at Kim Sha Beach, **Westport Watersports** offers powerful Jet Skis at $40/30 minutes for a single rider and $50/30 minutes for a double rider.

Kontiki Watersports at Orient Beach (see above) offers Jet Ski rentals for $40 per half-hour, $70 per hour. WaveRunner rental prices are $40 for a half-hour single rider and $45 for double riders, $70 an hour for single rider and $80 for double riders. Banana boat rides cost $10 per person.

Scuba Diving

St. Martin has 40 dive sites with clear water. Colorful, abundant sea life around shallow reefs is perfect for novice divers. An island marine park is in the works, designating separate areas for fishing and scuba diving to insure protection of the pristine coral reefs.

Scuba Fun Dive Center operates out of Marigot and at Ans Marcel. The center offers a two-hour snorkeling trip for $37.50, a one-tank dive for $56, and a two-tank dive for $106. The introductory course includes a 45-minute dive to a maximum of 15 feet. The $112.50 fee includes equipment and an open bar onboard for after-dive refreshments. Certified divers can rent equipment to be delivered anywhere on the island at no extra charge. Full equipment rental costs $35 per day. ☎ (011) 590-87-33-40 (Marigot location), (011) 590-87-36-13 (Anse Marcel location); www.scubafun.com. Scuba Fun opened a second operation just a short walk from the cruise ship dock at Great Bay Marina. They offer dives at 9 am, 11 am and 2 pm.

Dive Safaris runs boat dives from two locations – Bobby's Marina (near the cruise ship dock) and the Palapa Marina in Simpson Bay. This dive operation has contracts with cruise ship companies, therefore, you should book dives (except the shark-feeding trip) through your shore excursion desk. Call the dive shop direct to book the shark dive.In addition to the scheduled reef dives, a guided one-tank dive to feed gray reef sharks is offered on Tuesdays, Thursdays and Sundays at 2 pm. About 20-30 sharks come for lunch. Scratch and Big Mama are the largest and most frequent callers. ☎ (011) 599-545-3213 or 542-9001; www.thescubashop.net.

Ocean Explorers Dive Center is located at Kim Sha Beach in Simpson Bay. This full-service dive shop offers a two-tank dive costing $100, including all equipment. If you used a tender to get ashore, they request that you leave on the very first tender of the day, which departs at 9:30 am, in order to allow sufficient time. Certified divers must be at the shop 30 minutes before the dive to participate. Assuming you won't make the first dive, join the second, which leaves the shop at 11:30 am (be there at 11) and returns in plenty of time to get back to the ship before sailing. ☎ (011) 599-544-5252, fax (011) 599-544-4357; www.stmaartendiving.com; e-mail divesm-@megatropic.com.

Diving in Anguilla is available through **Shoal Bay Scuba & Watersports,** ☎ (264) 497-4371; www.shoalbayscuba.ai; sbscuba@anguilla-net.com. A one-tank dive costs $50, a two-tank dive costs, $80 including tank and weights; it's $10 extra for BCD and regulator rental. Snorkeling costs $25, including gear. Dives are scheduled at 9 am and 11 am, and the taxi cost from the ferry to the shop is about US $16. This full-service dive shop also offers parasailing, paddle boats, snorkeling and windsurfing activities. Take the ferry across from Marigot to explore some of the most beautiful uncharted and untouched coral reefs in the northern Caribbean (see *Self-Guided Tours*, page 110, for details). Dive packages are available upon request.

Sailing & Motor Cruises

Sailing the waters around St. Martin is a good way to avoid crowds, enjoy a day in the sun, or try snorkeling. The waters are warm and shallow, giving even novice snorkelers a chance to spy on the local undersea creatures around the reefs. Try one of the following excursions.

Offshore Sensations offers a full-day scorpion speedboat charter to Anguilla for $950 and a half-day charter for $550. This speedy option departs at 9:30 am from the Marina Royal in Marigot. You'll see Cap Juluca, the hotel of the rich and famous, snorkel at Sandy Island, visit Shoal Bay on Anguilla, have lunch (at your expense), swim at Scilly Cay, and swim along the shores of Scrub Island. Drinks and snorkeling equipment are included at $125 per person. For reservations, ☎ 590-690-651616, or e-mail yonathon@the900thdimension.com. Visit www.offshoresensations.com.

***Atlantis* Submarines** offers a semi-sub ride leaving from Grand Case in French St. Martin on Thursday, Friday and Sunday. A semi-sub is a glass-bottom boat with individual windows for each person. This cruise must be booked through the shore excursion department onboard ship.

The ***Lambada*** catamaran day sail costs $70 per person, plus a $7 port fee. The trip to Anguilla and Prickly Pear includes BBQ lunch (choice of chicken, fish or ribs), snorkeling and swimming. Bring your own bathing suits, towels and cash for drinks/tipping on the beach. Non-swimmers take a dingy to the beach for a relaxing day in the sun. Book at www.saint-martin-activities.com.

Random Wind Schooner offers sailing on a 54' schooner on Wednesday, Thursday and Friday to the French side of the island for magnificent scenery. Various snorkeling stops are made along the way. The $75 per-person charge includes snacks, quiche, salad, bread, cheese, all equipment (including fishing gear) and an open bar. The ship takes eight passengers maximum and can be booked privately for $800. Book at www.saint-martin-activities.com.

One-Day Itinerary

To thoroughly enjoy St. Maarten, rent a car by 9 am so you will have a full day to explore, and allow six to seven hours for your island tour. This is a full day's worth of sightseeing, including various stops at beaches, shopping areas and exclusive resorts. There's no need to worry about getting lost; there are plenty of road signs and friendly locals who will help you if needed. Take your time and enjoy the heavenly beaches, the delicious food in Marigot and the duty-free shopping in Philipsburg.

What to Bring

Be sure to bring a towel and a bathing suit if you plan to swim or sunbathe. Keep in mind that most of the secluded beaches have no changing facilities. Also pack suntan lotion and drinking water to protect against painful sunburn and dehydration.

Directions

Refer to the island map for numbers corresponding with the suggested sites described. If you were able to rent a car in Philipsburg, begin your tour there. If you rented a car at Juliana Airport, pick up the tour as it goes past the airport and on to Maho Bay Resort.

An Island Tour

Leave **Philipsburg** via the Walter Nisbeth Road or Long Wall Road, keeping the town and ocean at your back. The Walter Nisbeth Road circles the Great Salt Pond and continues parallel to Long Wall Road, exiting town. Both roads merge into **Bush Road**, where you take a left up and over Cole Bay Hill. Bush Road follows a coastal route for five-10 minutes until it comes to another intersecting route, **Welfare Road**. Take a left (toward Juliana Airport), which will take you past a series of spectacular views. (If you go right, the road will lead you directly to Marigot within about 15 minutes.) Continue along Welfare Road. You might want to stop near Simpson Bay Lagoon at Plaza de Lago for souvenir shopping.

Past the airport, Welfare Road enters Maho Bay Resort and, if you keep to the right, you will enter **Mullet Bay**. Stay to the right through the first Y in the road, then continue along the golf course to the second Y. Here, a sharp left through a guarded gate will take you to Mullet Bay Beach and a right leads straight to Lagoon Watersports. Stay to the left through the rear entrance and pass a few more hotels until you cross over to the French side (indicated by road signs written in French).

In approximately 10 minutes, past Cupecoy Beach, you should find a sign for **Baie Longue**. Take the secondary road on your left for your adventure to Baie Longue, one of the most beautiful beaches on the island. Follow the dirt road until you pass the entrance of La Samanna, an exclusive resort. Follow the road to the right of La Samanna and watch for a chain-link fence surrounding a parking area, approximately 100 yards on the left. There are many private homes along the road, but drive slowly and you will find the entrance without a problem.

Leave your car and hike down the pathway to the beach. (Do not leave valuables in the car.) Baie Longue is a mile-long beach with plenty of privacy – perfect for sunbathing. There are rocks along the shore in the water, so be very careful when swimming. If you are a sunworshipper, you might wish to stay here awhile to soak up the rays, but limit your time. Stay no longer than an hour if you want to see the rest of the island on schedule. When you're ready to go, head back to the main road, then make a left to get back on track.

Follow the main road for a few miles past private estates and small beaches. Take your time and enjoy the scenery. Within 15 minutes, the main road will direct you into the French capital, **Marigot**, and a left onto Rue de la République will take you straight down to the harbor, where parking is available in a lot on the left.

Unless you are planning to visit Martinique or Guadeloupe, Marigot may be the closest you come to visiting France in the Caribbean, so enjoy the town's foreign atmosphere. Browse through the stores along the waterfront. When you are ready for lunch, ask for directions to **Marina Port la Royale**. There are many restaurants here featuring exquisite French food, but try a crêpe – any kind will do – for a true French delicacy.

Marigot is only 20-30 minutes from Philipsburg, but if you take the route along the eastern coastline back to town, the journey will run

60-90 minutes (depending on traffic), non-stop. To stay on schedule, spend 1½ hours in Marigot for shopping, sightseeing and lunch.

Make your way out of Marigot via Rue de Holland leading past the main harbor to the right. The easiest way to know that you are heading in the right direction is to watch for the signs to Grand Case and Cul-de-Sac. Continue along this winding road for 20 minutes until you reach an open meadowland area and see the sign for Grand Case. Make a left onto the narrow street until it ends, then turn right on the main street. There is a dirt parking area on the right where you can leave your car.

Stroll back along the road toward the beach and lavish restaurants. **Grand Case** is known as the Restaurant Capital of the Caribbean and hosts some of the most expensive restaurants in all the islands. From Grand Case you can see Anguilla in the distance across the water.

Spend up to 30 minutes in Grand Case, then drive back along the road past the restaurants (do not turn down the one-way road you came in on) to the end of the restaurant strip and make a left onto the main road. The next few locations on the route feature topless beaches, spectacular coastal views and some hideaways found only on St. Martin.

Continue on the main road for about 10 minutes, past the French airport, Aerodrome de l'Esperance, until you reach a fork in the road. Follow the main road to the right, which will take you through the most rural part of the island and on to another beach resort. Stop at a lookout spot just past a large electrical tower on the right side of the road. The observation platform here overlooks **Orient Bay** and one of the most dramatic coastlines in the Caribbean.

Just a few yards down from the platform, a sign on the left will direct you to **Club Orient Hotel** and **Baie Orientale**, the most popular clothing-optional beach on the island. It has facilities for renting snorkeling gear, windsurfers and WaveRunners, two eateries and shopping tents full of bathing suits and T-shirts. To the right of the parking area is the nude beach. If you wish to avoid it, stay on the beach to the left of the shopping tents. If you did not spend much time at Baie Longue and are ahead of schedule, you may wish to stay at Baie Orientale for swimming and sunbathing. (Baie Orientale is 30 minutes from Philipsburg.)

Returning to the main road, turn left. You have now crossed back over to the Dutch side's farming area, so be watchful for goats, sheep and cows crossing the road. Follow the paved road for 15 minutes until you see a sign for **Oyster Pond** and **Dawn Beach**. Make a sharp left, a right and finally a left up a steep dirt road clearly marked for Dawn Beach and Oyster Pond. (Do not worry, it's an easy transition.) When you reach the top of the hill (15 minutes), take in the view overlooking the Atlantic coastline. From this vantage point you can see St. Barthelmey, an outer French island, and Dawn Beach, one of the best body surfing and snorkeling spots on the island.

Slowly make your way down the steep road until you reach the hotels below. Visitors are allowed to drive through the **Dawn Beach Hotel** to reach the beach. If you have time on your schedule, do some snorkeling, swimming or walk down the beach to visit the Oyster Pond Hotel.

When you have made it back up the steep winding road to the main road, make a left for the descent back into **Philipsburg**. As you travel down, you'll be able to see Philipsburg, the Great Salt Pond and your cruise ship. When you reach the edge of the Great Salt Pond, you can turn either left or right to get back into town. A left will take you back to the A.C. Wathey Pier and a right will lead you into downtown Philipsburg, or to Bush Road and the airport.

If you have time before your ship sails, walk through downtown Philipsburg and do some last-minute souvenir shopping.

Antigua

A Beach for Each Day of the Year

Island Description

Sicilian donkeys and ruins of windmills dot the rolling landscape, free of urban clutter. Antigua (an-tee-GUH) is a rural island formed of coral and limestone with few inhabitants. The roads, although wide and straight, are dotted with potholes, which the taxi drivers happily dodge while passengers may feel they have been on Mr. Toad's wild ride! The island's highest point is Boggy Peak, 1,360 feet above sea level. Antigua's claim to fame is 365 white sand beaches. It is the largest Leeward Island, covering 108 square miles.

During his second voyage to the New World, Columbus bestowed on the island the name, "Santa Maria de la Antigua." Antigua contained no gold or natural spring water, but it did have ferocious Carib Indians, so the Spanish did not attempt to colonize. The first successful settlement was established by a group of English who came from nearby St. Kitts in 1632. Although the Caribs waged attacks to eject the British, the settlers held their ground and began to cultivate cash crops, such as tobacco, indigo and ginger. In 1674 Sir Christopher Codrington came from Barbados and established the first successful sugar plantation, called Betty's Hope after his daughter. Betty's Hope, with its unique twin windmills, was recently established as a non-profit trust.

Codrington's success encouraged others to begin sugar production and over 150 sugar mills were built on Antigua's flat landscape, all manned by slave labor. Although slavery was abolished in 1834, sugar remained the primary source of income here until the 20th century, when tourism took its place. Agriculture is also a part of the economy, with miles of countryside dedicated to a variety of crops. Indeed, Antigua's black pineapple is famous for its sweetness.

Barbuda, Antigua's sister island, is 27 miles northeast of Antigua, about 20 minutes by air. It is known for its pink sand beaches and the Frigate Bird Sanctuary, a birder's haven, but remains difficult to reach on a one-day excursion.

Island People

The only "town" on Antigua is St. John's, the capital, while every other populated area is considered a "village." With a distinct sense of pride, locals will point out their village and name their relatives living in other villages. Villages are small, filled with tin-roofed wooden chattel houses on raised foundations as a protection against flooding. Chattel houses, which can be moved with the owners, were the original type of dwellings occupied by slaves.

The island's population hovers around 75,000, which keeps it rural and uncrowded. Antiguans have a friendly, peaceful nature, and the island is largely untouched by the hustle and bustle of urban chaos. Taxi drivers are trained to describe local plants, flowers and historical sites and very much enjoy becoming tour guides for their passengers.

The most important event on Antigua is **Carnival**, which commemorates the emancipation of slaves. Carnival is celebrated for 10 days, beginning at the end of July and ending with two days of nonstop parades, music and dancing on the first Monday and Tuesday of August. The festivities include beauty pageants, a Calypso King contest and a steel band competition. Carnival Monday features a costume contest with elaborate outfits full of sequins, feathers, beads and glitter paraded across the stage during a spirited competition. Carnival Tuesday, called the Last Lap, is the final day for street dancing, or jamming, which begins early in the morning and continues well past midnight.

Island Foods

- ⚓ **Breadfruit** was brought here from the South Pacific by Captain Bligh to feed to slaves. Today, it's a staple. Green and oblong in shape, it is grown on local trees and cooked as a vegetable or made into bread or pie.
- ⚓ **Cassava** was a staple of the Arawak and Carib Indians. This starchy root can be ground into meal to make bread, and the juice is often spiced with sugar, cinnamon and cloves to make cassareep, an ingredient used in West Indian dishes.
- ⚓ **Christophine:** A large squash with pale green flesh, which can be eaten raw or cooked as a side dish.

- **Dasheen** plants supply the West Indian diet with edible spinach-like leaves and tubers similar to potatoes. Soup made from dasheen is very tasty.
- **Fungee:** A savory pudding, made with cornmeal and okra, served as a side to flying fish or pepperpot stew.
- **Guava:** This tropical fruit is about two inches long with pinkish flesh. It can be steamed, eaten raw or used to make a delicious drink.
- **Maub** is a slightly fermented iced drink made from the bark of a tree, mixed with ginger and sugar.
- The **pawpaw** is more commonly known outside the Caribbean as papaya. It can reach weights of up to 10 pounds. It makes a delicious breakfast fruit.
- The Caribbean islands produce 13 varieties of banana, the largest of which is the **plantain**. It is less sweet than most banana varietals and has a starchy texture. It is used in casseroles, as a side dish, or fried in oil.
- **Roti:** This curried dish is made from almost any kind of meat, mixed with vegetables and spices, wrapped in a light dough before cooking.
- **Sorrel** is a small annual plant with red leaves, which are used to make a Christmas beverage.

Holidays

If cruise ships pull into port on Sundays and scheduled holidays, some shops in Heritage and Redcliffe Quays remain open.

Annual Holidays

For more details and precise dates, contact the island tourist board (see *Appendix*).

January	New Year's Day
April	Good Friday; Easter
July	Carnival starts
August	Carnival ends
November	Independence Day
December	Christmas; Boxing Day; Old Year's Day

Useful Websites

The tourist board's official website, www.antigua-barbuda.org, provides descriptions of the island, beaches and historic sites. There are links to Sailing Week, a calendar of events, a list of restaurant locations and phone numbers.

The **www.antiguatoday.com** site is sponsored by a tourism magazine and provides a score of links to local businesses. To access a complete list of shops, click on Shopping, then click on the Antigua & Barbuda Today, Places to Shop listing. Another site, **www.antigua-net.com**, includes a link to Carib Seek, which has information on many different islands.

The Pier

Cruise ships dock directly in the island's capital of St. John's at a specially designed pier. You can walk from the ship straight into the modern duty-free shopping center, Heritage Quay (pronounced key), which contains a casino, hotel, pizza parlor, car rental agency and a wide variety of shops. You can venture around St. John's on foot – there's no need for a taxi.

Pier Phones

Exiting the ship, you'll see two credit card phones on your right, outside the Heritage Hotel. A bank of phones can be found on the left, further inside the shopping mall. Antigua has a modern telephone system, Cable and Wireless, that can handle credit card or phone card calls. You can call the US using your AT&T calling card. Dial 1, then the area code and number.

The area code for Antigua is 268, and it's a long-distance call from the United States.

St. John's

A Cruise Ship Pier
B Heritage Quay
C Redcliffe Quay
D Museum
E Post Office

Friars Hill Rd
Independence Dr
Cross St
St. Mary's St
Redcliffe St
Nevis St
Tanner St
South St
New St
Temple St
Dickenson Bay St
Newgate St
Church St
Long St
High St
Corn Alley
Market St
Popeshead St
Thames St
Wopping Lane
Wilkinson Cross
St. John's Harbour
400 METERS
400 YARDS

In Town

Currency

Legal tender in Antigua is the Eastern Caribbean (EC) dollar, which is tied to the US dollar at approximately EC $2.65 to US $1. The US dollar, credit cards and traveler's checks are accepted virtually everywhere, although exchange rates are better at banks than with local merchants.

There's a variety of banks near Heritage Quay on High Street. Banking hours are Monday-Thursday, 8 am to 1 pm, and Friday from 8 am to 4 pm (some banks close for lunch on Friday). An ATM is at the airport. The Bank of Antigua and Swiss American Bank, Ltd. have branches at Nelson's Dockyard.

Postage

As an independent country, Antigua issues its own postage. The post office on High Street in St. John's is a short walk to the left of the cruise port. The cost to mail a postcard is approximately US 30¢. (Remember US postage is not accepted on mail.) The post office has a Philatelic Bureau inside the building to the left, offering a wonderful assortment of collectible stamps.

Museums & Historical Sites

The **Museum of Antigua and Barbuda** is on the corner of Market and Long streets. It occupies the Old Court House, built in 1750 of stone quarried from Antigua's northeastern coast. Opened in 1985, the museum visually displays the story of Antigua from its geological birth, through political independence to the present day. It was designed with children in mind, and displays are hands-on.

Special exhibits include a wattle and daub house model, pottery, steel pans, touchable artifacts and utilitarian objects. One of the most prized possessions of the museum, exhibited by the front entrance, is the cricket bat used by island native Vivian Richards, the famous West Indies cricket team captain. Admission is free, but donations are encouraged. The museum is open Monday through Thursday from 8 am to 4 pm, Friday until 3 pm, and Saturday from 10 am to 2 pm. A museum gift shop contains books, postcards and local handicrafts.

Nelson's Dockyard National Park. (Also see *One-Day Itinerary*, page 119.) The most unusual historical landmark on Antigua is Nelson's Dockyard at English Harbour, one of the five best protected natural bays in the world. The British Royal Navy recognized the value of the area and established the headquarters for its entire Caribbean fleet here. During the 150 years of use by the navy, the British built an astounding complex of naval facilities and fortifications.

Horatio Nelson was the military commander in the Caribbean from 1784 to 1787. Unbending when it came to following the naval rule book, Nelson earned the animosity of the locals. Regulations stated that only the goods produced on British colonies could be carried as cargo on British ships. Island merchants, who earned their livelihood by importing and exporting goods from all over the West Indies, were severely hampered by Nelson's strict adherence to regulation. The situation got so bad that Nelson feared for his life and refused to sleep on land while in port. Nelson's tenure was short and he never lived in the Admiral's House on the park's grounds, which was built in 1855. Nelson's later fame in the battle of Trafalgar made him a hero.

Today, the dockyard is the best preserved example of a British naval yard in the Caribbean. Many restored structures are currently used for yachting businesses similar to those that originally occupied the buildings. English Harbour hosts Antigua Sailing Week at the end of every April – more than 120 racing yachts compete in the regatta. Admission to the dockyard is $2.50 for adults; children under age 12 are free.

Shopping

Shops near the cruise port are open from 9 am to 5 pm, Monday-Saturday, and on Sunday if a cruise ship is in port. The only duty-free shopping is offered in Heritage Quay and Redcliffe Quay. Carry your boarding pass and picture identification to guarantee duty-free prices.

Heritage Quay

This is one of two duty-free shopping areas on Antigua containing the popular stores of **Diamonds International, Benetton** and **Colombian Emeralds.**

Caribbean Reflections is a uniquely Caribbean gift shop offering handicrafts and souvenirs perfect for gifts.

Island Arts sells a wide array of paintings, pottery, prints and wood carvings made or hand-painted by artist and filmmaker (*Star Wars, Superman*) Nick Mauley. The art is presented in a pleasing atmosphere.

The Land Shop is a manufacturer's outlet store featuring quality leather handbags, wallets, luggage and accessories all designed in Land's trademark colors, crafted from hand-cut cowhide with a five-year guarantee.

La Casa Habana sells tobacco products, including Cuban cigars. Please be aware that Cuban products are illegal in the US, so smoke your supply before heading through Customs!

Several clothing shops are also located in Heritage Quay, including: **Catwalk**, which features designer fashions for women; **Oshkosh B'Gosh** carries children's apparel, shoes and socks; **Sunseakers** sells swimwear in all sizes; **Beach Stuff** carries everything you may need at the beach;**Timberland, Nautica** and **Guess Jeans** offer sports clothes, jeans and outdoor wear.

Redcliffe Quay

As you reach the end of Heritage Quay shopping area, turn right on Thames Street and walk one block to Redcliffe Street, the entrance to Redcliffe Quay. This area was once a slave compound, but a project beginning in the 1980s transformed the ruins into a unique shopping and dining area, retaining the original architecture and old-world ambience. Shops are situated on Redcliffe Street and in the interior courtyard, which is entered through an alleyway off the street. Redcliffe is the other duty-free shopping area on Antigua.

☆ **Island Woman** has exquisite designer dresses made from filmy layers of fine batik fabrics. The collection includes designer swimwear, original hand-painted clothing, soft leather sandals from Jamaica, handbags, hats and accessories. if you want an original wardrobe, this is the place to come.

☆ **The Goldsmitty** sells the exclusive jewelry designs of owner Hans Smith, who has been called a modern-day Fabergé by *Gourmet* magazine. Hans was born in Holland, but has been living and working in Antigua since 1965. He uses gemstones, pearls and gold to capture the shimmering beauty of coral reefs, frothy surf and delicate spider webs in the most elegant pieces of jewelry on the island. All the jewelry is made on the premises.

Sunny Caribbee sells gifts, souvenirs and merchandise from all over the Caribbean.

Isis provides a unique assortment of Egyptian products, art, jewelry, leather, garments, linens and Pharonic art hand-painted on genuine papyrus.

Kate Design features the delightful works of Kate Spencer, a well-known artist from St. Kitts. Her original oils and watercolors are inspired by the scenery and people of the West Indies. If you're not in the market for originals, some of her art has been reproduced onto a line of greeting cards, place mats, silk pareos, scarves and jewelry.

A Thousand Flowers Boutique carries comfortable linen and natural fiber clothing and accessories. Next door at **Ego** you'll find a little of everything, with a selection of men's and women's linen clothing, pottery, and unique international household items.

Around The Island

Walk up the street from Redcliffe Quay to visit **The Map Shop**. The fascinating assortment of Caribbean literature here includes items on the life of an Antiguan worker to books on island flora and fauna. Across the street is an outlet for **Caribelle Batiks**, which were formerly sold only on St. Kitts and St. Lucia. The hand-dyed batiks are special, and the soft touch of sea island cotton is comparable to fine silk.

The **Scrimshaw Artist** located on the south-facing veranda of Nelson's Dockyard offers unique scrimshaw gifts created by Michael "Scrim" Strzalkowski. Scrimshaw is the ancient sailor's art of engraving intricate designs onto whale's teeth, bone and other exotic materials originally found on old ships.

Nelson's Dockyard gift shop contains a fine selection of local handicrafts and nautical items. **The Art Center** at the dockyard displays the largest collection of indigenous Antiguan and Barbudan art on the island. At the park's entrance is **Market Square**, where locals sell T-shirts, beaded jewelry, belts and handicraft items.

The Jolly Harbour shopping complex features **Things Antiguan**, which sells locally-made gift items. It also has an art gallery, clothing, jewelers, a cotton shop and **Aqua Sports** selling water sports equipment.

Friendly ladies at **tourist attractions** around the island sell beaded necklaces and bracelets, which they string themselves. Their jewelry makes excellent gifts at very reasonable prices. Don't be put off by these persistent women; their trade is their livelihood and a friendly bargaining session will leave you with fun memories.

Transportation & Excursions

Taxis

Island taxis line up directly in front of the pier area in vehicles ranging from minivans to small cars. Most are available for trips to the beaches, or an island tour to Nelson's Dockyard. Rates are for the whole taxi, seating one to four people. You can try to bargain for a round-trip ride, but most drivers stay within the established rate guidelines. The taxi rate for island tours is $20 per hour, with a minimum of two hours.

Taxi Chart

All prices are given in US dollars.

Destination *from cruise ship pier, St. John's*	**Cost** *one to four people*
Cedar Valley Golf Club	$9
Galley Bay	$12
Halcyon Cove	$7
Hawksbill Beach Resort	$12
Nelson's Dockyard	$21
Ramada Royal Antiguan	$12
Jolly Harbour Resort	$15
Runaway Beach	$7

Rental Cars

Driving is on the left. The roads are wide but in poor condition, which makes driving difficult. You must acquire a temporary Antiguan driver's permit for $12, available at rental agencies. Minimum age to rent a car is 21 and a major credit card is required. Rates vary between $40 and $50 for air-conditioned four-door cars and jeeps. Gasoline is not included, and a collision damage waiver is available for $10.

Car Rental Agencies

The area code here is 268, a long-distance call from the US.

Avis . . . . ☎ 462-2847; 800-228-0668
www.avis.com

Budget . . . . ☎ 462-6702, 800-626-4516
www.budget.com

Hertz. . . . . ☎ 481-4440/4460, 800-654-3131
www.hertz.com

Dollar Rent A Car. . . . . ☎ 462-0362/0123, 800-800-4000
www.dollar.com

Village Car Rentals. . . . . ☎ 461-3746

Self-Guided Tours

Nelson's Dockyard

Antigua has one of the most beautifully restored historical sites in all of the Caribbean. **Nelson's Dockyard National Park** has been permanently set aside for the protection of the natural environment and for preservation of its extraordinary historic buildings. Entering the dockyard is like stepping back into a time when sailors were explor-

Nelson's Dockyard & English Harbour.

ing the high seas and English Harbour served as the headquarters for the British Royal Navy. A scenic 20-minute drive, $17 by taxi for one to four people, will take you to the main entrance of the dockyard, where you can explore the grounds and experience the lifestyle of the deckhands and officers centuries ago. Admission includes a tour for $2.50 per person. (See *One-Day Itinerary*, page 133, for details.)

Organized Tours & Activities

Party Boat

Jolly Roger is one of the best party boats in the Caribbean, with day cruises scheduled on Monday, Tuesday and Wednesday from 9:30 am to 12:30 pm. The five-hour cruise can be arranged by calling the *Jolly Roger*, ☎ (268) 462-2064; e-mail jollyroger@candw.ag. The trip includes a barbecue lunch, dancing on the deck, walking the plank and having a swing on the pirate rope.

Cruises

The ***Kokomo Cat*** offers a variety of catamaran cruises throughout the week, leaving from various hotels.

- ⚓ On Tuesday, Thursday and Saturday a cruise around Antigua's shore is offered for $85 per person.
- ⚓ A Wednesday Snorkel Safari runs $70 per person.
- ⚓ A special Triple-Destination trip on Sunday includes beach-pickup, cruise to Green Island for lunch and snorkeling, a sail down to English Harbour and Nelson's Dockyard for sightseeing and, finally, a stop at Shirley Heights at sunset. The return trip to the Ramada is provided by taxi, for an all-inclusive price of $100 per person.

All cruises include a Caribbean buffet lunch, open bar and snorkeling gear for the scheduled two hours of snorkeling. Reservations are recommended. ☎ (268) 462-SAIL (7245); fax 462-8305; kokomo@candw.ag; www.kokomocat.com. Don't miss this opportunity to sail the clear blue waters with one of Antigua's best catamaran cruises!

Beaches

The author's favorite beaches are at Galley Bay and Hawksbill Beach Resort. Both have a beachside restaurant and bar for daily visitors and, best of all, they're just 15 minutes from the pier (a $12 taxi ride, one to four people).

BEACH CHART	Facilities	Windsurfing	Snorkeling	Scuba Diving	Wave Runners	Swimming	Parasailing	Sailing	Water Skiing	Nude/Topless
Galley Bay	☆	☆	☆			☆				
Hawksbill Resort	☆	☆				☆			☆	☆
Ramada Renaissance	☆		☆	☆		☆				
Halcyon Cove	☆	☆	☆	☆		☆		☆		

Galley Bay has a selection of picturesque thatched-roof Gauguin-style cottages that serve as primitive hotel rooms for adventurous travelers. The wide stretch of beach here is ideal for relaxing in the Caribbean sun. The pounding waves and rocky coast to the right create perfect conditions for windsurfing and snorkeling. If you're a strong swimmer, head out for some snorkeling at the sunken wreck, just off the beach. Snorkeling equipment is available for rent at $15/hour, along with windsurfers, at the office on the beach.

> TIP: The resort's beachside restaurant serves delicious island dishes, as well as continental cuisine. You can use the facilities if drinking at the bar or having lunch here. Galley Bay can offer some peace and quiet, or a day of watersports – take your pick!.

Hawksbill Beach Resort is the perfect beach for privacy, with four cove areas. The beach farthest to the left is reserved for nude sunbathing. The coves are just a short walk from the main resort. Hawksbill is spread out on a large piece of property with rooms and cottages set right along the beach. An old sugar mill situated in the middle is being used today as a hotel gift shop and may be the closest some passengers get to seeing a piece of Antigua's past. If you're interested in watersports, inquire at the social desk next to the beachside restaurant. A taxi ride to Hawksbill should cost $12.

A private cove at the **Royal Antiguan** is just a 15-minute taxi ride ($11 for one to four people) away. Cabs will drop you at the hotel's main entrance, and a short walk through the grounds leads to the beach. The hotel has a restaurant, restroom facilities and a watersports office right on the beach (it also rents chairs).

Hawksbill Beach Resort.

Halcyon Cove on Dickenson Bay is the best beach for watersports and beach activities, but it is quite popular and can be crowded on bright sunny days. A 15-minute taxi ride takes you to the resort ($7, one to four people). The beach area has a restaurant, beachside bar and watersports center open to all visitors. **Dive Antigua** has an office set up at the far right of the beach and you may want to join one of their daily dive trips. **Halcyon Watersports** rents paddleboats and windsurfing boards. Beach chairs here are reserved for the hotel guests, but as a day visitor, you can usually find a place along the mile-long stretch of white sandy beach. (See *Island Activities, In The Ocean*, below.)

Island Activities

On Land

Golf

Jolly Harbour Golf Club features an 18-hole, par 71 championship course designed by Karl Litton. Greens fees are $25 for nine holes and $40 for 18 holes. Cart rental is $15 for nine holes, $20 for 18 holes; Club rentals are $15 for nine holes, $23 for 18. The course, located adjacent to the Super Yacht Terminal, is set in a lush tropical park and includes a driving range, new clubhouse with pro shop, bar and locker room. For tee times, ☎ (268) 462-7771, ext. 608 or e-mail jollygolf!candw.ag. A taxi ride should cost about $15 to Jolly Harbour.

Just three miles from St. John's is **Cedar Valley Golf Course**, an 18-hole course designed by Ralph Aldridge. Daily greens fees are $30 and cart rental also runs $30. Clubs are also available for $10 per day. The 10-minute taxi ride will cost only $8 for the whole taxi, one to four people. Tee times can be arranged by calling ☎ (268) 462-0161.

Tennis

You can book courts at the **Royal Antiguan**, only 15 minutes from the cruise pier, where a tennis pro is available for lessons (approximately $15 per hour) and equipment can be rented. Contact the guest service desk at the hotel to arrange court times, ☎ (268) 462-3733.

Jolly Harbour Sports Centre overlooks the marina and the entrance is right on the docks. There are four tennis courts offering clay and artificial turf surfaces. There's also a glass-backed squash court, which allows spectators to watch exciting games. For reservations, ☎ (268) 462-6260 or e-mail fragil@candw.ag.

Bicycling

A safe and easy way to see the rolling hills of Antigua is on a mountain bike. **Sun Cycles** rents bikes for $15 a day. ☎ (268) 461-0324 to make prior arrangements. The quiet scenic island roads are much more enjoyable by mountain bike than by car or taxi! Pick up an island map from Sun Cycles and bring along only necessary items to minimize weight.

In The Ocean

Swimming with Dolphins & Stingrays

Dolphin Fantaseas Encounter is a new operation offered on the islands of Anguilla and Antigua. Animal behaviorists give detailed briefings and guidance for feeding and touching stingrays and dolphins. Although much misunderstood, stingrays actually enjoy having their satin-like wings touched. You feed the rays their favorite foods for 15 minutes under the guidance of staff. The dolphin encounter involves 30 minutes of up-close playtime and trainers teach you to feed them from your fingers. Bring your swimsuits and towels; lifejackets, booties and masks are provided. Group size is limited to 10 people age five and older (the dolphin encounter has two groups of five visitors). Your ship's excursion office may offer a package, including lunch and transportation. If you want to see more or make your own reservations ($140 per person), go to www.dolphinfantaseas.com or ☎ (268) 562-7946.

Windsurfing

Halcyon Watersports has a windsurfing school that guarantees students will be windsurfing in two hours. You'll learn about the equipment, practice on a land simulator, then perform the fundamentals of windsurfing in the water. Lessons are given from 10 am to 2 pm for $45 per person. Advance bookings are required through the hotels guest service desk or the watersports center, ☎ (268) 462-0256 or 462-0383 (answering machine); e-mail hchanu@rexresorts.net. Board rentals are also available for $15 an hour. Dickenson Bay is a great location for both beginners and advanced windsurfers.

Galley Bay is not usually crowded with tourists. Good winds in this crescent-shaped bay create excellent conditions for windsurfing. Rentals are $25 for 30 minutes through the rental group on the beach (just stop by).

Hawksbill Beach Resort, next to Galley Bay, rents boards ($20 per half-hour) at the shack near the restaurant on the beach. Both Hawksbill Beach and Galley Bay are quiet and secluded, with perfect conditions for beginners.

Jolly Harbour Resort (see above) offers windsurfing, paddle boats, surf bikes, float mats and snorkeling gear. Jet Skis rent for $15 an hour and banana boat rides cost $10 each. For more information, ☎ (268) 462-0061; e-mail info@jollybeachresort.com.

Water Skiing

Hawksbill Beach Resort offers water skiing for $11 an hour. You can make arrangements with the social desk near the restaurant.

Scuba Diving

Antigua's best dive sites are popular. Book early with any of the following operators to ensure space.

For the dive experience of your life, take a trip with John Birk of **Dive Antigua**. John carries a large writing slate that he uses throughout the dive to explain sea life or point out curious creatures. Dive Antigua operates out of the Halcyon Cove Hotel, and will pick up at various locations. The two-tank dive is $79 per person, leaving at 9:30 am and returning at 2 pm. The price includes tanks, weights, mask, fins and snorkels; you can also rent a BC and regulator with computer for $21. If you're a first-time diver, arrange a Resort Scuba Course at $88 per person, which includes a lecture, pool session and one open-water dive on the reef. All equipment is supplied, but you must arrange for the session before arriving on the island. Departure time is 9 am and return is time 2:30 pm.

Dive Antigua takes groups to unmarked locations that offer exceptional opportunities to view Antigua's sea life. Be sure to watch for 10-lb. lobsters and the occasional nurse shark resting under the coral reefs. Contact Dive Antigua, ☎ (268) 462-DIVE (3483); e-mail birk@candw.ag, or Halcyon Cove, www.diveantigua.com, to arrange for the ultimate dive adventure.

Deep Bay Divers is less than two minutes' walk from the pier. Its 34-foot dive boat, *The Life of Riley,* holds up to 14 divers and provides water and drinks aboard. A one-tank dive costs $74 with all equipment and a two-tank dive costs $95. (Deduct $21 if you require only tanks and weights.) Snorkel gear rents for $16 a trip. ☎ (268) 463-8000; e-mail deepbaydivers@candw.ag; www.deepbaydivers.com.

Jolly Dive Antigua Ltd. works with the *Kokomo Cat* tours (see *Cruises*, page 134). The dive rates are $45 for a one-tank dive and $74 for a two-tank dive. BCD and regulator rental is $21 and wetsuit rental costs $5. They offer 10% discount on cash payments. ☎ (268) 462-8305; www.jollydive.com.

Sailing & Motor Cruises

Adventure Antigua offers the following sailing excursions. Prices include snorkel gear, food and drinks. With advance arrangements, cruise passengers can be picked up at the dock at 10 am and returned at 4:15 pm.

- ⚓ An all-day **Eco-Historical Tour** stops at colonial towns, a mangrove habitat and Guiana Island to visit the last undisturbed ecosystem on Antigua. The cost is $90 per person.
- ⚓ The **Around-the-Island Tour** offers a tranquil swim in North Sound, and also explores Green Island, historic Nelson's Dockyard, and the unspoiled lush southwest coastline. The cost is $130 per person.
- ⚓ The **Barbuda Trip** visits the pink and white sand beaches on Antigua's sister island. It allows time for beach combing, snorkeling and swimming. After a lobster lunch, you visit the magnificent frigate bird colony. The cost is $150 per person.

Get a 10% discount by booking direct at www.adventureantigua.com. If the times of the listed tours don't fit with your ships departure schedule, Adventure Antigua also arranges private charters. ☎ (268) 727-3261; info@adntiguaadventures.com.

The yacht ***Sentio*** is available for full-day and half-day private charters. *Sentio* is a 50-foot, ketch-rigged sailing yacht that specializes in day sailing around the island. It accommodates from two to 10 guests and includes gourmet meals, snorkeling and sailing instruction (for those who wish to join the crew, rather than just lay back and enjoy a day relaxing). A full day's sail costs $550 and a half-day costs $450. Their website, www.sail-antigua.com, shows photos of the yacht and has an option for contacting Captain John Frazer for charter arrangements. Or you can e-mail sentio@candw.ag.

One-Day Itinerary

Antigua claims to have 365 beaches, and we've selected two of the best for this one-day itinerary. Allow between six and seven hours for touring the island, visiting Nelson's Dockyard and relaxing in the warm Caribbean sun. Rather than battling the rough roads, hire a taxi for the trip to English Harbour and the surrounding historical sites. You can either make arrangements for a round-trip journey with one driver or take multiple taxis from each location.

The following list gives the driving times from the cruise ship pier to the sites and the approximate taxi fare for single trips from stop-to-stop. The total taxi fare if you use one cab for the entire trip is $50, one to four people.

Taxi Chart	
Nelson's Dockyard and sites	20 mins., $20
Hawksbill Resort/Galley Bay	25 mins., $18
St. John's	15 mins., $12

What to Bring

Bring along a camera to capture one of the best panoramic views of English Harbour and Nelson's Dockyard from Shirley Heights. This is the island's most photographed site. Wear or bring a bathing suit if you want to spend time at the white sandy beaches and swim in the blue crystalline waters. Plan to have lunch at Hawksbill Beach Resort or Galley Bay. If asked politely, the hotel will usually allow passengers to borrow a towel for the beach to save you the trouble of bringing one from the ship.

Directions

Refer to the island map on page 143 and a map available from Nelson's Dockyard.

An Island Tour

Begin your journey from St. John's by 9 am to allow for plenty of time to explore. Hire a taxi just outside the cruise pier area to take you to **Nelson's Dockyard** at English Harbour.

At the main entrance, pick up a free map of the dockyard. You can hire the services of a guide (for just $2.50 per person), who will explain the history and preservation efforts of the national park while you explore the grounds. We've allowed up to two hours for wandering around Nelson's Dockyard, one of the best working examples of colonial Naval history that has been preserved in the Caribbean.

Pass through the **Market Place**, where vendors sell island crafts and T-shirts, to the Engineer's Office, which has been transformed into the **Admiral's Inn Hotel and Restaurant**. Take a walk through the lobby – it resembles an English pub – and try to visualize how the building might have looked when it was used as a pitch and tar storage area.

Outside the building is a walkway leading to the remnants of the **Boat House**. The giant stone pillars that once held up the Boat House are an amazing display of craftsmanship. Notice the man-made trough, where the ships would sail into the building to have work done on their masts. It is our hope that one day the dockyard will reconstruct the full Boat House.

Walk along the main street toward the **Admiral's House** on the right. Built in 1855, the house was originally constructed as a residence for the naval officer in charge and the storekeeper, although Admiral Nelson (or any other commanding admiral) never lived here. The ground-floor museum displays some interesting yachting mementos and naval relics used during the time of Lord Nelson's command. Yachting trophies won by local teams in the yearly sailing regatta are on display. A gift shop to the left of the building has a superb collection of souvenirs of the dockyard and surrounding sites on Antigua.

Next door to the Admiral's House is the large **Copper and Lumber Store**, a magnificent example of Georgian architecture that has been converted into a hotel and restaurant. The two large circular cisterns here were built over 200 years ago and still hold water today. Very little restoration has been needed on these structures because they were so expertly constructed by English tradesmen.

On the right side of the Copper and Lumber Store is the two-level **Officers' Quarters**. The upper level contains a Tea Shop Restaurant and Limey's Bar, Lord Nelson's Gallery, Art Center and Dockyard Photo Shop. The galleries have a wide assortment of paintings and prints from local artists, which make excellent gifts. The lower level contains the Customs and Immigration office, as well as the port authority office, where modern sailors entering English Harbour report for clearance.

One of the most intriguing sites in the dockyard is the **Capstan House**. Capstans were devices used to turn the ships on their side so repair work could be done to their undersides. Only the capstans themselves have been restored, but you can still imagine the amount of work required to turn one of the large sailing ships onto its side.

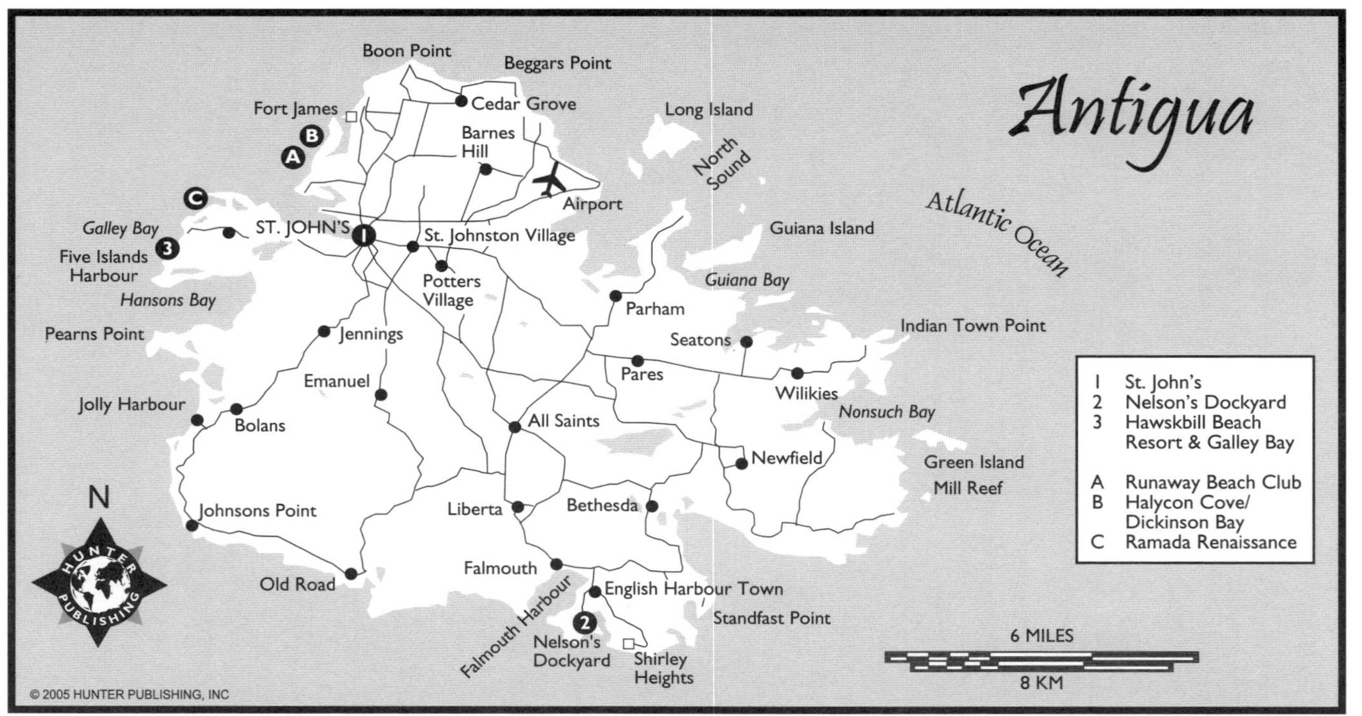
Antigua
Atlantic Ocean
Boon Point
Beggars Point
Fort James
Cedar Grove
Barnes Hill
Long Island
North Sound
Airport
Galley Bay
ST. JOHN'S
St. Johnston Village
Guiana Island
Five Islands Harbour
Hansons Bay
Potters Village
Guiana Bay
Parham
Pearns Point
Jennings
Seatons
Indian Town Point
Pares
Emanuel
Wilikies
Nonsuch Bay
Jolly Harbour
Bolans
All Saints
Newfield
Green Island
Mill Reef
N
Johnsons Point
Liberta
Bethesda
Falmouth
Old Road
English Harbour Town
Standfast Point
Falmouth Harbour
Nelson's Dockyard
Shirley Heights
1 St. John's
2 Nelson's Dockyard
3 Hawskbill Beach Resort & Galley Bay
A Runaway Beach Club
B Halycon Cove/ Dickinson Bay
C Ramada Renaissance
6 MILES
8 KM
HUNTER PUBLISHING

ANTIGUA

From this vantage point, you can see the next stop on the itinerary, the Clarence House, situated across the harbor up on the hill.

Leave the dockyard and take a taxi to the **Clarence House**, where a guide explains the history of past occupants (give your guide a tip). Spend about 20 minutes here and be sure to take a photo looking back at Nelson's Dockyard and the harbor.

The next stop is the recently built **Dow's Hill Interpretation Center**, offering a 30-minute multimedia presentation describing the history of Antigua and the British occupation of English Harbour.

The final historical site is **Shirley Heights,** where the most magnificent view of the entire Nelson's Dockyard National Park and English Harbour can be seen. The current structure was once used as a signal station where message flags were flown to warn troops at the dockyard of approaching ships. The Old Lookout Building has been restored and now contains a small restaurant and bar where you can enjoy a refreshing drink. Outside on the patio there is always a group of sweet (but persistent) ladies selling hand-strung beaded necklaces at very low prices.

The taxi ride to **Shirley Heights** passes old structures once used by British troops, which are now used for weekly musical gatherings by locals and visitors. The views of the Antiguan coastline and English Harbour are spectacular and make the trip from St. John's worthwhile.

When you are ready to head for the beach, decide whether you want privacy and relaxation or watersports and activities. **Hawksbill Beach Resort** has four beaches and you can usually find a peaceful spot. **Galley Bay** is a separate area offering a wide sandy beach with activities for sports enthusiasts and ocean lovers. Either trip will take approximately 20-25 minutes by cab from the English Harbour area. While crossing the countryside, be on the lookout for Sicilian donkeys, which inhabit most of the island. (Also see *Beaches*, page 135 127, for detailed descriptions of the two beaches.)

Allow up to three hours for lunch and relaxing on the beach, preparing to leave by 4 pm. A 15-minute taxi ride back to St. John's will allow you an hour or more for shopping in Redcliffe Quay or Heritage Quay before your ship departs.

St. Kitts & Nevis

The Sugar Plantations of the Caribbean

Island Description

St. Kitts was known to the Caribs as Liamuiga, the fertile isle, before Columbus dubbed it St. Christopher. The French, British, Dutch and Spanish were all aware of St. Christopher, but none braved the fierce Caribs to settle there until Sir Thomas Warner arrived in 1623 with a small group of English settlers. He claimed the island for the British, who shortened the name to St. Kitts.

Not long afterwards the French established a settlement at Basseterre, south of the British settlement near Old Road. The two cultures lived peacefully for a time in the same manner as the Dutch and French occupy St. Maarten today. However, the Carib Indians were unwilling to share their territory and attacked the British settlement, murdering many of the settlers.

Sir Thomas Warner escaped to recruit British and French troops, who banded together and mounted an attack to drive the Caribs from their stronghold in the hills. As a result, the picturesque island became the scene of one of the bloodiest battles in Caribbean history. An estimated 2,000 Caribs were slaughtered, causing the river to flow with blood for days. The site of the massacre was named Bloody Point, and island tour guides speak of the incident with a sense of remorse.

Having no common enemy to unite against, the British and French were not content to share St. Kitts for long. As early as 1690 the French captured Fort Charles to the north and the British mounted the first cannon on the promontory above Fort Charles in an effort to recapture the fortress. The site later became known as Brimstone Hill, the Gibraltar of the Caribbean, with its massive fortifications and unparalleled views of surrounding islands.

The British began the construction of **Brimstone Hill**, but were heavily outnumbered when 8,000 French soldiers attacked 1,000 British in 1782. The British fought valiantly and were able to hold out for over a month before surrendering. As a sign of respect, the French allowed the British soldiers and their commanders to march out of the fortress with all the honors of war, then return home to England. A year later the Treaty of Versailles returned St. Kitts to the British, who were able to retain control of the island from Brimstone Hill for over a century.

Today, restoration of the Brimstone Hill Fortress encompasses five bastions spread over 37 acres. It is the second largest (Haiti's Citadel is slightly larger) and most complete fortress in the Caribbean, built out of dark volcanic stone and topped by the colossal Citadel of Fort George on the topmost peak. Brimstone Hill is the most interesting fortress in the islands and well worth a visit.

Monkey Business

The French left a legacy on both St. Kitts and Nevis in the form of the **green vervet monkey**. The animals were imported by the French as pets and were turned loose when the adult monkeys became feral and too hard to handle. When the French left the islands, the monkeys remained in the wild and adapted quite well to island living, foraging for food in the dense rain forest and raiding plantation gardens. The breed thrived, and today islanders joke that there are more monkeys living on the island than there are people. The shy black-faced creatures are about the size of a large dog, with a white chest and a long tail used mainly for balance. They avoid contact with humans, but can often be sighted in the rain forest and on the road leading to the South Peninsula. Green monkeys have now lived on the islands for so long that they have evolved differently from their African cousins.

Shaped like a turkey drumstick, St. Kitts has a volcano, **Mt. Liamuiga**, at the northern end of the island (representing the fat end of the drumstick), which is surrounded by lush rain forest. The fertile lowlands in the central region are home to the island's small population and Basseterre, the capital. The arid Southeast Peninsula remained undeveloped until 1990, when the Dr. Kennedy Simmonds Highway was completed to provide access for future resorts. St. Kitts' sister island, Nevis, is just two miles away from the southernmost tip of St. Kitts and has its own volcano, Nevis Peak, and a tropical atmosphere.

About The Nearby Island of Nevis

Ask any local where Nevis got its name and they will probably begin to laugh. The joke on Nevis is that when Columbus saw the wispy white clouds perpetually clinging to the volcano he claimed it looked like snow. Columbus then named the island Las Nieves, meaning snow, perhaps because he'd run out of saintly names, or felt homesick for his own snow-capped mountains in the Pyrenees. When the British occupied the island, they shortened the name to Nevis (pronounced NEE-vus).

Almost circular in shape with its volcano in the center, Nevis looks like a cone from a distance and is more lush and tropical than St. Kitts, but shares the same basic history. The popular American patriot Alexander Hamilton was born on Nevis, and Lord Horatio Nelson met and married his wife Frances Nisbet on Nevis. Museums have been established to commemorate both events and are worthwhile tourist attractions. (See *Museums and Historic Sites*, page 151.)

Nevisians are quick to point out that Nevis is a much nicer place to live than St. Kitts, although the reverse is also claimed by Kittitians. The small agricultural island has a character of its own, almost old world in nature. Old plantation houses built from quarried volcanic stone have been converted into romantic guest houses and the coral reef surrounding the island creates intriguing white sand beaches, an oddity on volcanic islands.

The capital, **Charlestown**, is crowded only when the daily ferry arrives from St. Kitts and on Saturday mornings when farmers bring their goods to sell in the open-air produce market. Sea island cotton (used in Caribelle batiks) is grown on Nevis, while their ginger crop is used to make ginger beer and exported as a spice.

An agricultural island, St. Kitts is one of the few Caribbean countries still growing sugarcane. It is relatively untainted by tourism and possesses a picturesque charm. A drive through the countryside reveals acres of green flowing sugarcane fields, small farms with immaculate flower gardens and quaint Victorian cottages set against a backdrop of verdant forests rising to meet the angular, rocky face of a mist-covered mountain.

Island People

Kittitians are proud of their English heritage. Their capital city, **Basseterre**, may retain a French name, but the Circus in the center of town, with its tall green Victorian clock tower, is very British. Independence Square, surrounded by stately Georgian-style homes, was once a thriving slave market and the lines dividing the white section from the black still are visible, though unused today.

During Carnival, Independence Square becomes the center of festivities, with parades, calypso music and street dancing. The highlight of Carnival is to watch the clown dancers snapping their whips overhead. The male dancers dress in costumes of colorful cloth that dangles in long strips to represent the ragged garments their slave ancestors used to wear. The whips, made from long strips of palm fronds, symbolize the emancipation of the slaves, now free to brandish their whips in a mocking pantomime of their old slave masters.

Island Proverbs

"**Don't worry, be happy**," is the best-known island proverb. The West Indies slang, sometimes called Creole or Patois, includes unique sayings that will help you to understand the people and their special way of viewing the world. The following are just a few: "**no badduh me**," means leave me alone; "**Whatever in de old goat is in de kiddie**," meaning children often grow up like their parents; "**When de hog dance, rain's a coming**," means look for omens to foretell specific events.

Learning from the mistakes of other islands, St. Kitts is approaching the development of tourism cautiously. Their first major undertaking was to construct a duty-free shopping mall at the ferry pier near the center of Basseterre. The **Pelican Mall** is an attractive structure blending English and Caribbean architecture. It opened in 1991 with 26 duty-free shops and 10 offices for the Department of Tourism. During the second phase of construction, US $16.25 million was spent to build a connecting cruise ship dock.

A few plantation houses on St. Kitts and Nevis have been renovated and are open to the public as hotels and restaurants. These stately dwellings are surrounded by sugarcane fields and re-create an era of grace and elegance. Have lunch at the historic Rawlins Plantation on St. Kitts, or visit the many plantation estates on Nevis for a tranquil West Indian experience. (See *Self-Guided Tours* and *One-Day Itinerary*.)

Holidays

The ever-increasing number of passenger ships frequenting St. Kitts are important to the island's economy. Docking schedules are made public so everyone is aware of the arrival of their special daily guests. Businesses near the Circus make an effort to stay open during peak hours and taxis are always on duty.

Annual Holidays & Events

For more details and precise dates, contact the island tourist board (see *Appendix*).

January 1 . . . . New Year's Day
February . . . . Nevis Culture Day
March or April . . . . . Good Friday; Easter; Easter Monday
May . . . . Labor Day; Witt Monday
June. . . . . Queen's Birthday; St. Kitts Music Festival
August. . . . . August Monday (celebrates the freeing of slaves in the entire British West Indies)
September . . . . Independence Day
November . . . . Tourism Week
December . . . . National Carnival; Christmas; Boxing Day; Old Year's Day

Useful Websites, Internet Access

The official tourist board website for both islands is a colorful site with lots of pictures and good links to activities and historic sites, including names and phone numbers of guides. The diving and snorkeling pages describe dive sites in detail, complete with pictures of sea life. Visit it at **www.stkittsnevis.com**.

A very clever site you should check out is **www.nevis1.com**, which has some great links to places on Nevis. Be sure try out the recipes!

Internet Service

Sun N Surf Internet Café sits just off the Circus in the TDC Mall on Fort Street (downstairs). Open from 9 am to 8 pm. You can access e-mail while enjoying one of Mrs. Ottley's delicious cakes and pastries. ☎ 869-465-1998; sunsurfcafe@caribsurf.com

The Pier

Cruise ships arriving in St. Kitts will now be welcomed at the new pier adjacent to the **Pelican Mall** shopping complex in downtown Basseterre. The facility, completed in 1997, will allow larger ships to dock in Basseterre, which is very convenient for exploration of the island and the capital of St. Kitts.

Pelican Mall offers a variety of shops, a bank, post office and the islands tourism bureau for visitor information. The ferry that runs passengers to Nevis, the *Caribe Queen*, also operates from the same pier area.

Pier Phones

The **AT&T Direct** long distance service can be reached by calling ☎ (800) 872-2881 from St. Kitts when using an AT&T credit card. An international operator assists in making collect calls, which may be more expensive here than on other islands.

The **Cable & Wireless Company** offers a special phone number to use for calling the States. Dial 1-800-255-5872 (CALL USA) to make collect calls, or to make credit card or US calling card calls. Voice instructions guide you through the procedure.

The area code for St. Kitts and Nevis is 869, and it's a long-distance phone call from the United States.

In Town

Currency

The Eastern Caribbean dollar, tied to the US dollar at approximately EC $2.65 to S $1, is widely used in St. Kitts. Taxi drivers and tour operators often quote their rates in US dollars, so be sure to ask which currency is being used. Most merchants price merchandise in EC, but gladly figure the exchange rate and accept US currency, traveler's checks and credit cards.

You may get a better exchange rate at a bank or through your credit card company than with local merchants. If the cruise ship visits several islands using EC currency, consider cashing some traveler's checks at a bank to secure the better rate. Banks in Basseterre are located in the Pelican Mall and TDC Mall off Fort Street leading away from the Circus. Bank hours are Monday through Thursday from 8 am to 3 pm, Friday from 8 am to 5 pm, and Saturday from 8:30 am to 11 am.

Postage

There are postal facilities at the Pelican Mall and the St. Kitts Post Office is just next door in downtown Basseterre. It opens from 8 am to 3 pm daily, except Thursday, when it closes at 11 am. St. Kitts and Nevis both produce stamps bearing their island's name. To send an airmail postcard from either island costs about US 20¢. (Remember, US postage is not accepted.) A great selection of St. Kitts collector's issues are available at the Philatelic Bureau in the Pelican Mall. Also visit the Philatelic Bureau on Nevis, which is to the right of the ferry station, near the open-air market square.

Museums & Historical Sites

St. Kitts

A 25-minute drive will take you to the **Brimstone Hill Fortress National Park**, www.brimstonehillfortress.com, one of the most magnificent fortresses in the West Indies. The entry charge of US $10/adult, $5/child contributes to further restoration of the area. The national park is open 9:30 am to 5:30 pm daily. Eight sites are currently restored within the 37 acres of five bastions. Cannons are turned vertically on end, lining the narrow drive leading to the fort and set along the fort walls inside the massive entry gate.

The map (available at the entrance) identifies the sites with numbers that correspond with markers in the historic area. Climb up the long stairway to the Citadel and you'll be rewarded by unsurpassed views of the steep slopes, Sandy Point and the island of St. Eustastius in the distance. A small museum at the top of the fort contains Pre-Columbian artifacts and a variety of British, French and American garrison displays replete with clothing, weapons and military artifacts.

A book entitled ***Fire and Brimstone,*** written by British military historian Victor Smith, traces the history of Brimstone Hill from its inception to the present restoration. Copies of the book are on sale at the fort's gift shop and Wall's Bookstore in Basseterre.

Brimstone Hill Fortress.

The **St. Christopher Heritage Society (SCHS)** is on the corner of Bank and West Independence Square Streets in downtown Basseterre, not far from the Circus. A free exhibition details the history and natural environment of the country. ☎ 465-5584.

The site of historic **St. George's Anglican Church** on Canyon Street in Basseterre has a long history – churches occupied this site since 1625 and all but the current one has been destroyed by fire or hurricane. The present stone church (built in 1860) was recently ranked by The Organization of American States as a site of utmost national historic significance. The building is in bad shape, so the St. Christopher Heritage Society is raising funds to restore and protect the church and rectory.

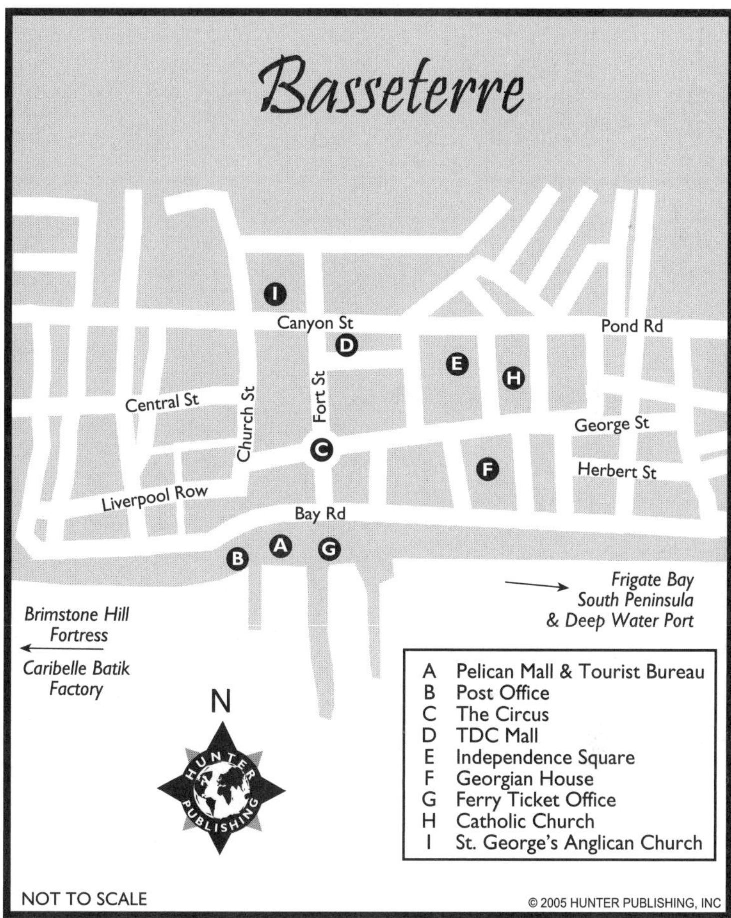

Nevis

Alexander Hamilton, who drafted the US Constitution and served as the US Secretary of the Treasury, was born on Nevis. Hamilton's likeness appears on the US $10 bill, but because Nevis was his place of birth, he was prohibited from running for the US Presidency. Nevisians are proud of their link with the United States and maintain Hamilton's birthplace as a landmark and the site of the **Nevis Historical Museum.** The museum is open Monday-Friday, 8 am to 4 pm, and on Saturday from 10 am to 12 pm, with no charge for admission. (See *Self-Guided Tours*, page 160.)

The **Morning Star Nelson Museum** (air conditioned) contains Nelson memorabilia, clothing worn by Nelson and his wife, portraits and historical displays. The museum is open Monday-Saturday from 9:30 am to 1 pm. The admission fee is $2 for adults and 75¢ for children. (Also see *Self-Guided Tours*.)

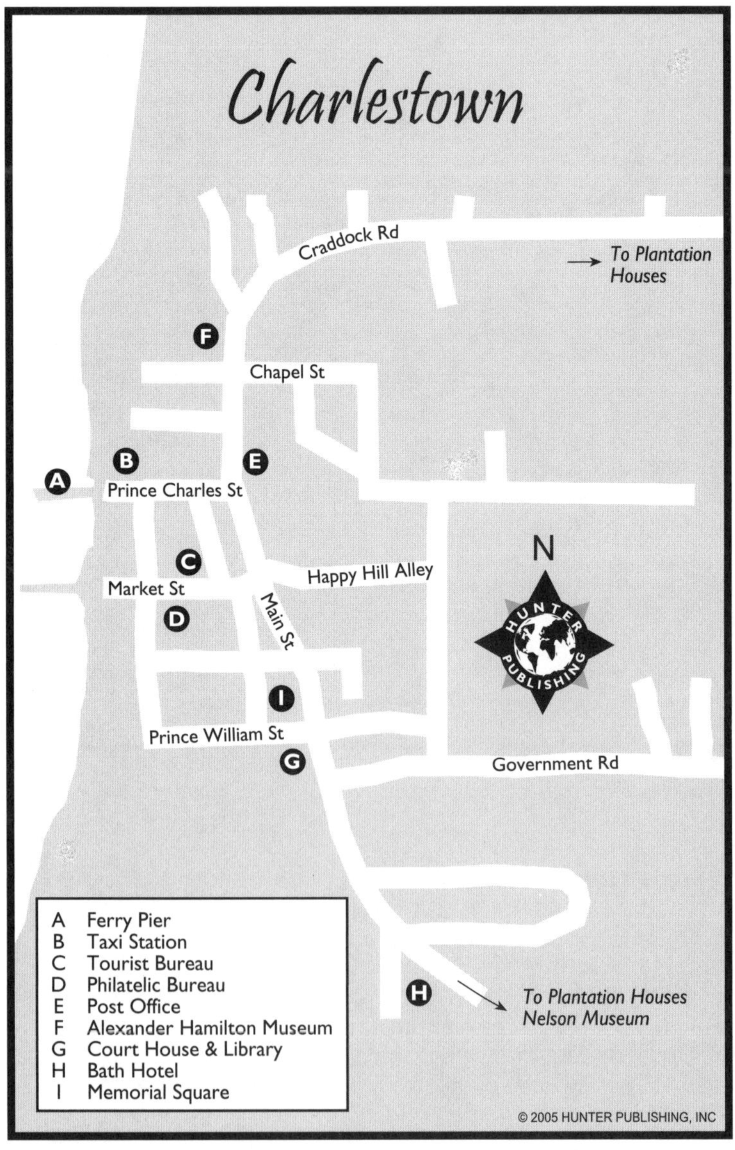

Shopping

Stores are open from 8 am to 4 pm, although some shops close during the noon hour for lunch. Most establishments are closed from midday on Thursday and all day on Sunday, unless cruise ships are scheduled to arrive.

Around The Circus

The Circus at the center of town reflects St. Kitts' British heritage with the most photographed landmark in the country, the **Berkely Memorial Clock**, erected in 1883 to honor T.B.H. Berkely, a local planter and politician. The area around the Circus includes shops, boutiques and small shopping malls that carry imported china, crystal, precision watches and quality jewelry. You won't want to miss the following retailers.

☆ **Island Hopper** sells West Indian crafts in a pleasant atmosphere. It offers an array of art, pottery, textiles and a wide selection of Caribelle batiks (ask to see the batik process samples). If you cannot get out to see the Caribelle factory, the Island Hopper is the next best choice. The prices are exactly the same and the quality of the finished pieces has attracted repeat customers over Caribelle's long history of production. Wall hangings with several overlays of color are intricate and take a great deal of time to produce, all by hand. The clothing is very comfortable, especially in the humid Caribbean climate, and always in style.

Crafthouse, in the Palms Arcade off the Circus, features locally designed handmade clothing and accessories, as well as a variety of island-made merchandise and souvenirs. Be sure to look for the "Island to Island" label, a line of upscale fashions designed and produced on St. Kitts by John Warden. His signature style is an elegant unstructured cut in white, off-white, black and taupe.

Kate Design is an outlet of Kate's art studio at the Rawlins Plantation, which is open to the public 11 am to 5 pm. The shop on the Circus features Kate's designs on silk pareos, cards, mats, jewelry, prints and papier mâché. Another outlet can be found on Main Street in Charlestown, Nevis.

A Slice Of Lemon on the Circus is a duty-free gift shop selling fragrances, cosmetics and skin care products, jewelry and Portmeirion pottery.

Ram's Duty Free is a large store just off the Circus on Liverpool Row. The shop carries Waterford crystal, Wedgewood china, Hummel figurines, Swarovski crystal, watches, leather goods, Lladro figurines and a large selection of T-shirts at very good prices.

Creole Publishing, also on Liverpool Row, publishes and sells unique island cookbooks, postcards, maps and books. You can also buy souvenir bags of island brown sugar. The red-and-white-trimmed building was built in the Caribbean gingerbread style and is a part of the historic zone in Basseterre.

Wall's Deluxe Record and Bookshop is on Fort Street (on the corner of Princess) and has a wide selection of Caribbean books, maps, postcards, film and souvenirs. They also have the best in calypso, reggae and steel band recordings.

The Chattel House Gallery (on Princess Street near Wall's) features the work of T. Allen Jones, an artist who creates scenes of Caribbean life. On sale are original works, prints and cards.

Glass Island, Princess Street, is the working art glass studio of Gianni Bracciali. The shop features unique kiln-formed art glass, large platters, jewelry and gift items made on site.

Spencer Cameron Art Gallery is situated in an historic structure on North Independence Square (a short walk from the Circus). It has gathered the best work of local artists, including the Dancing Clown paintings by Rose Cameron Smith. These colorful characters whirl, whip and dance in paintings that capture the spirit of Carnival. Rose Cameron Smith's clown paintings are also displayed (though not for sale) in the Tourist Information Center at the Pelican Mall. The gallery is open weekdays from 9 am to 4 pm and Saturdays until 1 pm.

Splash sells beach attire, towels and T-shirts for men and women.

Pelican Mall & Port Zante

This mall offers duty-free prices comparable to those in larger shopping ports, but without the swarms of people. About 26 shops operated by locals sell perfumes, jewelry, porcelain and crystal. Your browsing and buying will support them.

☆ The **Philatelic Bureau** has a wide selection of attractive stamps for the collector, all bearing the name of St. Kitts. This is a relatively new stamp-producing country and these beautiful editions make a great gift for any collector. Stamps bearing the Nevis name are available only at the Philatelic Bureau on Nevis.

IC Jewelers sells jewelry, Lladro, Swarovski, Mont Blanc and Beume & Mercier merchandise.

Brinley Gold Vanilla Rum offers island-made rum products.

The **Gold Plus Linen Shop** has a wide assortment of garments and products with prices comparable to those found on St. Thomas and St. Maarten. It is also a great place to find gold and silver jewelry.

Ashburry's Duty-free on Liverpool Row has watches by Baume & Mercier, Movado, Phillipe Charriol and Longines; jewelry by Monet, Swarovski and Christian Dior; fragrances by Hugo Boss, Gucci, Givenchy, Van Cleef and Yves Saint-Laurent, plus cosmetics and skin care products.

Smoke 'n Booze offers samples of quality tobacco and liquor products. All the major brands are available here, including Cuban cigars. Be aware that you are not allowed to bring Cuban products back into the US, so smoke them on the islands.

The **Tourist Information Center** employs a very helpful and friendly staff who supply free information and directions, plus island maps and brochures.

Don't miss investigating the **Driftwood**, which has two locations (in Pelican Mall and at the Frigate Bay Resort). This shop offers unique souvenirs, gifts and collectibles all hand-crafted or designed locally from calabash, coconut, bamboo, clay, ceramic, leather or wood. They also have great T-shirts.

Around St. Kitts

☆ **Caribelle Batik** occupies an historic 17th-century sugar plantation house, Romney Manor, which has five acres of gardens and the largest tree on the island – a 350-year-old saman tree. The work rooms where artists create vibrantly colored batik on Sea Island cotton are open to the public. A free tour and explanation of the batik process help you to understand the quality and value of the merchandise. Batik prices are based on the number of colors in the cloth, where each permanently dyed color represents a separate waxing and dying cycle. Sea Island cotton, which is grown on Nevis, feels almost like fine silk. The factory is open Monday through Friday from 8:30 am to 4 pm (closed weekends and annual holidays). Romney Manor suffered a disastrous fire in October of 1995, but has since rebuilt a bigger shop and demonstration area.

Kate Design Studio, between the Rawlins Plantation and the Golden Lemon, is Kate Spencer's studio and gallery of original art.

Kate is best known for her designs on silk pareos, cards, mats, jewelry, prints and papier mâché, which can be purchased at her shop in Basseterre. Her original watercolors and oils are not for sale here. Open to the public from 11 am to 5 pm.

Transportation & Excursions

Taxis

Taxis will be waiting outside the Pelican Mall to escort you on island tours, or on trips to one of the many resorts. Fares are regulated by a taxi association and priced for the whole taxi, one to four persons. Some island excursions are charged for the round-trip, so be sure to ask the driver for clarification. Some taxi drivers give quotes in US dollars, so be sure to confirm the currency before entering the taxi. The majority of drivers make enthusiastic tour guides, so take advantage of their friendly attitude for a wonderful day on the island.

Taxi Chart

All prices are given in US dollars.

Destination *from Pelican Mall, Basseterre*	**Cost** *one to four people*
Brimstone Hill Fortress (round-trip)	$38
Conaree Beach	$15
Frigate Bay	$8
Ocean Terrace Inn	$5
Rawlins Plantation (round-trip)	$60
Romney Manor/Caribelle Batik (round-trip)	$50
Royal St. Kitts Golf Club	$8
South Friars Bay	$12
Turtle Bay Beach (round-trip)	$40

Rental Cars

Cars are available for rent in downtown Basseterre. Driving is on the left. Unpaved island roads can be narrow and are not clearly marked. The continuous road that encircles the entire island (called "the main road") makes directions easy and takes about six hours to complete. From town, head west on Canyon Street.

Before renting a car, you must buy a $12 temporary driver's license at either the police or the fire station in Basseterre. Most rental agencies can assist in the process. A collision damage waiver is highly recommended and costs $5-$10 The minimum age for renting a car is 25 and a credit card is required to cover the deductible collision damage waiver. Rates vary between $35 and $60 per day, not including gas, for automatics and cars with a/c, but the cool island breezes on St. Kitts make this an unnecessary expense. Jeeps are fun to rent and usually run $35 to $70 per day, depending on size.

Car Rental Agencies

The area code for St. Kitts and Nevis is 869, a long-distance phone call from the United States.

Avis . . . . . ☎ 465-6507 or (800) 228-0668; www.avis.com
Sunshine Car Rental . . . . ☎ 465-2193 or (800) 621-1270
Delisle Walwyn Rentals . . . . ☎ 465-8449
www.delisleco.com; e-mail delwal@caribsurf.com
Thrifty-TDC Car Rentals . . ☎ 465-2991; www.tdcltd.com
Kantours. . . . . ☎ 465-3054; www.kantours.com
Nevis Car Rentals, Claude Nisbett . . . . ☎ 469-9837
Islandwide Scooter Rentals . . . . ☎ 466-7841
($25-$30/day free pick up) midasscooter@caribsurf.com
Tropical Tours . . . . ☎ 465-4167/4039/9649;
kisco@caribsurf.com

Self-Guided Tours

When St. Kitts was a flourishing sugar-producing island, plantations dotted the landscape. Today, you can visit several original Great Houses and old windmill ruins, including the immaculately restored and maintained Rawlins Plantation.

Rawlins Plantation

If you are venturing out on the island, the best stop for lunch is one of the oldest sugarcane estates on St. Kitts. The Rawlins Plantation has weathered many hurricanes and renovations and is now a beautiful estate property. The dining room was constructed over the ruins of the old boiling house and its chimney is in remarkable condition. One of the 10 guest rooms occupies an old sugar mill, remodeled to create a unique bedroom suite. The grounds are manicured and the buffet lunch is tantalizing. (You'll need to reserve a spot for an afternoon lunch.) The West Indian buffet is a feast not to be missed, featuring typical island delicacies and a sampling of fresh produce from the gardens of the Rawlins Plantation. Contact Paul or Claire Rawson, ☎ (869) 465-6221, to make a lunch reservation and book for a guided tour around the facilities. It will take 45 minutes to reach the plantation, and views en route are spectacular. Visit their website at www.rawlinsplantation.com; e-mail rawplant@caribsurf.com.

Nevis Day-Trip

A 45-minute trip to the sister island Nevis is definitely worthwhile. You can purchase tickets at the ferry reception desk, next to the cruise ship berth at the Pelican Mall in Basseterre. Tickets are $8 round-trip, per person. The current ferry schedule to Nevis is given below, but be sure to check at the desk for any changes.

Ferry Schedule

No service is offered on Thursday or Sunday.

Departs	**Arrives**
Monday:	
8 am Basseterre	8:45 am Charlestown (Nevis)
3 pm Charlestown	3:45 pm Basseterre
Tuesday:	
1 pm Basseterre	1:45 pm Charlestown
6 pm Charlestown	6:45 pm Basseterre
Wednesday:	
7 am Basseterre	7:45 am Charlestown
8 am Charlestown	8:45 am Basseterre
4 pm Basseterre	4:45 pm Charlestown
6 pm Charlestown	6:45 pm Basseterre
Friday:	
8:30 am Basseterre	9:15 am Charlestown
3 pm Charlestown	3:45 pm Basseterre
Saturday:	
8:30 am Basseterre	9:15 am Charlestown
2 pm Charlestown	2:45 pm Basseterre

Banana Boat Tours offers a private water taxi to Nevis for $35 per person, round-trip. The 34-foot rigid inflatable, certified and approved by the US Coast Guard, is fully equipped with the latest safety features. It travels up to 40 mph and departs from Port Zante. This operation also offers snorkeling, fishing and private charters. ☎ 465-0645; bananaboattours@caribsurf.com.

In Charlestown, take a walk around the small town starting to the left on Main Street. Two blocks down on the left is a small museum of Nevis historical memorabilia and the location where Alexander Hamilton was born. The museum opens its gates at 10 am and there is no entrance fee.

When you're done in town, hire a taxi for an island tour, which takes about 3½ hours and costs $55 for one to four persons. Also see the Nevis map on previous page for sites that should not be missed, including the following:

- **The Bath Hotel & Spring House**, just outside Charlestown, is the oldest hotel in the Caribbean. The property sits over a fault line with hot springs that have been used for baths for over 200 years. You can relax in the stimulating water for a nominal charge.
- **Morning Star, Horatio Nelson's Museum.** The Morning Star was a sugar plantation and the site of a 1706 battle between the British and the French. When Britain's most famous admiral, Lord Nelson, used Nevis as a base of operations, he fell in love and married a local islander, Frances Nisbet, in 1787. The museum has a wonderful collection of the couple's memorabilia. It is open Monday through Saturday, 9 am-1 pm, with an admission charge of $2 for adults and 75¢ for children.
- **Croney's Old Manor Estate.** One of the loveliest restored sugar plantations on Nevis has many sugar-producing items and historical buildings. There is a perfect view of the Nevis volcano from the grounds. If you can visit only one plantation, make it the Old Manor. Free.
- The **Nisbet Plantation** is a more modern plantation with one of the most gorgeous and artistic gardens in the entire Caribbean. A walk through the rows of royal palm trees leads to a mile-long stretch of white coral sand beach that cannot be matched. You are welcome to view the property, but you should advise the front desk personnel of your presence. The Nisbet Plantation is one of the most magnificently maintained plantations on Nevis. Free.
- **Oualie Beach Club**. If you get an early start, plan to have lunch at this enchanting beachside resort. Oualie Beach has a row of quaint cottages set along the beach with a wonderful view of the big island, St. Kitts. The private suites and cottages are specially designed to be distinctive to Nevis and they do not resemble a typical resort found anywhere else. Free.
- **The Botanical Garden of Nevis** was established in 1996 and contains beautiful plants from tropics worldwide, bronze sculptures from Thailand, ornamental

fountains and a magnificent conservatory styled after the Palm House at Kew Gardens in England. The central feature is Martha's West Indian Tea House, a restaurant and gift shop serving lunch and English tea, with scones and clotted cream.The entrance fee to the gardens ($8 for adults and $4 for children) is waived if you eat here or make a purchase at the gift shop.

Caribelle Batik Factory

A visit to this unique workshop and neighboring Brimstone Hill makes for a fun day. See *One-Day Itinerary, Shopping* and *Museums & Historical Sites*, pages 151, 157 and 171, for details.

Organized Tours & Activities

The following tours can be arranged through island hotels who will try to accommodate cruise passengers. Most sailing trips and island excursions begin at 9 am and return by 5 pm. For space availability and current times, contact the tour group directly.

Island Tour Groups

Tropical Tours, ☎ (869) 465-4167/4039, kisco@caribsurf.com, offers the following excursions:

- ⚓ The **Guided Island Tour** consists of a drive along the coastline through sugarcane fields to the Black Rocks, the Brimstone Hill Fortress & Museum and Romney Manors Caribelle Batik Factory. The entire tour lasts 3½ hours and runs $25 per person.
- ⚓ The **Queen City/Sister Island Tour** takes you on the ferry over to Nevis for a day of exploring the Nelson Museum, Alexander Hamilton birthplace, the Old Bath House and historical island sites. It leaves at 7:30 am and returns at 4 pm. Cost is $62, including ferry fees, lunch and refreshments (entrance fees to museums and security fees at ferry terminal are not included).
- ⚓ **Volcano Crater Tour**. A rain forest hike for the very fit adventurer to the extinct Volcano Crater Lake. You may see shy green vervet monkeys, exotic birds and fragrant

orchids. This tour incorporates a vigorous 2½-hour hike. It leaves at 7 am and returns at 5 pm. The $62 per-person rate includes lunch. A less strenuous half-day tour (leaving at 8:30 am and returning at 1 pm) walks through the rainforest for about an hour for $52 per person. The guide will set up sandwiches and soft drinks after the tour.

- ⚓ The **Horseback Rainforest Tour** leaves at 8:30 am and returns at 1 pm. It costs $62 per person, including drinks. Experience the beautiful flora and fauna, ride for an hour along trails through cane fields, then trek in lush rain forest.
- ⚓ The **Kayak Snorkeling Adventure** leaves at 8:30 am and 1:30 pm for a 3½-hour kayak trip along the scenic coast. The tour costs $52 per person, including refreshments and snorkeling. You'll see steep cliffs, remote bays and may spot sea turtles, pelicans, cormorants and green monkeys.

Rose and Jims Guided Tours, ☎ (869) 465-4694; e-mail rose_jim@caribsurf.com. We highly recommend Rose and Jim as guides. They bend over backwards to make your day on St. Kitts wonderful and arrange anything you need, including hikes in the rain forest. If you want a personalized tour, contact them ahead of time to reserve. The full-day island tour costs $66, the part-day to Brimstone Hill and Caribelle Batik, the Peninsula tour or the tour to Turtle Beach each cost $45, one to four people. Jim offers an excellent rainforest hike. He points out and explains the medicinal use of rainforest plants. You may see birds and wildlife, including green monkeys. The tour includes a visit to Romney Manor, the home of Caribelle Batik, so be sure to take your wallet. This excursion costs $35 per person and takes 2½-3 hours.

The **Scenic Railway** circles the island and a tour for cruise passengers is a combination train/bus trip that takes 3½ hours total (2½ hours on the train). You get great views from the large windows of double-deck cars, while the engineer narrates about island history and the natural wonders of St. Kitts. (There are no stops along the route, so a taxi tour is still the best way to see more of the island.) The cost is $89 for adults and $44.50 for children age three-11. ☎ (869) 465-7263; www.stkittsscenicrailway.com; scenicresrvations1@caribsurf.com.

Island Tours by Taxi

The **local taxi association** offers **island tours** leaving from the Pelican Mall and going to the Brimstone Hill Fortress, Romney Manor and Caribelle Batik Factory for $45, one to four people. There is an additional $5 entrance fee to the fortress. This tour lasts three hours. A complete island tour, including the fortress and batik factory, takes five hours and costs $66, one to four people. If you have time for the longer tour, it is worthwhile, but the mini-tour is just as interesting and allows you more time at one of the beaches or in Basseterre. The taxi drivers on St. Kitts are pleasant and informative.

Guided Hikes

Friendly and professional guides are available for all sorts of ecological, historical and archaeological walks or hikes.

- **Greg's Safaris** offers a four-hour tour of the St. Kitts Rain Forest for $40 per person, and a ½-hour off-the-beaten-path plantation tour ($45) that visits private great houses not normally open to the public. Greg transports guests in a modified Land Rover and offers a full island picnic with all tours. Visit www.gregsafaris.com for detailed descriptions of all available tours. ☎ (869) 465-4121/663-6008; e-mail g-safari@caribsurf.com.
- David Rollinson of **Eco-Tours Nevis** runs a three-hour rain forest tour on Nevis for $25 per person. He also offers a 1½-hour historic walk at $15 per person. His narrative is wry and informative. ☎ (869) 469-2091; e-mail droll@caribsurf.com.

Beaches

The Southeast Peninsula is a relatively undeveloped area of St. Kitts inhabited by hundreds of green vervet monkeys. At the south end of the island, closest to the sister island of Nevis, lies a special beach area known as **Turtle Beach**. If you want to spend the entire day on the sand, this is a good choice. It has a beachside restaurant, bar, scuba diving, free beach chairs and umbrellas, and a private stretch of sand; just offshore is a protected tropical reef perfect for snorkeling or scuba diving. Snorkeling equipment is only $10 for a full rental set. Relax on the beach, observe the monkeys and look for colorful tropical fish in the local waters. Turtle Beach has a volleyball court, shade trees and on Sundays it hosts an exceptional lunch buffet with a steel band from 12:30 to 3 pm. There's also an outdoor freshwater shower, changing rooms, gift shop and a feeding station where green vervet monkeys come to get a handout (very entertaining). It's just 25 minutes from Basseterre by taxi ($40 round-trip, one to four persons). The journey out to the beach along the Atlantic Ocean is breathtaking. There is so much space here that you may feel entirely alone, even if others are on the beach.

BEACH CHART	Facilities	Windsurfing	Snorkeling	Scuba Diving	Wave Runners	Swimming	Parasailing	Sailing	Water Skiing	Nude/Topless
Turtle Beach	☆	☆	☆	☆		☆		☆		
Conaree Beach	☆					☆				
South Friar's Bay	☆					☆				
Frigate Bay	☆	☆	☆		☆	☆		☆	☆	

A long, wide white sandy stretch with few people is **Conaree Beach**. A hurricane in 2000 damaged this area, but repairs are underway. Check with your taxi driver or the tourist board on current conditions before making a trip. You can hire a taxi to take you to the Sun 'n Sand Beach Village, then a stroll through the grounds will lead straight to Conaree. The beach is situated on the Atlantic side of Frigate Bay, with pounding waves that are both dramatic and powerful. Swimmers should stay close to the shore, but can have an adventurous time playing in the waves. The beach is large enough to accommodate all the passengers on your ship without feeling cramped. Be sure to wander through the Sun 'n Sand complex, complete with a restaurant, grocery store and small gift shop. This is definitely one of St. Kitts loveliest beachside resorts. Taxi drivers are always available at the hotel and the ride is 15 minutes from downtown Basseterre ($9 one-way, one to four people).

Twenty minutes from town on the Southeast Peninsula is **South Friar's Bay**, a popular destination for cruise ships like the *Windstar.* South Friar's Bay is set down a long road away from all other hotels, which means you can enjoy a day at the beach in privacy. Watersports are available when cruise ships are in port. A taxi ride here will run $25, round-trip.

The Caribbean-side of Frigate Bay is home to **Timothy Beach Resort** and **RG Watersports**. You can take a $8 one-way (one to four people), 15-minute taxi ride to the beach and have some fun in the sun. The Sunset Café at the resort offers lunch and facilities. **Mr. X Watersports** (☎ 869-465-5166) near Timothy Beach has Jet Skis, beach chairs, snorkeling equipment, water skis and windsurfers for rent (see *Watersports*, page 168, for rates).

Island Activities

On Land

Golf

The **Royal St. Kitts Golf Club** is only 15 minutes from Basseterre. This lush 18-hole championship course was designed by five-time British Open champion Peter Thomson, and borders both the Atlantic and Caribbean beaches. The club has greens fees of $25 (nine holes) or $35 (18 holes). Cart rentals are $30 (nine holes) and $40 (18 holes). Clubs are available for $10 (nine holes) and $15 (18 holes). Advance booking for tee times is recommended during the peak season, January through March. A taxi one way costs $8 for one to four people.. ☎ (869) 465-8339 or 5776; a toll-free number is available in Chicago, ☎ (800) 582-6208; and a local number in New York, ☎ (212) 535-1234.

The **Four Seasons Resort** (Nevis) has a beautiful golf course, 10 tennis courts and a spa. The course was designed by Robert Trent Jones and opened in 1991. Greens fees are $175 for 18 holes, $110 for nine holes, and reservations can be made at ☎ (869) 469-1111; www.fourseasons.com/nevis.

Horseback Riding

The **Nevis Equestrian Centre** offers a variety of rides for all levels, geared to the least experienced person. The most popular ride lasts 1¾ hours ($50/adult, $35/children age seven-13). It starts on the beach, goes up a mountain trail, through the bush, among plantation ruins and villages, then returns to the beach. Refreshments are served at the end. The stables are on the Main Road at Fort Ashby. Children under six are allowed to ride in the arena. Helmets are provided and are mandatory for children. Private guided rides can be arranged for an additional $25 per person. Scheduled 1½-hour rides depart at 9:30 am and 3 pm. Check out the petting zoo filled with rabbits, guinea pigs, turtles, birds, fish and monkeys. Call ☎ (869) 469-8118, fax 469-3106 or e-mail guilbert@caribsurf.com.

St. Kitts Frigate Bay & West Farm offers a four-hour rainforest ride leaving at 8:30 am and 2:30 pm for a minimum of four riders and maximum of eight riders. ☎ (869) 465-2222.

Mountain Biking & ATVs

The **Wheel World Cycle Shop** has outlets in Basseterre's Flamboyant Mall in Bassetere (☎ 869-466-3251) and on Main Street in Charlestown, Nevis (☎ 869-469-7137). They rent mountain bikes for $20-$35 per day, as well as BMX road bikes and in-line skates. A security deposit or passport is required for all rentals.

Fun Bikes offer guided tours on four-wheel ATV bikes, leaving at 8:30 and 11:30 am and return at noon and 2:30 pm accordingly. ☎ 869-466-3202 or 662-2088 for rates and reservations.

In The Ocean

Watersports

Frigate Bay, on the Caribbean Sea side of the island, is only 15 minutes from the pier and has calm seas that make learning easy. **Mr. X. Watersports** (☎ 869-465-5166) offers Hobie Cats ($30/hour), snorkeling gear ($10/day), kayaks ($15/hour), windsurf boards ($15/hour), Sunfish ($20/hour), and bicycle rentals ($15/day). They also offer a snorkel reef trip for $25, including equipment, and a Friar's Bay trip for $5 per person.

The open bay on the Caribbean side of St. Kitts has wonderful conditions for learning or playing in the surf.

On Nevis, the **Oualie Beach Resort** (see below) rents windsurfing equipment for $95 a day.

Ocean Kayaking

The newest activity available at the **Oualie Beach Resort** on Nevis is ocean kayaking. A three-hour kayak and snorkel tour travels along the coast from Oualie Beach to Pinney's Beach with a stop for snorkeling over virgin reefs and another stop to enjoy tropical drinks, local pastries and fresh fruit. The trip ends next to the Four Season Resort. Views of Mount Nevis rising into the sky and St. Kitts across the channel are breathtaking. An enjoyable tour for novice or experienced kayakers. The $45 fee and includes refreshments, instruction and an expert guide. ☎ (869) 469-8503; www.beach-works.com.

Scuba Diving

Pro Divers offers a dive leaving from the cruise ship dock at Port Zante at 9 am and returning at 1pm. The one-tank dive costs $60 and the two-tank dive costs $90 (both dives include equipment). Specially trained instructors take extra precautions to protect the natural beauty of the underwater world on St. Kitts. To capture the dive on film, underwater cameras with strobe are available for $20 and a dive computer runs $10.

The 3½-hour training session includes lessons, a boat trip, two shallow-water dives, equipment and soft drinks. If you're interested only in snorkeling, Pro Divers also offers half-day snorkel trips, 3½ hours long, to three different sites, with equipment and drinks included for a cost of $35 per person. For bookings and inquiries, ☎ (869) 466-DIVE (3423); www.prodiversstkitts.com.

St. Kitts Scuba operates from the Bird Rock Hotel, about a mile southeast of Basseterre. Boat excursions run $50 for a one-tank dive, $80 for a two-tank dive and $35 for snorkeling. Dive gear rents for $10 and includes octopus, regulator, gauges and BCD vest. ☎ (869) 465-1675; fax (847) 699-7583; brbh@caribbeans.com.

On Nevis, diving is offered at **Scuba Safaris**, operating out of the **Oualie Beach Resort**, ☎ (869) 469-9518; fax (869) 469-9619; e-mail scubanev@caribsurf.com. Visit www.divenevis.com and read about some of the dive sites they visit. A snorkel safari costs $35, plus $10 for snorkel gear, a one-tank dive costs $35, and a two-tank dive costs $80. Equipment rentals are $8 for regulator and $5 for a BCD vest. A one-way trip by powerboat from the cruise ship dock in St. Kitts costs $150 for up to six people, and it's much faster than the ferry.

Ocean Sailing & Motor Cruises

Tropical Tours also runs a full-day catamaran trip, which includes a visit to Nevis for a beach barbecue and snorkeling. Transportation, open bar and snorkeling equipment are all included in the price of $77 per person. Visitors can have a great time swimming, dancing, snorkeling, or walking the plank. The tour leaves at 9 am and returns at 4:30 pm. For more information, ☎ (869) 465-4167 or 4039; e-mail Kisco@caribsurf.com.

Banana Boat Tours offers a three-hour snorkeling tour for $160 for the whole boat (one-four people), with all equipment, snacks and drinks, including the famous Banana Slide Rum punch. Guests must bring their own suits and towels. Fishing trips for two-six people are $90 per person, including rods and bait. A three-hour cruise along the coastline costs $35 per person with a six-person minimum. All tours leave from the Port Zante dock. Reservations can be made by e-mail, bananaboattours@caribsurf.com.

Sea Nevis Boat Charters offers day sailing/snorkeling trips onboard the *Sea Dreamer*, a beautiful 44-foot sailboat, sailing out of Nevis. A half-day trip (1 to 4 pm) costs $95 per person, while a full day (10 am to 4:30 pm) is $125 per person. There's a minimum of four and maximum of 10 passengers. Both trips include snacks, open bar and snorkeling equipment. Private charters are $500 for the full day. ☎ (869) 469-9239 or 663-2084 (cell); fax (869) 469-9522; seadream@caribsurf.com.

Blue Water Safaris owns two 65-foot catamarans. They offer full-day itineraries at $65 per person, leaving port at 9:30 am and returning by 4:30 pm. The price includes an open bar, snorkeling equipment and a BBQ lunch of chicken, salads, fresh banana bread and a delightful dessert. You'll snorkel off the St. Kitts' coast, sail across the narrows to Nevis, then swim, snorkel or beachcomb at Pinney's beach. A half-day snorkeling excursion costs $40 per person, with two daily trips scheduled (8:30 am to 12:30 pm and 1:30 to 5:30 pm). Deep-sea fishing costs US $360 for a half-day or US $700 for a full-day charter, including bait, tackle and drinks. No more than six anglers are permitted, and it's "bring your own box lunch." For reservations, ☎ (869) 466-4933; fax 465-3366; or e-mail waterfun@caribsurf.com.

One-Day Itinerary

St. Kitts' friendly and informative taxi drivers make the best tour guides. To arrange an excursion, speak with a few drivers until you find one willing to give a site-specific island tour. The cost of the taxi for a full day should be between $125-$150. This may be more expensive than on other islands, but well worth the money! To help in planning, we've profiled the sites and given time allowances for each location below. The total island tour from Basseterre to Conaree Beach should take 5½ hours. Allow 15 minutes for the cab ride ($9) back to the ship.

Taxi Chart	
Romney Manor & Caribelle Batik Factory	30 mins.
Brimstone Hill Fortress	1 hour
Black Rocks	30 mins.
Rawlins Plantation	1½ hours
Sun 'n Sand Hotel/Conaree Beach	2 hours

What to Bring

A camera with lots of film is a necessity. St. Kitts is impressive, with rolling fields of sugarcane and dramatic coastlines. Bring a bathing suit for the beach. Lunch should be pre-arranged at Rawlins Plantation (have the taxi driver call ahead, or contact Paul or Claire Rawson yourself at ☎ 869-465-6221).

Directions

Refer to the island map on page 173.

An Island Tour

Begin your island adventure at the **Pelican Mall** at 9 am. The driver will first drive through the capital of Basseterre, then travel up the coast to **Romney Manor,** home to the **Caribelle Batik Factory** (open Monday-Friday, 8:30 am-4 pm; ☎ 869-465-6253). Ask the driver to point out the unusual Indian petroglyphs on rocks in a yard along the road.

At the factory you will see the process of producing high-quality batik. First, a design is sketched onto a piece of white cotton, then molten wax is applied by a pen-like tool that pours out the wax onto the areas that will remain uncolored by the first dye. Wherever wax is placed, the color will not be absorbed. Next, the fabric is colored either by painting or dipping into the dye. Every color on the batik requires a separate waxing and dying process. A wide selection of colorful prints, lightweight fabric clothes and other dyed items are sold at the store inside the factory.

The next stop on the coastline is **Brimstone Hill Fortress National Park** ($5 for adults, $2.50 for children), The Gibraltar of the West Indies. Of all the forts and historical ruins in the Caribbean, Brimstone Hill Fortress is the best and most complete example of British and French fort architecture open to the public. The entire grounds can be explored within an hour. Be sure to hike up the steep stairs to the top of Fort George, which affords excellent views of the surrounding countryside and the outer island of St. Eustastius – a photographer's dream come true. The **Fort George Museum** at the top of the stairs displays British, French, American and Pre-Columbian artifacts in the rooms of the old barracks. Built in the mid-1600s, the fort is a definite highlight of St. Kitts.

A tour of the coastline would not be complete without a stop at the dramatic **Black Rocks**. These jagged crevasses were formed by a prehistoric volcanic eruption. Large sprays of water frequently explode from the massive rocks as waves crash against the volcanic terrain. These waterspouts create impressive shots for video camcorders and still photographers.

With prior arrangements, lunch at **Rawlins Plantation** (☎ 869-465-6221) is the next stop for the day. The gourmet West Indian buffet lunch offered between 1 and 2 pm contains an assortment of local dishes, including fresh fruit and produce grown on the property. Highly recommended! Take a stroll through the manicured gardens and view the remains of the sugar mill, once the center of activity on the plantation. Spend up to 1½ hours here, then proceed down the coast back through Basseterre.

If you're searching for a wide stretch of coral-white sand, head to **Conaree Beach**. However, check on beach conditions before going, as this area sustained hurricane damage in 2000. If it's open, have the taxi driver stop at the entrance of the Sun 'n Sand Beach Village, then walk through the grounds to the beach. Row after row of pounding Atlantic waves hit the crescent-shaped cove – it's dramatic to watch and excellent for playing in the surf. Even good swimmers

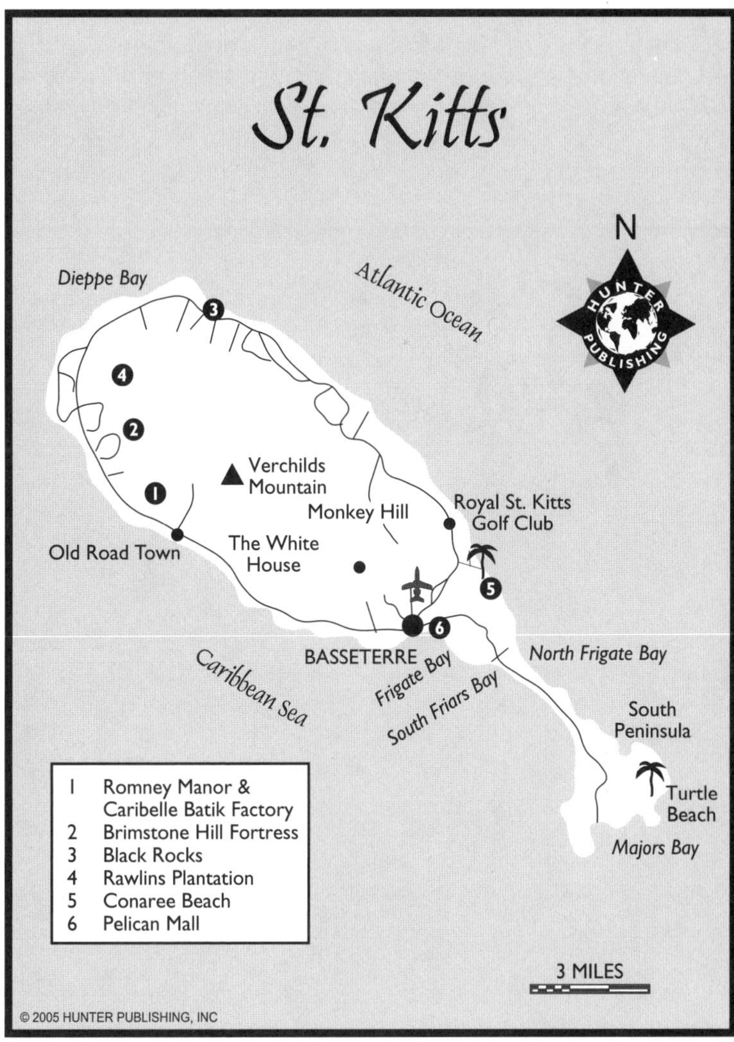

should stay close to the shore here. The long beach is a great spot for relaxing in the sun, with enough sand for everyone.

An alternate choice for a day at the beach is Frigate Bay, on the Caribbean side of St. Kitts (just a few minutes from Conaree Beach). This bay is not subject to pounding waves or strong Atlantic currents. The beach is delightful, the swimming is tame and watersports activities are available.

Arrange for the driver to return to the beach in a few hours, or dismiss him and hail a taxi from the hotel for the drive back into town. If you have time, go to Pelican Mall for some last-minute souvenir shopping. This island sightseeing tour runs between five and six hours.

Dominica

Caribbean's Nature Island

Island Description

Columbus sailed past Dominica (pronounced DOM-en-eeka) on a Sunday, so the island was named after that day of the week. To describe the land when he returned to Spain, Columbus crumpled a piece of stiff paper and placed it on a table, telling his audience that Dominica was an island of jagged peaks rising from the sea – an apt description, since it is composed of towering mountains, deep river gorges, cascading waterfalls and boiling lakes and was formed by the eruptions of several volcanoes.

At least two-thirds of Dominica's land area is covered by forest or other vegetation, with two mountain peaks over 4,000 feet. Thousands of acres are under the protection of the National Park Service, an example of Dominica's farsighted government. The mountainous terrain is dissected by deep valleys and gorges, with some 365 streams and rivers, a hiker's paradise and a gardener's dream. With almost 350 inches of rain each year, almost anything will grow in the rich volcanic soil.

Dominica's inaccessible territory produced a turbulent history for the island, which changed ownership between the English and French many times. Both armies found it difficult to wage a successful land campaign, as the steep cliffs prevented conventional invasions. An invading army was forced to trudge through miles of extremely rugged land to wage a sneak attack on the enemy. Two armies once passed within a mile of each other without meeting, and the forces of nature could defeat both armies before a battle was actually waged.

The dense jungle proved beneficial to those who wished to hide from the dominating armed forces. Rebel slaves, called **maroons**, ran away from their masters, disappearing into the tropical forest. Their resistance against slavery took the form of raiding estates and burning crops. The maroons were defeated in 1815 in the Maroon War, but their influence on many islands was an element in the collapse of the economics of slavery in the Caribbean.

Today, agriculture is the primary source of income for the majority of island inhabitants. Bananas are the largest export crop and can be seen in large groves on the steepest of mountains. The banana plant is unique because it produces one large stalk of bananas and then must be cut down to allow another plant to sprout from its roots. Blue bags, which can be seen covering the stalks, protect the bananas from insects and filter the sun's rays to improve growth. Another large source of income is the coconut, which is made into hand soap, shampoos and lotions in a local factory. One small factory packages guava, passion fruit and hot sauce from plants grown by locals.

Island People

Dominican culture is the closest to true native Caribbean life found in the islands and is almost untainted by tourism. The island did not have paved roads until 1970, when a new road system was engineered to link the villages that were once completely isolated from each other. Until that time, men undertook the arduous land journey to the big town of Roseau rarely and only for business.

A villager could be recognized by his distinctive appearance, his family name and his accent, all linked to a village archetype. Children from the countryside who were sent to school in Roseau at great expense and sacrifice to their families were considered backward by their town-bred schoolmates. When paved roads linked the island and made travel easier, inter-village marriages became more common and the island began the process of melding into a modern society. The villages are slowly becoming a part of the whole country of Dominica, though individual village pride and identity are still displayed in community festivals and yearly religious events.

Today, tourism has not infringed upon the island lifestyle to any large degree and you will find few enterprises existing strictly for your pleasure. The government has shown its commitment to protecting the natural environment and is developing tourism slowly. World economic factors may change attitudes as European trade agreements threaten to eliminate British price protections, which have traditionally favored Caribbean agriculture. Dominica may be forced to play the tourism game for economic survival, but the island as a whole will continue efforts to protect its fragile environment.

Opposite: Caibbean-style architecture, courtesy Sint Maarten Tourism

REGGAE
Cafe
Love Laugh

Above: Marigot Harbour from Fort St. Louis, courtesy Sint Maarten Tourism

Below: Caneel Bay, St. John, courtesy USVI Dept. of Tourism/Steve Simonson

Above: The rare jacquot parrot, St. Lucia, courtesy Middleton & Gendron

Below: St. Lucia's Pitons, courtesy Middleton & Gendron

Above: Green vervet monkeys, Barbados © Laura Rapp

Opposite: Mahogony Run Golf Course, St. Thomas, courtesy USVI Dept. of Tourism

Below: Harrison's Caves, Barbados © Laura Rapp

Above: Cruz Bay, St. John, courtesy USVI Dept. of Tourism

Opposite: Morningstar Beach, St. Thomas, courtesy USVI Dept. of Tourism

Below: Bayside Riding Club, courtesy Sint Maarten Tourism

Smiling school children on Dominica.
(Image courtesy Dominica Tourist Office, NY.)

Island Proverbs

When a dog sucks an egg, he blamed fer everything.
Those who do bad things are blamed automatically.

What hurt de turkey dont hurt de duck.
What bothers one doesnt bother another.

How it go?
How are you doing?

Make sure better den cock sure.
Know the truth rather than making assumptions.

Home drum beats first.
See to your own family first.

De truth come out when the spirit go in.
Alcohol loosens the tongue.

Opposite: Nevis landscape

Holidays

As tourism has not become a major industry on Dominica, shops still close on public holidays. However, taxis, tour guides and dockside vendors are available whenever a cruise ship is in port.

Annual Holidays

For more details and precise dates, contact the island tourist board (see *Appendix*).

January . . . New Year's Day; Merchants Holiday (shops close)

February . . . . Carnival (Monday-Tuesday preceding Ash Wednesday)

April . . . . Good Friday; Easter Monday

May . . . . May Day; Whit Monday (Pentecost)

July. Domfesta (festival of the arts)

August . . . . August Monday (the freeing of slaves in the entire British West Indies)

October. . . . . Heritage Day; Jorne Creole (celebrates French Creole ancestry with music and festivals)

November . . Independence Day; Community Service Day

December . . . . Christmas; Boxing Day

Useful Websites

The official tourist board website, **www.dominica.dm**, offers colorful pictures, maps, descriptions of Dominica's natural attractions and history of the island. We found the most informative site to be **www.caribline.com/islands/dm**, which offers good maps of the island and its largest towns, plus a list of shops and car rental businesses (for those brave souls willing to navigate the steep mountain roads!). One great website with links to local tours and activities is www.avirtualdominic.com. You can download a walking tour of Roseau for $5, and be sure to click on the "What to do in one day" for suggestions that are tailored to cruise ship passengers.

The Pier

There are two docking locations – the relatively new pier area in downtown Roseau (pronounced rose-oh) and the Cabrits pier near Portsmouth. The Roseau pier, completed in 1995, receives the majority of cruise ships. The local Tourist Information Office occupies the Old Post Office building at Bay and King George Streets. The Cabrits facility was specifically designed for the tourist trade. It contains a small museum with displays of artifacts and local crafts, public telephones, a souvenir shop and a theater with audio-visual programs. The Cabrits pier is a short walk from Fort Shirley, which affords views of Portsmouth Bay and gives you a sense of the colonial military importance of this location. As the majority of cruise ships dock at the port in Roseau, the remainder of the chapter will use Roseau as a starting point for tours and excursions.

Pier Phones

The area code for Dominica is 809.

A new island phone system makes phone calls easier with high-speed Internet available.

Public phones are available along the pier area in Roseau and in the Old Market Craft Centre. However, island phone cards may be required for local calls. Look for telephone card dispensers, check with the tourist information desk to purchase island phone cards, or ☎ (800) 872-2881 to connect with the AT&T Direct service. The modern docking facility at the Cabrits pier has a bank of public telephones expressly for cruise ship passengers.

The **Cable & Wireless Company** offers a special phone number to use for calling the US. Dial 1-800-255-5872 (CALL USA) to make collect calls, or credit card or US calling card calls. Voice instructions guide you through the process.

Cornerhouse Café, near the Old Market, serves coffee and lunch along with high-speed Internet access. For $3 you can log onto the Web for 30 minutes while enjoying great food. ☎ (767) 449-9000; cornerhousedom@hotmail.com.

In Town

Currency

The **Eastern Caribbean dollar** (EC) is the official currency of Dominica, tied to the US dollar at approximately EC $2.65 to US $1. Tour guides and taxis accept US currency, but it is wise to use EC currency for making purchases in town and on the Carib Reserve. Be sure to carry bills in smaller denominations as you may not be able to get change in rural areas. Credit cards and travelers' checks are widely accepted by merchants in Roseau.

Banks in Roseau are located on Hillsborough Street and across from the new post office. Banks are open Monday through Friday from 8 am to 1pm and Fridays 3 to 5 pm. Passengers can cash traveler's checks at banks and receive a better rate than they can get in stores.

Postage

If you are a stamp collector, or wish to make a big hit with one at home, buy the collector editions on Dominica. Some of the most beautiful stamps in the Caribbean are sold at the main post office in Roseau, located along the waterfront at the corner of Bay Street and Kennedy Avenue. A special window is provided for the Philatelic Bureau and many of the stamps available for purchase are displayed on the wall. Dominica's extraordinary stamps show tropical fish, exotic birds and historical events that appeal to collectors. An airmail postcard costs US 20¢. (Remember, US postage is not accepted.)

Museums & Historical Sites

T he Botanical Gardens are located at the edge of town at the end of King George Street. Taxi drivers and tour guides often drive their passengers through the gardens, but it's an easy walk from the pier and you'll get to see the colorful flowers and lush vegetation up close. Be sure to visit the exhibit in the middle, which features the elusive and nearly extinct Sisserou parrot, the national bird of Dominica, along with two colorful but endangered Amazon parrots. The Sisserou parrots are quite striking, with purple chest feathers accented by a multitude of green and blue feathers. The parrot exhibit was established to increase awareness of the plight of the endangered birds. Too many parrots have been captured, smuggled out and sold to collectors abroad, while the remaining birds have vanished deep into the forests.

The Old Sugar Mill Cultural Center. The remains of a water-driven sugarcane mill with large wheels are a short ride from the cruise ship port in Roseau. The Old Mill was one of the largest and longest running on the island and it operates today as a cultural center and museum. Before heading out there, ask the taxi driver if it's open, since it might be closed for annual renovations.

The estate was bought by millionaire Andrew Green in 1908 and many of his old photographs are on display. Mr. Green reorganized the mill operations with steam crushers and electricity. Artifacts and displays give you an overview of the island's history, geography and folklore. If you feel like a walk, head up the hill to the right of the mill and visit the woodcrafters. Their shop, set in the former overseer's house, is open for viewing. Watch the artists carving superb pieces. The second-story showroom is filled with elegant finished pieces.

Fort Shirley. Dominica was the last island in the Caribbean to be colonized and the forbidding topography limited the number of choice sites for construction. Fort Shirley, once the most important military outpost on the island, is a short walk from the new Cabrits cruise ship port in Portsmouth. The unrestored structure is an excellent example of 18th-century British military defense and offers a wonderful view down into the harbor.

View of Cabrits from Fort Shirley.

The Carib Reserve. The dense forests and impassable terrain of Dominica saved the Caribs from extinction. When Europeans began settling in the north at Cabrits and in the south at Roseau, the Indians withdrew into the dense forest, waging a guerilla war against anyone foolish enough to follow. Unhappy slaves often disappeared into the forest in much the same way, living off the land, raiding estates and eluding their white masters. The Caribs were virtually eliminated on all other Caribbean islands, but today the Carib Reserve is home to approximately 3,000 Carib descendants. The modern group engages in agriculture, fishing and native crafts, such as canoe carving and weaving intricate straw goods.

The reserve is more like a township or province occupied by a particular ethnic race than a typical reservation for Indians. The property is owned by the entire tribe, which has the right to build houses and raise crops on almost any part of the land they choose. Caribs have distinctive physical characteristics that set them apart from their West Indian neighbors. Like many American Indian tribes, the Caribs have broader facial features, straight dark hair and olive color skin. The Caribs are shy, but their natural curiosity may cause them to stare at white tourists with the same wonder that causes the tourists to stare at them.

Be sure to stop at their small roadside craft shops, where delicately woven baskets, carved wooden snakes that look almost real, canes covered in woven matting and carved gourds are for sale. The shy shop owner might hesitate to tell you the price and, in many cases, you may have to force them to sell you something. (See *Shopping*, below.)

Roseau

The **Tourist Information Center and Museum** occupies the antique building that was formerly the post office at the corner of Bay and King George Streets. Stop in and pick up an island map and other information.

Old Market Craft Center. The cruise ship pier is adjacent to the commercial area of Roseau, so taxis are not needed for a trip into town. Ships dock at Bay Street and the historical market square off Bay Street and King George Street has been converted to the Old Market Craft Center. There are three units on the bottom floor **Columbian**

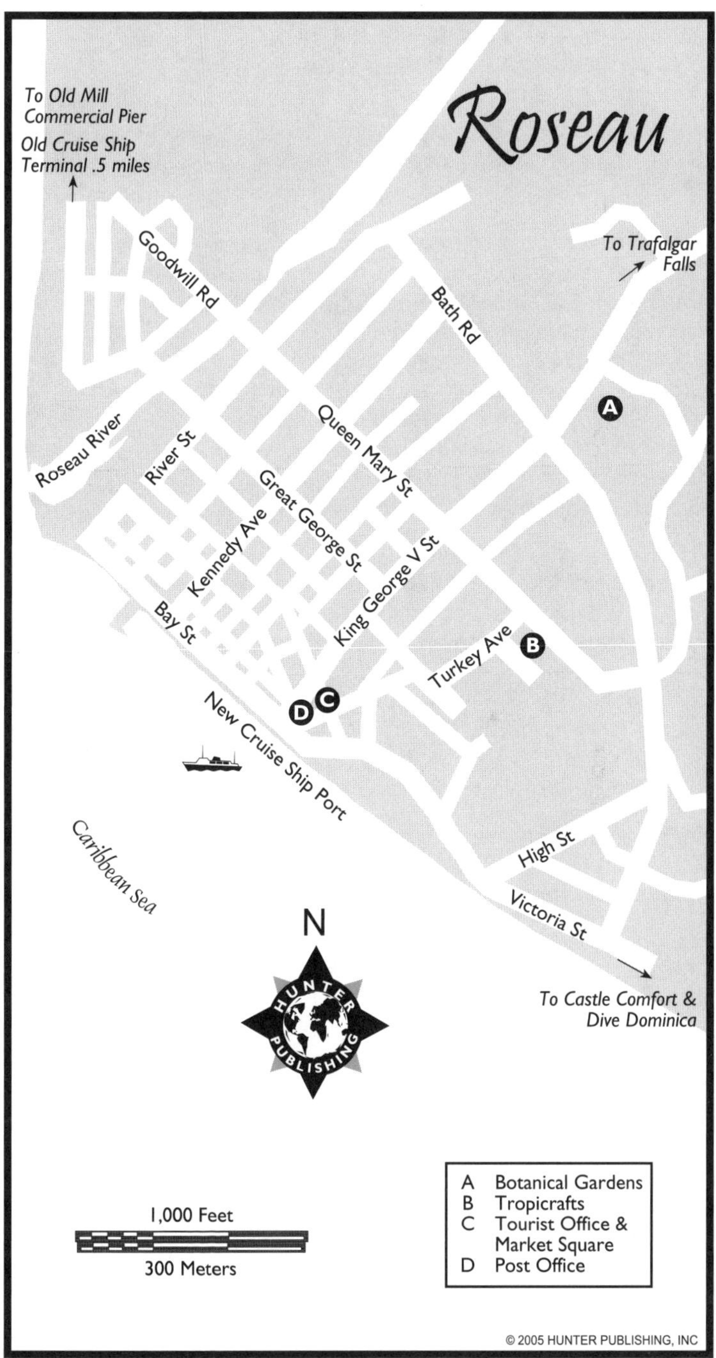
Roseau
To Old Mill
Commercial Pier
Old Cruise Ship
Terminal .5 miles
To Trafalgar
Falls
Goodwill Rd
Bath Rd
Queen Mary St
Roseau River
River St
Great George St
Kennedy Ave
King George V St
Bay St
Turkey Ave
New Cruise Ship Port
Caribbean Sea
High St
Victoria St
To Castle Comfort &
Dive Dominica
N
HUNTER
PUBLISHING
1,000 Feet
300 Meters
A Botanical Gardens
B Tropicrafts
C Tourist Office &
Market Square
D Post Office
© 2005 HUNTER PUBLISHING, INC

Emeralds, Ashburry Perfumes and a dive center, **Dive Dominica** (see *Organized Tours* and *Scuba Diving*).

The best buys on Dominica are locally made goods, and the craft center sells a variety of them. Straw goods, including hats, baskets and mats, are for sale, along with boxes, wood carvings, pottery, candles and coconut-oil soaps, handmade cigars, preserves, hot sauces and syrups. Carib Indian products are also sold here.

Roseau has not yet awakened to the commercial allure of duty-free shopping, so you will find yourself in the midst of a true West Indian town without the glitz and glamor of a duty-free mall designed for tourists. Roseau was built over years to handle the daily business of an agricultural island and to serve as its governmental capital. Take time to walk the narrow streets here and you'll see how business on a small scale is conducted in curio shops, bakeries and restaurants. Notice the buildings constructed with second-story verandas, a reflection of the French influence Dominica.

Tropicrafts, near the Botanical Gardens, is another place to find an assortment of local merchandise. The prices are reasonable, the quality exceptional and the variety of products is nicely displayed. The store carries Carib Indian baskets, coconut soap, guava jam, passion fruit concentrate, original artwork, books about the island and the Caribbean, and wood carvings. You can watch local women weaving large grass floor mats – they enjoy meeting visitors who stop in to admire their craft. The shop is well organized and accepts credit cards and traveler's checks.

Dominican Pottery (near the courthouse on Long Lane) sells hand-painted notecards and pottery sculpted from local clay (some pieces were made by inmates in the prison work program).

PhotoWorld (on King George V Street, about three blocks inland from the cruise ship dock) can meet all your photography needs. They sell film, batteries and a full line of Kodak products.

Caribana (on Fields Lane off Great George Street) carries artwork by well-known Dominican artists, including Earl Etienne. Exhibits include fine wood carvings and other high-quality crafts. Refreshments are available!

Baroon International (on Kennedy Avenue off Long Lane near the courthouse) offers duty-free jewelry made from 18K gold and silver, diamonds, rubies and semiprecious stones such as hematite, jade, malachite and red and pink coral. Baroon's creates interesting custom designs, too.

Ego Boutique (on Hanover Street off Hillborough) offers internationally and regionally made linen and cotton clothing. They have crafts from Europe, Asia and Africa, as well as quilted and applique cushions handmade on Dominica.

Frontline Cooperative (on Hillborough off Independence) has local newspapers, postcards and Caribbean literature, including works by Dominican authors Lennox Honeychurch and Jean Rhys. Their T-shirts, music and Dominican cookbooks make great souvenirs.

Outside Roseau

Old Mill Woodcrafters is to the right of the Old Sugar Mill Cultural Center (see *Historical Sites*, page 181, for location) and offers wooden sculptures made on-site by local artists.

Carib Indian Reserve Shops, 30 minutes from Roseau off the Central Forest Reserve road, is in the Carib Reserve. Here you can visit a small strip of local shops run by the shy Carib Indians, offering a selection of woven baskets, handmade items and carved canes. You may need to ask the cost of merchandise that interests you, as the owners do not like to intrude on your privacy. Prices are given in EC; small denominations of EC currency is best. Be sure to ask about the wife leaders, a special instrument used by the ancient Caribs in raids to steal Arawak women and bring them home to be wives. (The women were valued for their height.) The tool is sure to be a conversation starter (or stopper) at home!

Transportation & Excursions

Taxis

At Roseau pier you'll see a great number of taxis, all available for trips around the island. Fares are regulated by the local taxi association and based on the entire taxi, usually seating one to four people.

Be aware that the drivers of taxis or tour vans rely heavily upon their fares. They will not try to cheat daily visitors, but will do their best to show them their spectacular island. The locals around the island are among the friendliest and most honest of all the Caribbean islands.

Upon completion of an island tour or excursion, it is customary to tip the driver.

Taxi Chart

All prices are given in US dollars.
Note: The island government imposed a $2 sightseeing tax per attraction visited ($5 for the entire day); add that fee to the following taxi rates.

Destination *from Roseau cruise dock to*	**Cost** *one to four people*
Castle Comfort/Dive Dominica	$6
Emerald Pool	$30
Portsmouth	$50
Trafalgar Falls	$20

Rental Cars

Driving is on the left in Dominica and only the exceptionally brave should attempt to drive on this mountainous island. Of all the Caribbean islands, Dominica has some of the best conditioned roads, but they are also the narrowest and steepest. Local tour guides and taxi drivers know all the bends, drive cautiously and are the safest and most reliable form of transportation. You should rent a car or four-wheel-drive jeep only if you are confident driving on the left side of the road, have the patience to drive slowly around sharp corners, and are willing to honk when approaching blind curves. Remain very alert!

Most agencies offer a free pick-up and return to the port, a collision damage waiver at the rate of $6 per day and require a credit card to cover the $400 for damage or loss to the vehicle. You must also buy a temporary driver's permit for $11 and must be over the age of 25 to rent a car. Rentals start at $35 and prior arrangement is not necessary.

Car Rental Agencies

The area code for Dominica is 809.

Avis	☎ 448-0413 or (800) 228-0668
Budget Rent-A-Car	☎ 449-2080 or (800) 626-4516
Courtesy Car Rentals	☎ 448-7733
Wide Range Car Rentals	☎ 448-2198

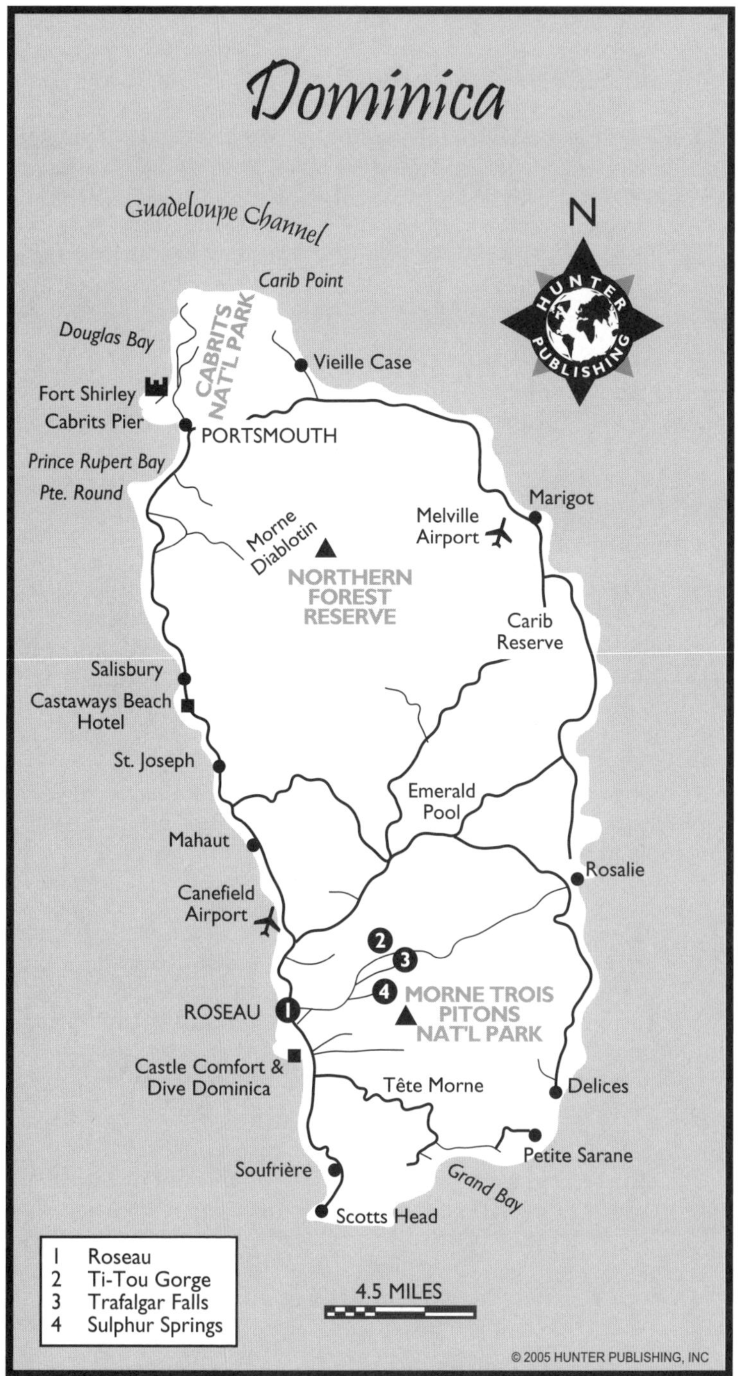
Dominica
Guadeloupe Channel
N
HUNTER PUBLISHING
Carib Point
Douglas Bay
CABRITS NAT'L PARK
Vieille Case
Fort Shirley
Cabrits Pier
PORTSMOUTH
Prince Rupert Bay
Pte. Round
Marigot
Melville Airport
Morne Diablotin
NORTHERN FOREST RESERVE
Carib Reserve
Salisbury
Castaways Beach Hotel
St. Joseph
Emerald Pool
Mahaut
Rosalie
Canefield Airport
MORNE TROIS PITONS NAT'L PARK
ROSEAU
Castle Comfort & Dive Dominica
Tête Morne
Delices
Petite Sarane
Soufrière
Grand Bay
Scotts Head
1 Roseau
2 Ti-Tou Gorge
3 Trafalgar Falls
4 Sulphur Springs
4.5 MILES
© 2005 HUNTER PUBLISHING, INC

Organized Tours & Activities

Dominica is a very rural and unspoiled place that does not have attractions specifically designed for tourists. Its natural landscape and rain forest allow you to appreciate how Caribbean islands once appeared to British and French explorers. The island may not appeal to everyone, but a walk through the rain forest or a climb over rocks to reach a breathtaking waterfall is likely to bring out the adventurer hidden within. You will probably be quite impressed with what you discover.

The island government has imposed a $2 sightseeing tax per attraction visited ($5 for the entire day), so add that fee to the taxi rate quoted.

Recommended Tour Company

Ken's Hinterland Adventure Tours & Taxi Service provides the most interesting and informational excursions on the island. The tours listed below are approximately five hours long, but with advance reservations they can be customized to your ship's schedule. The cost is for one to four people – a $140 tour may sound expensive, but it's just $35 per person. Trips use a comfortable, air-conditioned minivan with a local island guide. Ken's tours are available only by reservation, so book before arrival in Dominica. ☎ (767) 448-4850 or 3517, fax (767) 448-8486; www.kenshinterlandtours.com; e-mail khatts@cwdom.dm.

- ⚓ Take a trip to **Emerald Pool** and a drive through the **Carib Indian Reserve**. The pool is one of the first areas on Dominica to be developed as a tourist attraction. It features a 20-foot waterfall cascading into a shimmering pool below. The water is cool and refreshing; you may feel compelled to jump in and splash around! Ken's always supplies a knowledgeable guide who will point out particular vegetation unique to the Caribbean and Dominica.

  The second part of the tour takes you through the only specially designated reserve in the Caribbean where original descendants of the Carib Indians still live and prosper on their own land. Stop at the craft stores here and purchase handmade straw and wooden souvenirs directly from the Carib Indians. The prices are unbelievably low and the quality superb. A trip to the reserve takes you by the rocky eastern coastline and the lush vegetation along the inland roads.

The tour guide will make stops along the roadside to point out the wide variety of bananas, passion fruit and cocoa trees, encouraging you to taste different fruits. The total tour will show you the natural side of Dominica with all its culture and beauty. The cost for Tour #1 is $120 for one to four people, and $30 for each additional person.

⚓ The second tour option goes along the west coast to the smaller cruise port area and the second major town on Dominica, **Portsmouth**. First, it stops at the mouth of the **Indian River** for a boat trip into the tropical jungle, not unlike floating up the Amazon in South America. Fortunately on this river trip you will not have to worry about alligators or poisonous water snakes; simply sit back and enjoy the peace and tranquility of the rain forest. The boat ride usually costs US $10 per person, but that fee is included in Ken's tour price. If you enjoy your time afloat, tip the guide.

The second stop is at the **Cabrits pier**. The terminal has been specially designed for cruise passengers and has a collection of island artifacts on display. A short walk takes you to **Fort Shirley**, a massive fortress that once protected the island from invaders. Wander through the ruins and imagine how the populated fort may have looked in the 18th century.

Tour #2 involves little walking, but plenty of sightseeing and the unique experience of traveling up the tranquil Indian River. The drive along the west coast is dramatic, with views of high cliffs, crashing waves and small fishing villages. It costs $140 for one to four people, plus $35 for each additional person.

⚓ **Whale-Watching Tour.** The waters surrounding Dominican have gained recognition as one of the best areas in the Caribbean to view whales. **Dive Dominica** offers a whale-watching excursion. The $50 per-person trip, offered only on Wednesday and Sunday, leaves at 2 pm and lasts about 3½ hours. There are no guarantees, but they are successful in seeing marine wildlife on 90% of their trips. Most often, they spot sperm, pilot and false killer whales, plus spotted, spinner and bottlenosed dolphins. Listening devices are lowered into the water so you can hear characteristic whale noises, clicks and groans. We highly recommend this unique tour. ☎ (888) 414-7626; www.castlecomfortdivelodge.com.

The **Anchorage Hotel and Dive Center** offers whale-watching tours on Sunday and Wednesday for $50 per person. They also offer private whale-watching charters for $80-$150 per hour. ☎ (767) 448-2638; www.anchoragehotel.com.

Island Tours by Taxi

The **local taxi association** also provides **island tours** for $20 per hour (one to four persons). These taxis are available at the pier, where you can arrange the price and ask about the sites to be covered. A tour that takes no more than three hours will go the Botanical Gardens, the lookout point over Roseau and up to Trafalgar Falls; it should cost $10 per person. An island tour that includes a trip to the Emerald Pool, the Botanical Gardens and the lookout point overlooking Roseau, should cost $15 per person and takes no more than four hours. Excursions along the west coast to Portsmouth and the Indian River take no more than five hours and cost $35 per person, including the boat ride.

Beaches

Dominica is a volcanic island. Its beaches are dark to silvery-grey in color and are not especially as pleasant as coral islands for beachcombing. Dominica's specialty is its lush tropical rain forest but, if you are intent on going to a beach, the **Castaways Beach Hotel** has the closest one to Roseau, the only beachside resort on the island. A 30-minute drive ($25) along the west coast will bring you here. You are welcome to use the facilities here, including windsurfing, snorkeling, diving, a restaurant and bar. Dominica receives over 300 inches of rain per year, so you may encounter an occasional rain shower during the day. ☎ (767) 449-6244 to arrange for these activities in advance.

Island boats nestle along Dominica's shore.
(Image courtesy Dominica Tourist Office, NY.)

Island Activities

In The Ocean

The government adds a $2 per-person marine reserve fee to each dive or snorkeling tour.

Scuba Diving

Scuba diving reached new levels on Dominica when Derek and Ginette Perryman began **Dive Dominica**. The Perrymans have the most organized, professional and friendly dive operation in the Caribbean. Its underwater guides and instructors are highly qualified and the dives they offer can't be matched. They are based just 15 minutes from Roseau at Castle Comfort, and will make special arrangements with you. Boat dives include tanks and weights; the rates are $45 for a one-tank dive and $75 for a two-tank dive. If you want to learn, take a Resort Course, which includes all equipment, a short lecture and two dives for $130 per person. A buoyancy vest and auto inflator are available for $8, regulators for $8 and a dive computer for $10.

A number of locations are open to certified divers. The hot bubbling reef at **Champagne**, the thriving sea life at **The Pinnacle** and the swim-through holes at **Soufrière Pinnacle** are among the best spots along the southern coastline. Spotted drum fish are abundant, as are bottom-dwelling snake eels, so keep your eyes open. Even snorkelers will enjoy every minute in the water; there is a great deal to see. Contact Dive Dominica before your ship arrives in port to ensure a space on their daily boat departures. Trips cost US $25 per person, including equipment rental. If you want to go along for the ride and not get wet, the charge is US $10. Derek and Ginette Perryman can be reached at ☎ (767) 448-2188; fax (767) 448-6088; (888) 414-7626; dive@cwdom.dm; www.castlecomfortdivelodge.com.

The **Anchorage Hotel and Dive Center** offers a one-tank dive for $50, a two-tank dive for $65 and a three-hour snorkeling trip for $30. ☎ (767) 448-2638; anchorage@cwdom.dm; www.anchoragehotel.com.

On Land

Horseback Riding

High Ride Stables offers a one-hour guided ATV Jungle Safari tour (after full instruction) for $50 per person, and a two-hour ride for $70. The fee includes all safety gear, helmets, goggles, rain gear, refreshments and return transportation to the cruise ship dock. They also offer a one-hour horseback ride ($40 per person) through the rainforest. Again, the fee includes helmets, refreshments and a ride back to the cruise ship dock. Call in advance and they will arrange for transportation from Roseau for $10 per person. At www.virtualdominica.com/highrideadventures/index.html a map shows the rides and offers trail descriptions. ☎ (767) 448-6292 or 440-2117; highriders@cwdom.dm.

One-Day Itinerary

To truly appreciate Dominica's natural beauty, you must hike. **Ken's Hinterland Adventure Tours** has a magnificent three-four-hour tour to Trafalgar Falls and Ti-Tou Gorge. If there has been excessive rain before you arrive, the water flow into Ti-Tou Gorge and at Trafalgar Falls can make access impossible, so rely on the judgment of your guide. Both these sites are amazing, and this particular tour is designed for the nature lover who wants to explore. Be prepared to get wet and have the best day of your entire cruise! The cost is $100 for one to four people ($25 each additional person). Reservations must be made prior to arrival on the island. Ken's can arrange to pick you up at the pier. Contact Ken George Dill, ☎ (767) 448-485/ 3517 (after hours); fax (767) 448-8486. The Hinterland Tours website is www.kenshinterlandtours.com, e-mail khatts@cwdom.dm.

What To Bring

While hiking in the rain forest you are likely to encounter rain, so bring along a light rain jacket and wear clothes that dry quickly. Rather than carrying an umbrella, wear a baseball hat or a hat with a wide brim, which will allow the rain to run off. Wear comfortable walking shoes or old tennis shoes with good traction for climbing over slippery rocks. Sandals with a strap around the ankle and thick gripping soles are also excellent for walking through the streams and climbing rocks. Finally, wear a bathing suit beneath your clothes and bring a towel for drying off after the swim up Ti-Tou Gorge and a dip in the hot springs at Trafalgar Falls. Bring a camera only if it is water-resistant. Do not bring valuables (which would be left in the tour van). Just bring yourself and a sense of adventure.

Directions

Refer to the island map on page 187.

An Island Hike

1. If you contact Ken's before arriving in Dominica, the tour van will be waiting near the pier for your arrival.

2. The itinerary is very flexible so, depending upon the weather conditions, the first stop is **Ti-Tou Gorge** (meaning little throat hole). Situated 20 minutes into the tropical rain forest above Roseau, Ti-Tou Gorge is a fascinating place where you can swim up the narrow throat of the mountain and marvel at the twisted rock formations carved out by the powerful river. Keep your shoes on during the swim because unseen rocks on the river bottom can be quite sharp. After a short swim through a narrow slit in the mountain, you will be enchanted by the sculpted beauty of the gray canyon walls and will feel like an explorer forging a new path. The gorge opens into a misty cavern with a thundering waterfall that maintains a constant current of fresh water, which also makes for a fun and easy swim back out of the gorge.

3. The next stop is **Trafalgar Falls**, the most magnificent falls on Dominica. There are actually two waterfalls at Trafalgar, which you

can view from the lookout point at the end of the 15-minute hike into the lush forest. The fall on the right is not easy to reach and is best viewed as a backdrop for pictures. The taller of the two falls, to the left, is the most popular. Cascading 200 feet down a rocky cliff face, the water gathers into small pools and pockets at the base. A stream of hot spring water trickles down the left side near the bottom, distinguished by bright orange streaks covering the rocks. The orange substance is created by a chemical reaction as the hot water brings out the color of iron-ore deposits in the volcanic rock. The thundering falls and hot springs are truly an unforgettable experience.

Trafalgar Falls is 20 to 25 minutes from Ti-Tou Gorge and entails a 15-minute walk from the parking area to the viewing spot below the falls. If you're in good shape and can handle the climb to the base of the falls, the fun begins there. The tour guide leads and helps you up and over rocks to the pools at the base of the falls. Here, you can jump onto the rocks to find your own pocket of hot spring water. The guide will point out the cold and the hot areas of the fall, as well as the safest way of climbing the rocks to reach your own private area. Once you have found your spot, allow the hot spring water to flow over your neck and back for a natural massage. You should feel refreshed and rejuvenated. Be careful on the hike down.

4. The drive along the steep winding roads of Dominica will give you the impression you have entered a tropical jungle deep in South America. The fabulous views of jagged mountains dropping straight down to the coastline and the dense vegetation of the rain forest shrouded in mist will intrigue you. The trip should take approximately five hours and your guide will deliver you directly to the pier terminal. Ken's guides are the most informative and the friendliest on the island; they will work hard to earn an extra tip at the end of the day.

5. If you have extra time, add a visit to **Emerald Pool** (making the trip five-six hours total). You walk through a rainforest to the most photographed pool on Dominica, where you can swim. This additional stop adds $60 total for one-four people to your tour price, but it is worthwhile.

The French West Indies

Guadeloupe & Martinique

Visiting either Guadeloupe or Martinique is like taking a trip to France, as both islands are Overseas Departments of France. In 1974, they were given the further status of "Region," with full representation in the French Parliament in Paris.

Spanish treasure hunters were successfully repelled by the indigenous Carib Indians and did not settle on either island. The first settlements were established in 1635 by the French, who fought the Caribs and drove them to neighboring islands. The French introduced cash crops, which thrived in the rich volcanic soil. The slave system enhanced the profitability of sugarcane and banana production.

The French and English battled over control of the islands until 1763, the year that France relinquished all rights to Canada in exchange for the French West Indies. The tug-of-war continued until 1815, when the Treaty of Paris designated both islands as French.

The British still claim ownership of the Rocher du Diamant (aka Diamond Rock), a small rock island rising 600 feet from the sea just off the west coast of Martinique. The British used this as an "honorary sloop of war" in 1804 and manned it for 17 months. Legend says the wily French invaded the rock, first with barrels of rum as bait and then with regiments to cast out the British. Since then, the site has been jokingly called H.M.S. *Diamond Rock*, but it looks more like a green egg floating on the surface than a once-valuable military landmark.

The abolishment of slavery in the French West Indies occurred in 1848, largely through the efforts of Victor Schoelcher. Schoelcher later donated 5,000 books and a strange-looking house that became a library to the island of Martinique. After the slave system ended, indentured Indians from Calcutta and Pondicherry were imported to replace the low level laborers; many stayed when their contracts had ended.

Guadeloupe and Martinique are both volcanic islands with recent volcanic activity. The town of St. Pierre in Martinique was completely destroyed by an eruption of the Mont Pelée volcano in 1902, but today the volcano appears harmless. Guadeloupe's volcano, La Soufrière, is considered dormant, but fumaroles emitting wisps of sulfurous vapor can be seen from miles away. Volcanology museums have been established on both islands to visually demonstrate the catastrophic effects of an eruption.

The rain forests, natural by-products of volcanoes, are currently protected by the French Government in a Parc Naturel Regional (Natural Regional Park) on each island. They are a part of the Green Tourism Program, which protects beautiful sites, landscapes and architecture and provides facilities for visitors to enjoy them.

Island People

The island culture of the French West Indies can be described as French, but with a difference. As with most Caribbean islands, the people are a blend of ethnic strains from Africa, Europe, South America and India. The mother country may be France, but the islands are 4,000 miles away and are influenced by an atmosphere that adds spice to the French way of living.

Over three centuries, the disparate cultures have merged to create a new social structure and new customs. Traditions like Carnival are similar to those on other Caribbean islands, but savory cuisine and cosmopolitan attitudes are exclusively French, contributing to a distinctive island culture.

Language

French is the official language and **Creole** is the common slang, which is understood by West Indians in general. If you don't speak French, you may prefer to confine your shopping to the larger cities and stick with the international hotels where English is spoken frequently. If you plan to venture out of the major towns, carry a French phrasebook to help with communications.

Currency

The **euro** is now the official French currency, with an exchange rate of about 1.25 euros to US $1.

To obtain the best exchange rate when shopping or renting a car, use a credit card. Banks are open from 8 am to noon and from 2 to 4 pm weekdays. Some banks in Guadeloupe are open on Saturdays from 8 am to 12:45 pm and banks in Martinique open as early as 7:15 am, but are not open on Saturdays.

Postage

The islands of the French West Indies use the same postage as France, with no special island issues. Post offices in Guadeloupe and Martinique are crowded, confusing and not user-friendly. They conduct many types of business at the post office, so very long lines are common. Buy stamps on the ship or in small shops rather than attempting to go to the post office. Local cafés-tabacs, newsstands and some souvenir shops also sell stamps. The postage rate to mail a postcard is about US 85¢. (Remember, US postage is not accepted.)

> Don't be surprised to see topless women featured on postcards here; the French do not consider nudity immodest.

Guadeloupe

Land Of Beautiful Waters

Island Description

The Indian name for Guadeloupe was "Karukera," meaning Island of the Beautiful Waters, and a visit to one of the islands waterfalls will convince you that the name was appropriate. Guadeloupe is actually two islands separated by a very narrow saltwater river, the Salée River, but connected by a bridge. Grande-Terre, where most of the large hotels are situated, is a large flat land mass with white sandy beaches. Basse-Terre is mountainous and contains the Parc National rain forest and Soufrière volcano. Together, the two halves look like a big green butterfly.

Agriculture is an important part of Guadeloupe's economy. Bananas are the primary cash crop, as well as sugarcane, various fruits, spices and flowers, which are exported to France. Rum production is important to the economy and distilleries are still operating. Tourism is becoming more vital each year.

Holidays

The French close their businesses on national holidays and sometimes half a day before the scheduled holiday. Shops at the pier complex may be open while a ship is in port even on a holiday, and taxis and tours are still available. But shopping in the commercial district and out on the island might be scarce during a holiday period. During Carnival, all business comes to a halt for five days, but the festivities more than make up for anything you might miss!

Annual Holidays & Events

For more details and precise dates, contact the island tourist board (see *Appendix*).

January. . . New Year's Day; Three King's Day or Epiphany

February . . . . Carnival, Mardi Gras (peak of Carnival), with parades & street dances; Ash Wednesday

March or April . . . . Easter Sunday; Easter Monday

May . . . . Labor Day; VE Day; Slavery Abolition Day; Ascension Thursday; Pentecost Monday

July . . . . . Bastille Day; Schoelcher Day (Victor Schoelcher negotiated the signing of emancipation proclamation)

August . . . . Assumption Day

November. . . All Saint's Day (tombstones are illuminated with candles); Armistice Day (fireworks)

December . . . Christmas Eve (dancing, revelry); Christmas Day; Young Saint's Day (costume parade); New Year's Eve

Useful Websites

The best website we found is **www.frenchcaribbean.com** (click on Guadeloupe). It's easy to navigate and provides good information. The "Activities" section gives names, addresses and local phone numbers for tour operators (for some, it offers prices too). You may notice that tour prices and entrance fees for attractions fluctuate. This is done in line with exchange rate so that the operators net the same return.

Another website, **www.antilles-info-tourisme.com** (click for the English version), offers helpful links, one of which describes hikes, and another describes places to surf. There are good maps, plus a link to car rentals (click on the British flag for English). Most lists include phone numbers and e-mail links.

The Pier

Cruise ships dock at the **St. John Perse** complex in the heart of downtown Pointe-à-Pitre's commercial center. The French West Indies-style complex was built specifically for cruise passengers, combining traditional colonial architecture and a modern French design in a unique style found nowhere else in the Caribbean. You can walk off the ship and straight into the duty-free shopping plaza or to town.

The complex at the dock has currency exchange center with ATMs, a bakery, cigar store and restaurants. A Tourist Information Center is located near the taxi stand to the right, near Victory Plaza. The English-speaking staff offers complimentary maps, magazines, valuable directions and shopping suggestions. Look for the pamphlet titled "Guadeloupe Excursions," which describes itineraries for driving tours to be taken by cab or in your rental car.

Pier Phones

Public telephones near the pier are scarce. As you disembark, you'll see one phone to the right near a restaurant and another to the left at the end of the dock building. Ask at the Tourist Information Center for new phone locations and where to purchase **Telecartes**, prepaid discount phone cards that can be used in special booths marked Telecom. Telecartes can be purchased from outlets marked "Telecart en Vente Ici." To access **AT&T**, ☎ 0800-99-00-11 by using a phone card.

To call Guadeloupe, dial 590 (the international access code), then 590 (the country code), then the local phone number.

In Town

Shopping

The best buys on Guadeloupe are luxury items made in France, including perfumes, china, crystal, champagne and wine. Guadeloupe has a Value Added Tax (VAT) of 20% on store-bought goods. However, if you pay with traveler's checks or major credit card, your purchases are exempt. Some prices listed in US dollars may already reflect the 20% discount, so be sure to ask the clerk.

> ➠ TIP: Paying by credit card is a good idea as the companies secure a decent exchange rate, but be sure the credit card slip is marked , for euro, to establish the correct currency type.

The French invented the concept of chic boutiques and define the meaning in elegant small shops filled with merchandise from worldwide sources and talented local artisans. If you're a shopper, you'll appreciate the unusual and sophisticated offerings. Shops are open weekdays from 9 am to 1 pm, and from 3 pm to 6 pm; most are also open Saturday mornings and are closed Sundays and holidays. Personnel in the pier shops make an honest effort to speak English and offer assistance.

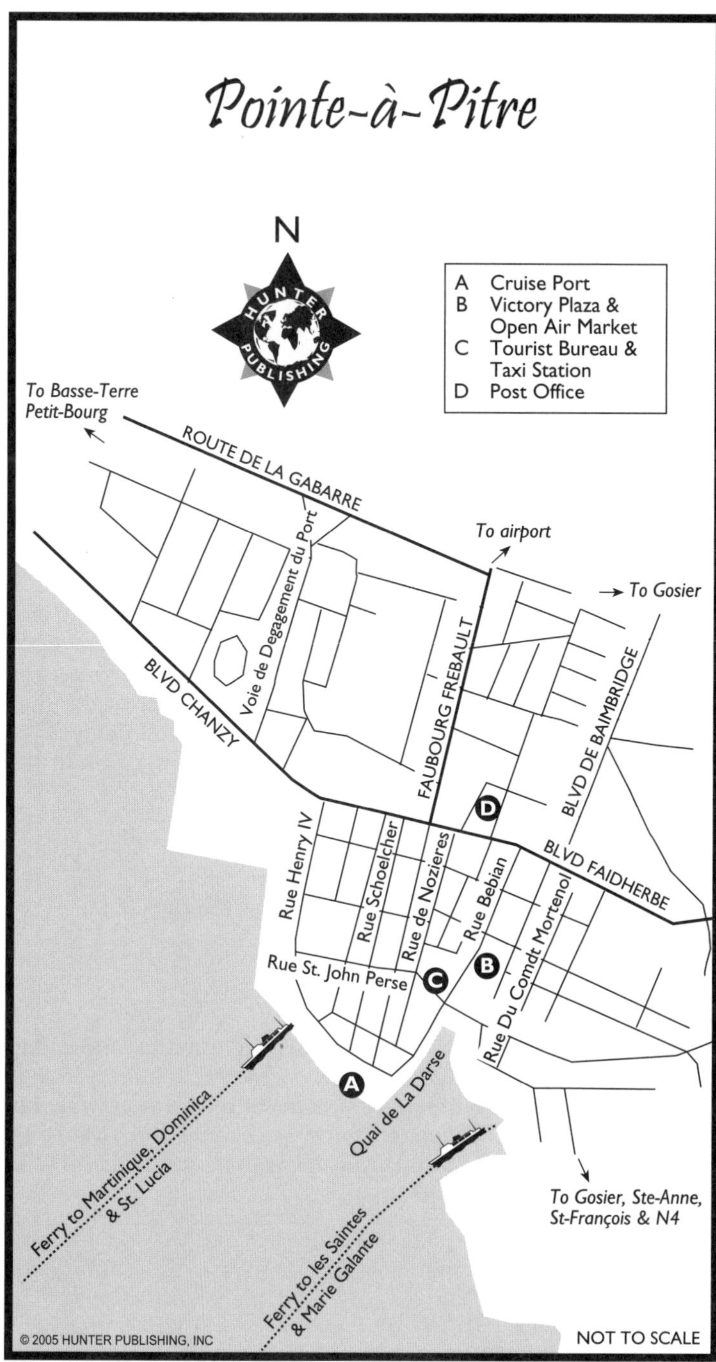
Pointe-à-Pitre
N
HUNTER PUBLISHING
A Cruise Port
B Victory Plaza & Open Air Market
C Tourist Bureau & Taxi Station
D Post Office
To Basse-Terre Petit-Bourg
ROUTE DE LA GABARRE
Voie de Degagement du Port
To airport
To Gosier
BLVD CHANZY
FAUBOURG FREBAULT
BLVD DE BAIMBRIDGE
BLVD FAIDHERBE
Rue Henry IV
Rue Schoelcher
Rue de Nozieres
Rue Bebian
Rue Du Comdt Mortenol
Rue St. John Perse
Quai de La Darse
Ferry to Martinique, Dominica & St. Lucia
Ferry to les Saintes & Marie Galante
To Gosier, Ste-Anne, St-François & N4
NOT TO SCALE

St. John Perse Complex

Shops here feature locally handcrafted souvenirs unique to Guadeloupe. There's a bookstore, cigar shop, café and bakery. Savvy shopkeepers here attempt to speak English, and their merchandise is always interesting. The French appreciate exotic jewelry (look for the word *bijoux* on shop signs), and on Guadeloupe this translates to unique jewelry created from seashells, coral, gems and gold. Don't hesitate to buy a piece of jewelry, as you're not likely to find its duplicate on the next island. Expect high prices attached to unique pieces.

Point-à-Pitre

The majority of duty-free stores are situated on **Rue Frébaut**, which leads away from the pier complex. Only a hardy shopper should confront the traffic-choked commercial district. If you decide to do so, plan your shopping from the cruise ship's list of recommended stores. If you dislike city congestion, shop in the St. John Perse Complex, then take a taxi out of the city. Boutiques in the smaller beach towns are a better choice for leisurely shopping.

The **open-air market** where locals buy fresh fruits, vegetables and spices can be reached on foot heading right along the waterfront heading right to Victory Plaza (starting with your back to the ship). Caribbean-style open-air bazaars are lively and offer a glimpse into the French West Indian culture. Even if you're not buying, take a walk around here.

Transportation & Excursions

Taxis

Taxis wait at the pier, set to transport you on island tours and on trips to outer island attractions. Taxis either use meters in francs, or negotiate fares (regulated by the government) based on the whole taxi, which seats one to four people. The vehicles range from Mercedes-Benz cars to minivans, and the drivers take great pride in them. This is reflected in higher taxi rates.

Most taxi drivers do not speak fluent English, but they do attempt a few words for basic communication. Negotiating a taxi fare with drivers can be more difficult due to the language barrier, but be sure to establish a rate in francs or US dollars before entering the taxi. To eliminate misunderstandings, use a notepad to write down the number and show it to the driver while negotiating. A half-day island tour costs US $90-$115, one to four persons.

Taxi Chart

Call for a taxi at ☎ 20-74-74, 82-96-69 or 83-09-55. The following prices are one-way estimates based on distance. All prices are in US dollars.

Destination *from St. John Perse Complex*	**Cost** *one to four people*
Airport	$10
Carbet Falls	$55
Gosier	$15
Pigeon Island	$30
Saint-Francois	$38
Sainte-Anne	$25

Rental Cars

Due to the high cost of taxis fares, we highly recommend that you rent a car. Driving on Guadeloupe is on the right, easy for Americans. The roads and highways are well signed and they can be driven with the assistance of an island map.

You can rent a car at the airport by taking a taxi ($10) or call an agency prior to arrival and they will arrange to have a car waiting for you at the port.

> TIP: When calling Guadeloupe, ask for someone who speaks English before trying to make arrangements. Most agencies at the airport employ English-speaking clerks.

Daily rentals range between $60 and $90, depending on the type of vehicle. A valid driver's license is needed and agencies usually require a credit card to cover the damage deposit. When you pay for the car, be sure the agency writes the total amount on the credit card slip with to indicate euros.

French motorists drive very fast, so drive defensively. Don't pull off the road in the rain forest unless there is a cleared parking area covered with gravel. Grassy areas are always soft and muddy; unknowing tourists can easily get stuck. The agency should provide you with a map.

Car Rental Agencies

To call Guadeloupe, dial 590 (the international access code), 590 (the country code), then the local phone number.

Blue Carib (free delivery) . . . . ☎ 24-68-54; blue.Kariblocation@wanadoo.fr

Avis . . . . ☎ 82-02-71 or (800) 821-2847; www.avis.com

B&B Grande Remise (chauffeured limos) . . . . ☎ 83-56-08 berdier@caramail.com

Budget . . . . ☎ 21-13-49 or (800) 472-3355 or 626-4576; info@budget-p.com; www.budget.com

Hertz . . . . ☎ 82-00-14, 82-88-44 or (800) 654-3131; www.hertz.com

Thrifty. . . . . ☎ 91-55-66 or (800) 367-2277

Self-Guided Tours

Tour of Basse-Terre

Touring this region means you can explore the **national park**, a lush rain forest. Worthwhile sites off Route de la Traversée include Cascade aux Ecrevisses (Crayfish Falls) and the Parc Zoologique et Botanique (Zoological & Botanical Park). The 30-foot **Crayfish Falls** is an easy five-minute walk from the gravel parking area off the main road and the cool refreshing pool is ideal for a dip. The **Zoological & Botanical Park** has mongooses, iguanas and the island's own variety of raccoon. At the end of Route de la Traversée is **Ilets Pigeon** (Pigeon Island), where Jacques Cousteau has established a scuba-diving preserve that offers daily boat trips for divers and snorkelers. The total trip from Pointe-à-Pitre to Pigeon Island, with stops at the falls and zoo, takes between 1½ and two hours.

Another trip to the southern section of Basse-Terre guides you to **Chutes du Carbet** (Carbet Falls), one hour from Pointe-à-Pitre. There are three hikes through the rain forest, all of which lead to the extraordinary cascading waterfalls. The driving route to the trailheads passes through small seaside towns, a street lined with

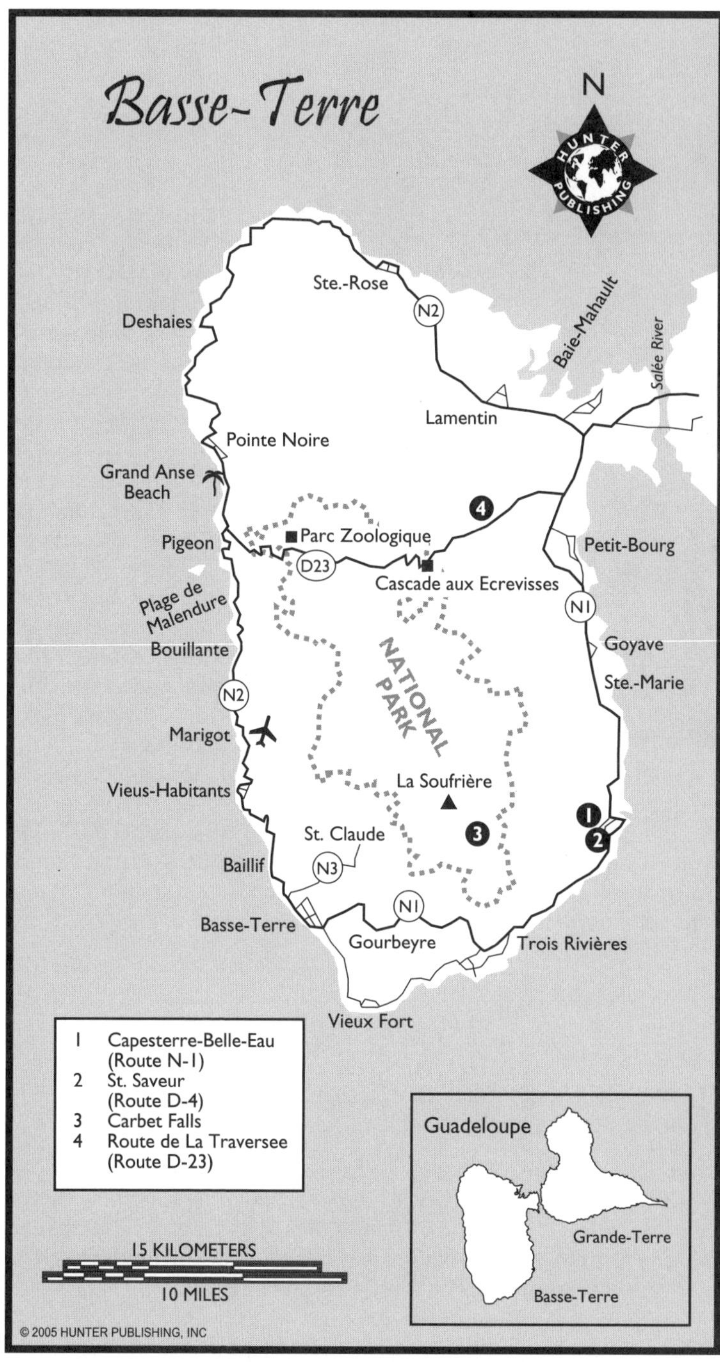
Basse-Terre
N
HUNTER PUBLISHING
Ste.-Rose
N2
Deshaies
Baie-Mahault
Salée River
Lamentin
Pointe Noire
Grand Anse Beach
4
Pigeon
Parc Zoologique
D23
Cascade aux Ecrevisses
Petit-Bourg
Plage de Malendure
N1
Goyave
Bouillante
NATIONAL PARK
Ste.-Marie
N2
Marigot
La Soufrière
Vieus-Habitants
1
3
2
St. Claude
Baillif
N3
N1
Basse-Terre
Gourbeyre
Trois Rivières
Vieux Fort
1 Capesterre-Belle-Eau (Route N-1)
2 St. Saveur (Route D-4)
3 Carbet Falls
4 Route de La Traversee (Route D-23)
Guadeloupe
Grande-Terre
Basse-Terre
15 KILOMETERS
10 MILES
© 2005 HUNTER PUBLISHING, INC

Crayfish Falls, a worthwhile stop on your tour of Basse-Terre.

flamboyant trees and a section with tall royal palms. The scenic drive is beautiful, and the Carbet Falls are spectacular.

An easy half-hour walk brings you to the **lower waterfall**. The **Premiere fall** takes 2½ hours to reach on foot and is recommended only if you're in good shape and have six to seven hours. Another hike to **Grand Etang** and **La Soufrière volcano** is an arduous 3½ hours; we don't recommended it. All three hikes go through shaded rain forest pathways. The picturesque falls make exceptional locations for an afternoon picnic and spectacular photo subjects. Food vendors at the beginning of the trails sell light refreshments. This is Guadeloupe's most spectacular attraction by far.

Beaches

Guadeloupe discourages complete nudity on the beach but, as in France, topless sunbathing is quite common.

The white sandy **Canella Beach** in Gosier, along the southern edge of Grande-Terre, is our top choice. Taxis can drop you at one of the beachside hotels (15 minutes, $8, one to four people), where you can enjoy any number of watersports and have lunch. The nearby marina has shops and some smaller tourist restaurants.

BEACH CHART	Facilities	Windsurfing	Snorkeling	Scuba Diving	Wave Runners	Swimming	Parasailing	Sailing	Water Skiing	Nude/Topless
Canella Beach	☆	☆	☆			☆		☆	☆	☆
Sainte-Anne	☆		☆			☆		☆		☆
Grande Anse	☆					☆		☆		☆

Farther along the southern edge of Grande-Terre is the small town of **Sainte-Anne**, with a public beach stretching along the coastline. The beach here, a 30-minute drive from Pointe-à-Pitre, is great for snorkeling or sailing (Sunfish boats rent for US $30-$40 per hour). A picturesque stop en route is the **Relais du Moulin hotel,** set off the road between Gosier and Sainte-Anne. The turn-off to the hotel is clearly marked with a billboard and the old sugar windmill used as their reception area is visible from the road. The beautiful property is covered in multicolored bougainvillea vines and the windmill is an ideal subject for photographs. It has a wonderful restaurant, but the one drawback is that the staff does not speak English. You can take a taxi direct to Sainte-Anne and back, but a better plan would be to make it part of a three- to four-hour island tour by taxi.

Grande Anse, on the western coast of Basse-Terre, is the most popular and beautiful beach on the island. Drive 45 minutes on Route de la Traversée, turn right at the end of the road and go for another 10 minutes along the coastline (N2). This will bring you to the Grande Anse turn-off on the left. A sign shows the way to this wide and very long stretch of sand, which is always alive with people picnicking, sunbathing or enjoying watersports. We recommend you stop here only as part of an island tour. If it's just beach you want, stay closer to home and get a cab to Canella (above).

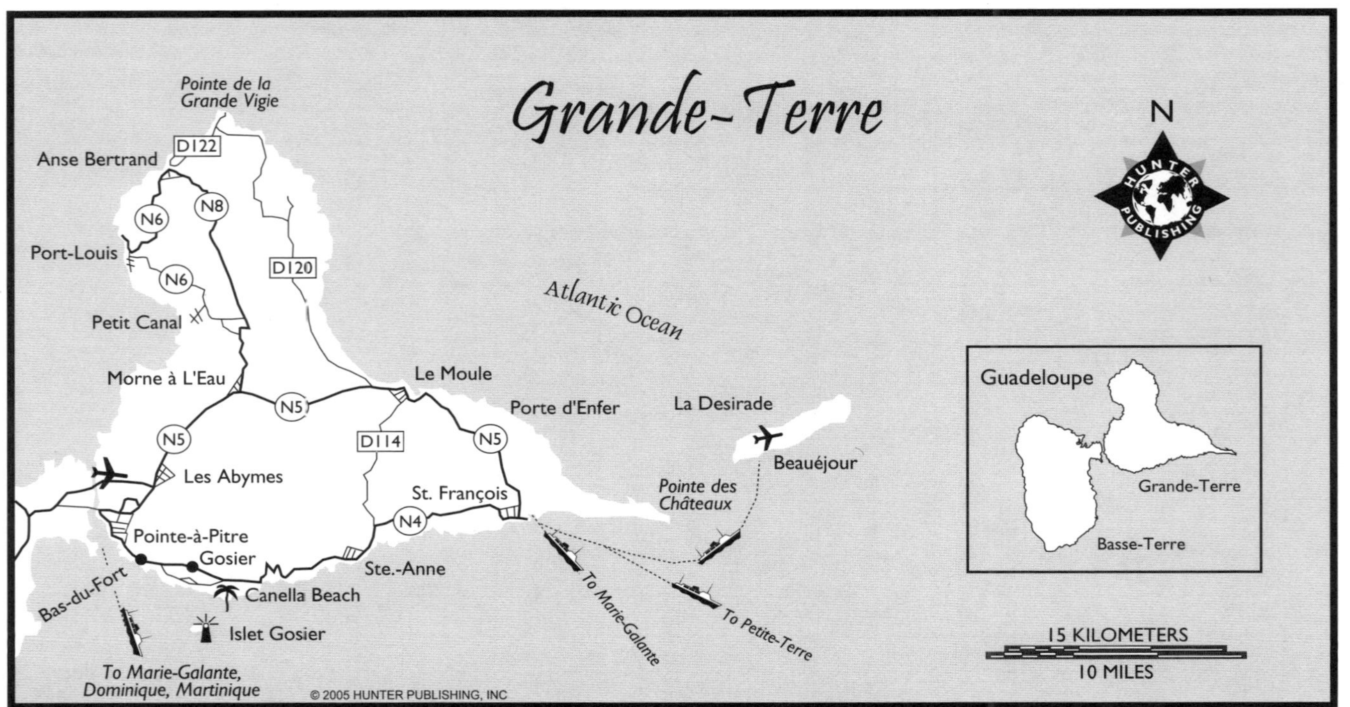

Grande-Terre
N
HUNTER PUBLISHING
Pointe de la Grande Vigie
D122
Anse Bertrand
N8
N6
Port-Louis
D120
Petit Canal
Atlantic Ocean
Morne à L'Eau
Le Moule
N5
Porte d'Enfer
La Desirade
D114
Les Abymes
Beauéjour
Pointe des Châteaux
St. François
N4
Pointe-à-Pitre
Gosier
Ste.-Anne
Bas-du-Fort
Canella Beach
Islet Gosier
To Marie-Galante
To Petite-Terre
To Marie-Galante, Dominique, Martinique
© 2005 HUNTER PUBLISHING, INC
Guadeloupe
Grande-Terre
Basse-Terre
15 KILOMETERS
10 MILES

Island Activities

On Land

Aquarium

The **Aquarium de la Guadeloupe** is a new attraction for those who wish to see fantastic ocean creatures without getting wet. Ask at the shore excursion desk for details.

Golf

The 18-hole **Golf de St. François** course is 45 minutes from the port in the Saint-François region of Grande-Terre. It was designed by Robert Trent Jones and offers a shop, lockers, bar, restaurant and an English-speaking pro. Greens fees are $50, cart rentals are $44 and club rentals are $20. A taxi ride will take approximately 40 minutes. The course is quite far from Pointe-à-Pitre, so consider combining a trip to Saint-François with an island tour, or plan to spend time at the nearby beaches. To arrange tee times, ☎ (590-590) 88-41-87.

Tennis

There are two tennis clubs near the port area at the **Marina Club** (☎ 90-84-08) and the **Centre Lamby-Lambert** (☎ 90-90-97) in Gosier. Both are just 15 minutes by taxi from the pier. Court fees range between $15 and $20 an hour.

In The Ocean

Unless you speak French, renting sports equipment can be difficult. Visit the hotels along the beach in **Gosier**; they have equipment available for rent and often have personnel who speak some English to help get you started on the water.

Watersports at Canella Beach

The following can be found along **Canella Beach** in Gosier:

Windsurfing rates begin at $20 an hour from many operators along the beach. Water skiing starts $20 for 15 minutes and can be negotiated for three or more people. Hobie Cats are available for $45 an hour, Sunfish for $20 an hour and pedal boats for $15 an hour. The price for parasailing is between $45 to $75, depending on length of ride.

Snorkeling

Excellent reefs are located off the beach in Gosier, at the St. François Reef and Ilet du Gosier. Equipment is available for $15 per set and hourly rates can be arranged through the hotels.

Scuba Diving

The best scuba diving on Guadeloupe can be found off Pigeon Island, at the **Jacques Cousteau Underwater Reserve**. **Plaisir Plongée Caraibes** (formerly Chez Guyet Christian) has a diving operation on Pigeon Beach, ☎ (590-590) 98-82-43. If you don't speak French, we recommend that you contact them prior to arrival to arrange for an English-speaking dive instructor. Even certified divers not using a dive computer should have an English-speaking guide. The rate for a one-tank dive is $45.

The reserve is well protected and has striking coral reefs, enormous barrel sponges and large schools of jacks. The underwater sites here are unmatched.

Les Heures Saines offers a one-tank dive for about $45, a two-tank dive for about $80, and snorkeling for about $15. Transportation can be arranged for about $25 if you call ahead. ☎ 98-86-63; heusaine@outremer.com. Ask for an English-speaking guide.

> TIP: Consider using a French phrasebook when making arrangements and checking the current schedule of dives.

Cruise ship companies are now offering a drive through the national park followed by a glass-bottom boat ride to Pigeon Island. This might be the best way to see the island's best attractions without language hassles.

The **Eden Plongée** dive shop is located at 17, Bd Achille René Boisneuf in Port-Louis. This town is north of the cruise ship dock and is closer than Pigeon Island. Their website lists a one-tank dive at about US $50 and snorkeling for US $25. There are nice beaches here, with Jet Skis and watersports available. To make reservations,

☎ (590) 228-727; e-mail edenplongee@chez.com; www.chez.com/edenplongee.

One-Day Itinerary

Guadeloupe may prove challenging to those who don't speak any French, but exploring the wonders of nature requires no language skills. Guadeloupe's national park contains spectacular waterfalls and the drive down the coast to the Carbet Falls is quite picturesque. To begin the adventure, you should rent a car, which will give you the freedom to experience Basse-Terre on your own. This itinerary will take between four and five hours.

What to Bring

Hiking shoes or shoes with a gripping sole are important for the trek to the waterfall. A packed lunch and bottled water is vital because only snacks and pastries are available from the vendors at the beginning of the trail. Occasional rain showers are common to the rain forest, so bring a hat and light jacket. If you're interested in taking a dip at the base of the fall, wear a bathing suit. Other than these few items, bring your spirit of adventure and a camera to capture the spectacular sites of the day.

Directions

Refer to the island maps on pages 205 and 208.

An Island Tour

Reserve your car before arriving on Guadeloupe and start your excursion as early as possible. Leave **Pointe-à-Pitre** by the main highway (N1, Route Nacional) heading west toward Basse-Terre. Watch for signs to Petit-Bourg, still on N1. The road passes through Goyave to the town of **Sainte-Marie,** where Columbus once landed. A statue commemorates his historic visit. On the road towards Capesterre-Belle-Eau you pass through the **Allée des Flamboyants,** a lane with overhanging flamboyant trees covered in bright red flowers from mid-June through September. At Capesterre-Belle-Eau, you will encounter the famous **Allée Dumanoir**, a road lined with century-old royal palms.

After 45 minutes of driving, shortly after the row of palms, look for St. Sauveur and a sign to the right for **Chutes du Carbet**. Road D4 (Habituée Road) will direct you through a large banana plantation on

GUADELOUPE

a narrow road which dead-ends at the trail to the falls. Follow the signs for 15 minutes. Park along the road and begin the hike up to one of the falls.

> ➠ Drive cautiously. Watch for other drivers and honk when approaching blind curves.

Carbet Falls has three hiking trails to tiered waterfalls and one to the Grand Etang and La Soufrière volcano. We suggest you hike to the first waterfall, a 65-foot cascade that is most impressive for photographs. The 30-minute trek through the tropical rain forest on a well-traveled path leads along the creek bed past giant ferns, palms and flowering bushes. At another smaller waterfall to the left of the Carbet Fall, you may see locals climbing with ropes. The base of the fall is a good spot to picnic, surrounded by the tranquil rain forest. Spend up to an hour exploring the grounds around the waterfall, then begin the half-hour journey back down the trail.

A 15-minute drive back to the main highway and 45 minutes to Pointe-à-Pitre will return you to the port. If you have more time free, consider driving the **Route de la Traversée** for more sightseeing (see *Self-Guided Tours*, page 204). The total trip, counting stops, should take between four and five hours. Guadeloupe's best attraction is its natural beauty, which can be appreciated only by getting out to explore the island.

One of Guadeloupe's old mills.

Martinique

Isle Of Flowers

Island Description

The Carib Indians called Martinique "Madinina," meaning Isle of Flowers. The people endeavor to protect the lush atmosphere for which their island was named. Martinique is the larger of the two French islands, elongated in shape with two large natural harbors. The largest port at **Fort-de-France**, the capital, is always filled with yachts, sailboats and visiting cruise liners.

The second harbor, along with the most beautiful beaches, are at the southernmost point on the island near Sainte-Anne. A volcano and rain forest are at the northern end of the island, near St. Pierre, while the island's center consists of several mountain masses linked by hills called "mornes." The mountains make the roads steep, winding and lined with lush tropical foliage, which makes the drive most enjoyable. The coastline, perfect for fishing and boating in the calm Caribbean waters, has been Martinique's main asset. **St. Pierre** was known as the Paris of the West Indies until it was destroyed in a volcanic eruption by **Mont Pelée** in 1902. Today, the village is charming and just as beautiful, although chilling reminders of the natural disaster have been preserved.

Two sites unique to Martinique are the birthplace of Napoleon's wife, Josephine, and the site where the French painter Gauguin lived for five months in 1887. A special museum commemorates each historical figure.

Holidays

Martinique residents take national holidays seriously and close their businesses sometimes half a day before the scheduled holiday. Taxis and tours are always available when cruise ships are in port, but shopping may not be an option on national holidays. At Carnival time, businesses close for five days.

Annual Holidays & Events

For more details and precise dates, contact the island tourist board (see *Appendix*).

January. . . New Year's Day; Three King's Day or Epiphany

February . . . . Carnival; Mardi Gras (peak of Carnival, parades & street dances); Ash Wednesday

April . . . . Easter Sunday; Easter Monday; Aqua Festival Du Robert (festival of the sea)

May . . . . Labor Day; Slavery Abolition Day; Ascension Thursday; Pentecost Monday; in St. Pierre a month-long program of theater, dance, music & art commemorating city history

July. . . . . Bastille Day; Festival of Fort-de-France, a program of theater, dance, music and art commemorating the city's history

August . . . . Assumption Day

November. . . . . . All Saint's Day (tombstones illuminated with candles);Armistice Day (fireworks); Semi-Marathon, a 22-km race; International Guitar Festival during the last part of the month

December . . . Christmas Eve (dancing, revelry); Christmas Day; Young Saint's Day (costume parade); New Year's Eve

Useful Websites

The tourist board's official website is **www.martinique.com**, and it has a section dedicated to the needs of cruise passengers. You can read about available tours, as well as options for booking through the cruise ship. The sports section lists phone numbers of hotels with tennis courts. The shopping section describes good buys and lists names and addresses of shopping centers.

Another recommended site is **www.frenchcaribbean.com** (click on Martinique). This site is easy to navigate and provides good information.

NOTE: Because taxis fares are high on Martinique, it may be less expensive to book tours while onboard the ship.

The Pier

The cruise ship terminal in the commercial district is a 15- to 20-minute walk from Fort-de-France. If you choose to walk into town, stay to the left upon leaving the pier until you arrive at the Place de la Savane Park. The park contains historical statues and an open-air market across from the main downtown shopping area.

Facilities at the pier include a Tourist Information Office, a telephone, a shady area where taxis wait and a fine duty-free shop selling French perfume, champagne, wine and other island products.

Pier Phones

There are a few phones in the terminal building. Keep in mind that calls from Martinique are costly. To access **AT&T,** ☎ 0800-99-00-11 using a phone card or Telecarte. The prepaid Telecartes can be used only in special booths marked Telecom and can be purchased from outlets marked "Telecart en Vente Ici." Ask the Tourism Office at the port for the nearest locations to buy and use Telecartes.

To call Martinique from the US, dial 596 (the international access code), then 596 (the country code), then the local number.

Shopping

La Maison Créole, near the cruise terminal, carries top brand names in perfume, writing instruments, silk, leather goods, fancy jewelry, gold crafts, wine, champagne and tobacco at duty-free prices. The staff is well trained, friendly and speaks English. Regulations require delivery of purchases at La Maison Créole directly to the ship before departure. You can then pick them up from the ship's purser or cruise director.

In Town

Museums

The **Martinique Departmental Museum**, opposite La Savane Park, is an archeological museum with exhibits focusing on the culture of the Arawak and Carib Indians and the role they played in island history. It's open from 9 am to 1 pm, then from 2 to 5 pm on weekdays and from 9 am to 12 pm on Saturdays. Admission is about US $3.50.

The **Schoelcher Library** is at the top corner of La Savane Park. The striking polychrome Byzantine-Romanesque building was designed by architect Henri Pick. It was prefabricated in France and the parts were then shipped here for completion in 1893. The building houses a collection of over 10,000 books donated by Schoelcher. It is open Monday, 1-5:30 pm; Tuesday-Thursday, 8:30 am to 5:30 pm; Friday, 8:30 am to 5 pm; and Saturday, 8:30 am to 12 pm.

The small **Gauguin Museum** honors the French painter who spent five months on the island in 1887. It contains Gauguin's personal documents, letters and reproductions of his paintings, displayed in the heart of the landscape he loved. Located in Carbet on the route to St. Pierre, the museum is open daily from 9 am to 5:30 pm. Admission is US $3.50.

The **Museum of Volcanology** in St. Pierre is on the site of a former battery overlooking the sea. Through photographs and other media, it tells of the tragic eruption of Mont Pelée in 1902. Only one person in the entire town survived the disaster, a prisoner who was locked in an underground cell. On display are photographs, oxidized glass, distorted musical instruments from the town's theater and other items recovered from the ashes. The museum was founded by the American volcanologist Franck Perret in 1932 and is open daily from 9 am to 5 pm. Admission is about US $2.

La Pagerie Museum in the Trois-Ilets district sits on the spot where the Empress Josephine was born in 1763. Before she married Napoleon and ruled as the empress of France from 1804 to 1809, Josephine was married to Alexandre de Beauharnais. There was no love lost between them, as Alexandre had actually wanted to marry one of Josephine's more attractive sisters. The museum is a small exhibit of mementos, including her childhood bed, paintings and a passionate love letter from Napoleon. The collection was compiled by Dr. Robert Rose-Rosette and is displayed in the former kitchen of the estate. The kitchen is the only room still standing, after the rest of the estate was destroyed by a hurricane. Wander through the grounds, which contain the ruins of an old sugar mill alongside thousands of colorful flowers. Open Tuesday-Friday, 9 am to 5:30 pm; weekends from 9 am to 12:30 pm. Closed on January 1, May 1 and 22, and December 25. Admission is US $3.50.

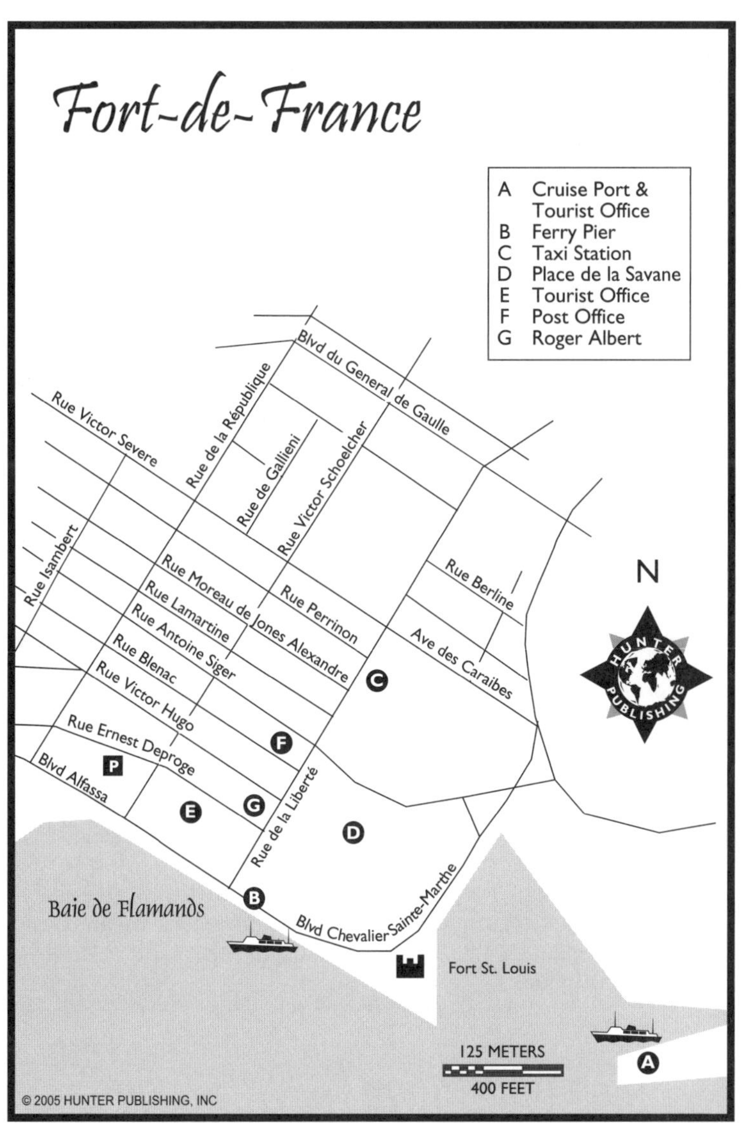

Shopping

Fort-de-France is a miniature Paris in the heart of the Caribbean, with great buys on imported French fashions, perfumes, champagne, wine, crystal and china. The **Roger Albert** store at 7 Rue Victor Hugo, across from La Savane Park, is the best place to buy perfume, Lalique crystal and French designer merchandise – Cartier, Lacoste, Yves Saint Laurent and Dupont. You will save 20% if you make your purchase with traveler's checks or a credit card. The staff at Roger Albert is friendly, speaks English and is specially trained to provide service.

The best clothing shops are on the streets that lead away from La Savane – Park Rue Victor Hugo, Rue Moreaude Jones, Rue Antoine Siger and Rue Lamartine. Top jewelers are located primarily between Rue Isambert and Rue Lamartine. Look for their unique gold "knot necklaces" and "slave chains."

Local craftsmen create exotic coral and shell jewelry, bamboo objects and basketry, which can be purchased in an open-air market across from Roger Albert in La Savane Park. Madras cloth, silk batik scarfs, enameled jewelry boxes, pottery from Poterie de Trois-Ilets and baskets from Morne-des-Esses are local specialties found in the boutiques.

Gourmands might stop in at a local *supermarché*, where French delicacies such as canned quail or foie gras may seem a true bargain. Be sure that any agricultural or food products are packaged in sealed containers, or Customs may not allow them to be transported into the US.

French Restaurants & Sidewalk Cafés

A visit to the French West Indies would not be complete without sampling true French cuisine. Stop by one of the following restaurants for superb pastries, baguettes or an assortment of mouthwatering crêpes: **Le Lafayette**, Rue de la Liberté; **Le Desnambuc**, Rue de la Liberté; and **La Crêperie,** 4 Rue Garnier Pages (corner of Rue de la République).

Transportation & Excursions

Taxis

The pier in Fort-de-France is always swarming with taxi drivers waiting to take visitors out on the island. Although some drivers use minivans, those that you see around town operate as collective taxis for island locals.

Taxis fares, which are metered and regulated by the taxi association, run pretty high. Costs depend on driving time and all fares are based on the entire car, seating one to four people.Before entering a taxi determine if the rate is in francs or US dollars. Outer island excursions will often take three or more hours, at about US $40 US per hour. You can call for a cab at ☎ 63-63-62 or 63-10-10.

Martinique's Department of Tourism has arranged special tour prices for cruise passengers who book tours through their ship. You can save money with these special prices, but if you prefer to go out on your own, we recommend renting a car. The following taxi prices are one-way estimates based on distance from the ship.

Taxi Chart

All prices are given in US dollars.

Destination *from cruise ship pier*	**Cost** *one to four people*
Balata Gardens	$40
Fort-de-France	$8
Pointe du Bout	$45
Saint Pierre	$50
Sainte-Anne	$30
Trois-Ilets	$35

Rental Cars

Driving is on the right, so American drivers will be comfortable. The roads outside of Fort-de-France are easy to navigate, although local residents drive very fast. Drive defensively and take your time and you'll enjoy a pleasant day on the island.

Rental cars are available in downtown Fort-de-France at agency offices near Roger Albert and the ferry terminal. You can either walk or take a taxi into town.

A valid driver's license is necessary to rent a vehicle and the minimum age is 21. Agencies are open weekdays 8 am to 12:30 pm and reopen from 2:30 to 5:30 pm. Most are closed on Sundays, but are open 8 am to noon or 1 pm on Saturdays. Rates run $50 to $90 per day, depending on type of car.

Reservations are recommended. During the high season, cars are in short supply and can be difficult to obtain on the day of arrival, so book ahead. Few agencies have English-speaking personnel.We recommend that you use a credit card for the rental. Ask for an island map, too.

Car Rental Agencies

To call Martinique, dial 596 (the international access code), 596 (the country code), then the local number.

Avis . . . . ☎ 70-11-60, (800) 331-1084; www.avis.com
Budget . . . . ☎ 70-06-10, (800) 626-4516; (ask for dock location) www.budget.antilles.com
Hertz . . . . ☎ 60-64-64, www.hertz.com
Europcar . . . . ☎ 73-33-13

Self-Guided Tours

Botanical Gardens

Just outside Fort-de-France, on the road to Morne-Rouge, is the **Jardin de Balata** (Balata Botanical Gardens). Martinique is named the Isle of Flowers and the garden displays every type of tropical vegetation, including many flowering plants and trees. Colorful hummingbirds dart around the park. There is a self-guided nature walk along the shaded pathways and the old Creole house on the grounds offers a glimpse into the island's French colonial past. This is a great escape from the congested city streets of Fort-de-France. Admission is $6.50 for adults and $2.50 for children. It's open daily from 9 am to 5 pm, and will take 25 minutes to reach by taxi along winding roads.

Pointe du Bout

Another way to escape from Fort-de-France is by taking a ferry across the marina to **Pointe du Bout**. The boats leave from Alfassa Boulevard, next to Place de la Savane, the park near the Roger Albert store. You can walk 15 minutes from the pier to the ferry area, or take a five-minute taxi ride for $8. Ferries cost $4 per person for a round-trip and leave Fort-de-France and Pointe du Bout at the times shown below.

Ferry Schedule

Check the ferry terminal building for any time changes before departing.

Fort-de-France	Pointe du Bout
6:30 am and 12:15 pm	6:10 am and 12:05 pm
7:30 am and 12:45 pm	6:45 am and 12:45 pm
8:00 am and 1:15 pm	7:15 am and 1:45 pm
8:30 am and 2:30 pm	8:00 am and 2:30 pm
9:00 am and 3:00 pm	8:30 am and 3:30 pm
10:00 am	9:00 am 4:00 pm
11:00 am	9:30 am and 4:30 pm
11:45 am	10:30 am and 5:00 pm
11:30 am	5:30 pm

Once in Pointe du Bout, hire a taxi to take you to the Trois-Ilets area, home to three unique museums. **La Pagerie Museum** is the birthplace of Empress Josephine and contains mementos from her home and family. The **Maison de la Canne** (Sugar Cane Museum) explores the distillation process of sugarcane used in making rum products. You can also spend time at Bakoua Beach, the only beach near the port area. Sandwich shops near the ferry dock serve great baguettes for lunch and there are also a few boutiques for shopping.

Organized Tours & Activities

The Department of Tourism has established a number of fixed-price tours that can be booked through the shore excursion office. You can read full descriptions of these and and other available tours at www.martinique.com (click on "Cruises"). Prices are not provided, so check with your ship for the latest fees.

- **Martinique Walking Tour** (1½ hours). Learn about the history, architecture and plant life of Fort-de-France as a guide leads you through its bustling streets. Stop for a refreshing drink of sugarcane juice, then use your free time to shop and make your own way back to the ship.
- **Martinique Snorkeling Tour** (2¼ hours). After a 35-minute ride on the boat *Sea Punch*, you arrive at a snorkeling lagoon. Here you have time to enjoy the wonders of undersea life, colorful coral and brilliantly colored fish. Minimum age: eight years old.

- **St. Pierre by Land and Sea Motor** (4 hours). A party boat takes groups along the western coast of Martinique en route to St. Pierre. Tour the village by tram and learn about the eruption of Mt. Pelée in 1902. You return to Fort-de-France by taxi through the rain forest, calling briefly at the Balata church, a replica of the Sacred Heart basilica in Paris.

- **Balata, Botanical Garden and the Route de la Trace** (3 hours). Visit the rain forest along the Route de la Trace, originally carved out of the mountainside by Jesuit monks. Stop off and wander through the Balata gardens where over 100 species of tropical plants are displayed in a natural setting (labeled in English, French and Latin). Finally, call at the Balata Church before returning to the ship.

Several distillery tours are also available, often including a visit to a nearby museum or beach. These tours vary in duration, from two to five hours, and always offer free rum samples followed by time to purchase your favorites.

Beaches

BEACH CHART	Facilities	Windsurfing	Snorkeling	Scuba Diving	Wave Runners	Swimming	Parasailing	Sailing	Water Skiing	Nude/Topless
Pointe du Bout	☆	☆	☆	☆		☆		☆		☆
Les Salines	☆		☆			☆				☆

The only beach close to the pier area is across the harbor at **Pointe du Bout.** You can take the ferry there and walk 10 minutes to your right down to the beach. It is not a spectacular stretch of sand, but it's a good place to enjoy the sun. There's a small area near the Meridien Hotel called **Bakoua Beach**, and although you're allowed to use the beach, the hotel facilities are out of bounds. Watersports equipment rentals are available from the hotel and there are sandwich shops near shore.

➡ Note: Nude sunbathing is not allowed here, but topless sunbathing is quite common.

The best beach is an hour's drive from Fort-de-France to the southernmost point on the island in the region of Sainte-Anne. **Les Salines** is the longest stretch of white sand on the island and the cove here is ideal for body surfing, snorkeling and swimming. Shaded benches are great for picnic lunches, and the restroom facilities are a unique experience in themselves ("squat" toilets with a simple hole in the floor). Les Salines is certainly worth the drive, but you should combine the trip with an island tour to make the most of your time and money.

Island Activities

On Land

Golf

Across the harbor from Fort-de-France is the 18-hole golf course at Trois-Ilets. The course, designed by Robert Trent Jones, is one mile from the Pointe du Bout ferry dock, accessible via a 25-minute taxi ride from the cruise ship pier. The **Golf de l'Imperatrice Josephine** offers an English-speaking golf pro, a pro shop, a bar and a restaurant. Greens fees are $54, cart rentals $50 and club rentals $20. Tee times can be arranged, ☎ (596-596) 68-32-81. This is one of the most beautifully designed courses in the Caribbean. If you want to play it, contact the golf club in advance or immediately upon arrival.Special prices are allotted to hotel guests and cruise passengers. You can opt to book your golf excursion through the ship to secure transportation, greens fees and a shared golf cart in the package price.

Tennis

There are three tennis courts at the **Golf de l'Imperatrice Josephine** golf course (☎ 596-596-68-32-81), the **Meridien Hotel** (☎ 596-596-66-00-00) has three courts and two courts at **Le Bakoua** (☎ 596-596-66-02-02) are available by reservation. All three locations are across the harbor from Fort-de-France in Pointe du Bout. You can play by making arrangements in advance. Rates vary, but range between $15 and $25 per hour.

Hiking

A private guided hike will give you a true appreciation for the rain forest environment. These treks require good physical fitness as trails can be slippery and steep. Guided half-day hikes can be arranged through **Caraibe Aventure**, ☎ (596) 79-68-70, or **Madinina Tours**, ☎ (596) 70-65-25; e-mail Madinina.tour@wanadoo.fr. Both agencies are located in Fort-de-France and charge an average of $40 per person.

Four-Wheel Drive Adventure

Discover the very heart of Martinique by traveling in a Jeep along picturesque routes away from the traditional tourist byways. A four-wheel-drive adventure (maximum six people at $50 each) can be arranged through **Caraibe Aventure** in Fort-de-France, ☎ (596) 79-68-70. Decide on the circuit yourself with the help of a guide who's eager to please.

In The Ocean

The beachfront hotels on **Bakoua Beach** at Pointe du Bout have watersports, although most operators do not speak English. The language barrier can make renting equipment difficult.

Windsurfing

Rates range between $15 and $20 an hour and 30-minute lessons are offered for $20.

Snorkeling

The coastline around **Pointe du Bout** and nearby **Anse Mitan** has excellent reefs. Snorkeling gear is often limited. Rates range between $15 and $20 per hour. A special ferry from Fort-de-France takes visitors straight to Anse Mitan, and certain ferries to Pointe du Bout also make a second stop at Anse Mitan. Ask the ferry attendant which ferry you need to take.

Ocean Kayaking

The waters surrounding Guadeloupe are perfect for paddling in a kayak. Contact **Madinina Tours** in Fort-de-France, ☎ (596) 70-65-25, e-mail Madinina.tour@wanadoo.fr, or **The Ship Shop**, ☎ (596) 74-70-08, at Le Marin.

Scuba Diving

The following scuba dive operations are in Pointe du Bout, across the harbor from Fort-de-France.

- ⚓ **Balaou Club** likes to work with Americans and will gladly pick you up at the dock. A one-tank dive costs $57, and a two-tank dive costs $92. Both trips include lunch. Contact Balaou Club at Anse Mitan in Trois Ilets, ☎ (596) 66-07-61, e-mail balaouclub@cgit.com.
- ⚓ The **Espace Plongée Martinique**, located at the Masi Creole Hotel near Carbet, offers scuba. The first dive boat departs at 8:30 am, returning at 11:45 am, and the second leaves at 2 pm, returning at 5:30 pm. Be sure your ship's departure schedule works with these times. One-tank dives cost $50 per person and reservations should be made ahead of time, ☎ (011-596) 66-01-79, e-mail E.P.M@wanadoo.fr.
- ⚓ **Tropicasub Plongée** is located at 17 Plage de la Guinguette in Saint-Pierre. If you plan to drive north to see St. Pierre and the Mt. Pelée volcano, make dive reservations with this PADI-certified group. They are wreck specialists, offering first dives for $40 and second dives at $15. ☎ (596) 78-38- 03; e-mail tropicasub@hotmail.com; www.tropicasub.com. This dive group offers English-speaking staff to make your dive safe and enjoyable.

If you do not have your own dive computer, request an English-speaking dive instructor. If none is available, plan to dive on another island.

Day Sailing

Martinique is a paradise for sailing. ***Le Toumelin*** leaves from the Meridien Hotel, ☎ (596) 49-35-01, fax (569) 74-88-12, and offers a half-day excursion with drinks and snorkeling (US $87 per person). ***L'Ile Blue***, ☎ (596) 66-06-90, and the ***Micaline***, ☎ (596) 66-09-10, leave from Point du Bout, and can be booked for day sailing trips or picnic excursions.

One-Day Itinerary

Mont Pelée, a volcano at the northern end of the island, is a unique historical site. In 1902 it erupted and destroyed the coastal town of St. Pierre. The town has since been rebuilt, but an area of ruins has been preserved. You can view remnants from the eruption in the Museum of Volcanology in St. Pierre, and the volcano itself can be explored with a guide (see *Hiking*, above). Allow three hours for the hike.

The drive to St. Pierre takes 45 minutes to an hour and the total itinerary lasts six to seven hours. The best way to explore the island is by renting a car. Be sure to get a road map.

What to Bring

If you're going to spend the whole day on the island, carry small US bills or francs to pay for lunch and entrance fees to the museums. Also, bring a camera to capture the beauty of Martinique's northern countryside.

Directions

Refer to the island map on next page.

An Island Tour

Rent your car at 9 am to get an early start on the day. With the assistance of a map and directions from the rental agency, take the N2 road out of Fort-de-France heading north. You will soon see signs for Schoelcher, Case-Pilote, Bellefontaine and Morne-Vert, small fishing villages with magnificent coastal views. Approximately 30 minutes from Fort-de-France, you will enter Le Carbet and should begin looking for the sign to the **Gauguin Museum**, set on the right side of the road.

A narrow dirt road takes you to the entrance of the museum, which commemorates the one-time inhabitant of Le Carbet. The Gauguin Memorial Art Center was built to honor the famous French painter and has a collection of personal letters and photographic reproductions of works from Gauguin's Martinique period. The museum also houses a collection of traditional island costumes, headdresses and artwork made by local artists. The admission fee is about $3.50 and it is worth a 30-minute stop on the journey to St. Pierre. Open 9 am to 5:30 pm.

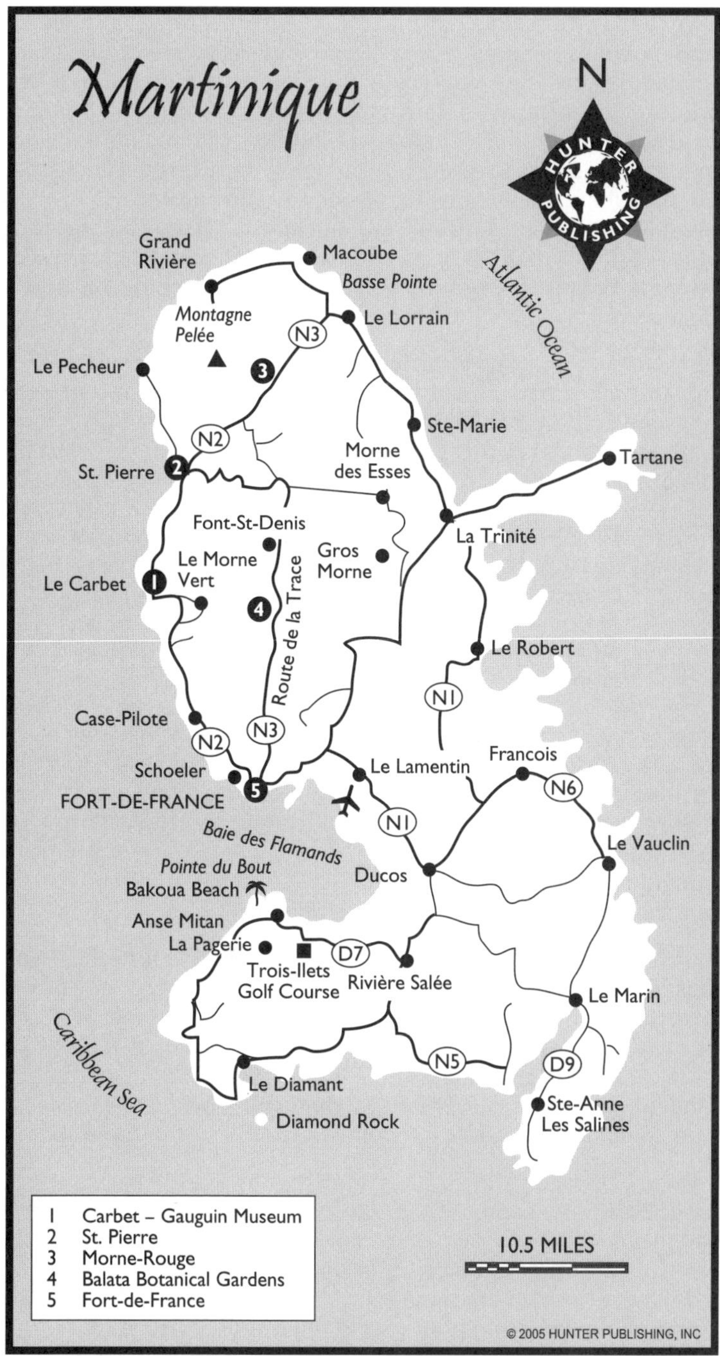
Martinique
N
HUNTER PUBLISHING
Atlantic Ocean
Caribbean Sea
Grand Rivière
Macoube
Basse Pointe
Le Lorrain
Montagne Pelée
N3
Le Pecheur
3
Ste-Marie
N2
Morne des Esses
Tartane
St. Pierre
2
La Trinité
Font-St-Denis
Le Morne Vert
Gros Morne
Le Carbet
1
4
Route de la Trace
Le Robert
N1
Case-Pilote
N2
N3
Francois
Schoeler
5
Le Lamentin
N6
FORT-DE-FRANCE
N1
Le Vauclin
Baie des Flamands
Pointe du Bout
Ducos
Bakoua Beach
Anse Mitan
La Pagerie
D7
Trois-Ilets Golf Course
Rivière Salée
Le Marin
N5
D9
Le Diamant
Ste-Anne Les Salines
Diamond Rock
1 Carbet – Gauguin Museum
2 St. Pierre
3 Morne-Rouge
4 Balata Botanical Gardens
5 Fort-de-France
10.5 MILES
© 2005 HUNTER PUBLISHING, INC

Leave the museum and turn right for a 15-minute drive to **St. Pierre**, once known as the Paris of the West Indies. As you enter the town, the roads become one way. Follow the signs to the **Museum of Volcanology,** open between 9 am and 5 pm. Admission is US $2. Plan to arrive here no later than 11 am and allow 30 to 45 minutes for viewing the photos, distorted musical instruments, a cracked liberty bell and other items. When the Mont Pelée volcano erupted in 1902, the devastating heat and suffocating ashes killed almost everyone living in the coastal town of St. Pierre. The only survivor was a prisoner who was buried in an underground cell; it was found after the rubble was taken away.

If you want to tour St. Pierre, jump on the ***Cyparis Express*** (named after the sole survivor of the eruption), a colorful train that gives hour-long English-language tours on weekdays and half-hour tours on the weekends. Cost is $10 for adults, $5 for children. Catch the train on the boardwalk at the base of the Museum of Volcanology.

> ➠ TIP: The authors' favorite spot is the **Supermarché** near the waterfront pier, which has a superb deli offering sandwiches or baguettes. There are plenty of street-side cafés too. Ask for a sandwich to go and enjoy it as you explore the coastline. Plan to be en route for Morne-Rouge by 1 pm.

It takes only 15 minutes to reach **Morne-Rouge**, which has an excellent view of Mont Pelée. The quiet town is typical of rural communities throughout the island, and from here you'll begin your slow journey back to Fort-de-France. Signs leading south on N3 to Fort-de-France are posted along the road and the highway becomes a winding pathway through the tropical rain forest, the *parc naturel* common in the northern part of Martinique.

After 20-25 minutes of driving, a sign for the **Balata Botanical Gardens** will direct you to the right. The majestic gardens offer views of Carbet Peak and the bay of Fort-de-France. Beautiful pathways are lined with tropical plants, trees and flowers. You should arrive at the Botanical Garden between 2 and 2:30 pm. Spend about 40 minutes wandering through this tropical wonderland. The entrance fee is about $6 for adults and $2.50 for children. Ticket sales stop at 4 pm.

A 15- to 20-minute drive back into Fort-de-France will take you through the east end of town. You'll probably need to use a town map to guide you safely when returning the rental car. Walk through the Market Square at **Place de la Savane** and enjoy the beautiful park. At the completion of the tour, you will have spent between six and seven hours admiring the outer regions of Martinique.

St. Lucia

Helen Of The West Indies

Island Description

Nobody knows who bestowed the name of St. Lucia on this beautiful island; historians doubt it was discovered by Columbus. The first known European to settle here was the pirate **François De Clerc**, known as Wooden Leg. Legend says the peg-legged pirate buried his stolen Spanish gold on Pigeon Island, which later became the site of a British fortress.

St Lucia's famous Pitons.
(Image courtesy Middleton & Gendron.)

When the English arrived in 1605, after being blown off course on their way to Guiana, they bought land from the Carib Indians to begin a settlement. Of the 67 English settlers who arrived on the island, only 19 survived subsequent Carib attacks and were able to flee in a stolen Carib boat. The second wave of English settlers, led by **Sir Thomas Warner**, were also killed or driven out by the Caribs in 1639. A successful settlement was eventually established at **Soufrière** in 1746 when the **French West India Company** bought the island from the British in 1651.

The French choice of location for their settlement may have been fortunate. Soufrière is near the **Sulphur Springs**, which were deeply feared by the Indians who believed the boiling pools were occupied by the god of death. The nearby twin peaks, the **Pitons**, represented the goddess of birth and the giver of food. These gods were perceived as both powerful and dangerous to the Indians. The British soon declared war on the French for helping in the American Revolution and St. Lucia was considered a prize, changing hands 14 times before the English prevailed.

A crucial naval battle for the English was waged from St. Lucia in 1782 when **Admiral George Rodney** learned of French plans for joining forces with the Spanish Armada to drive the English out of the Caribbean. Admiral Rodney kept watch daily from the fort on Pigeon Island for a signal of the French fleet sailing from Fort Royal in Martinique. Finally, 150 French ships containing 10,000 men departed from Martinique and within two hours Rodney sailed with his own fleet of 100 ships in hot pursuit. The resulting defeat of the French fleet in the **Battle of Iles des Saints** secured British supremacy over the seas and its position of power in the Caribbean.

Castries, the capital of St. Lucia, was destroyed many times by hurricanes, military attacks and catastrophic fires, so there are few historic structures remaining. Castries' large harbor, framed by stately mansions perched on hills facing the Caribbean, became a favorite port in colonial days. St. Lucia's natural vegetation, dramatic volcanic mountains and fertile fields earned the island the name, Helen of the West Indies, comparing it to the beautiful Helen of Troy.

In 1863 the coal industry was introduced to St. Lucia to fuel the coal-driven steamships that called upon Port Castries. Indentured East Indians arrived during the next 30 years to provide manpower for the industry and many remained as island residents after their terms of indenture ended.

Agriculture is still St. Lucia's largest source of income and a large portion of the countryside is cultivated with bananas. This single crop accounts for 80% of the island's economy and has earned the nickname "green gold." The islanders prefer to call their farms "estates," rather than plantations. Some privately owned estates are still in operation, offering tours to the public.

In an attempt to lure more tourists, St. Lucia opened the Pointe Seraphine Shopping Mall adjacent to the cruise ship port a few years ago.

This is a beautiful, modern shopping haven that offers some of the most stylish shops and boutiques.

The Island People

St. Lucians are a mixture of British, French, African and Indian, forming a unique West Indian culture. Island native **Eudovic** uses his skills as a master wood-sculptor to express elements of the unique people. His "tree of life" wall carvings show the face of a man, a house and a garden, all sheltered under the branches of a coconut tree.

The Cycle of Life

According to Eudovic, when a baby boy was born, his father took the infant's umbilical cord and planted it along with a coconut. When the coconut palm grew, it would mark the area that would be the boy's land during his lifetime. When the boy became a man, he would build his house, raise his crops and his family would live on the land under his tree. When the man died, the tree was cut down, symbolizing an end to the dual-life cycle.

Craftsmen like Eudovic care deeply for their island, their people and their art. To find materials for his craft, he trudges through the rain forest in search of choice pieces of dead wood, and he plants new trees to help replenish the land. Eudovic also teaches the skills he has learned over a lifetime to apprentices so that his art will be kept alive. He welcomes visitors to his work studio (see *Shopping*, page 238) with a childlike pleasure and his warm hospitality exemplifies the West Indian character.

The government is aware of the island's natural attractions and beauty. It is building new roads to link the major towns and tourist attractions with the cruise ship port, but at the same time realizes the value of its natural resources; a number of protected marine areas have already been established.

Sports in the form of soccer and cricket are important events. It is not unusual for a traffic jam to occur near the local soccer field on a Saturday morning, and locals take pleasure in discussing the latest sporting events in the same way Americans talk about football or baseball. Island sports figures become national heroes, even though their nation is smaller than most states in America.

Island Proverbs

Fishermen don't say de fish stink.
People don't notice the bad in themselves.

Who help you buy de big mule, don't help you feed it.
The one who helps get you in trouble doesn't help get you out.

Head not made fer hat alone.
Use your brain.

Holidays

Pointe Seraphine's shops are open whenever a cruise ship is in port, and ship arrival dates and times are known by local merchants and taxi drivers. St. Lucia loves a party and most of their holidays give rise to a festival, which makes visiting St. Lucia especially enjoyable during these times.

Annual Holidays & Events

For more details, contact the tourist board (see *Appendix*).

January . . . New Year's Day; fiesta held in Vigie Playground, Castries. Locals sell delicacies, masquerade bands

February. . . . . Early February, starting the Sunday before Ash Wednesday is Carnival, lasting over a week; Independence Day

April . . . . Good Friday; Easter; Easter Monday

June. . . . . St. Peter's Day is a Fisherman's Feast (local fishermen dress their boats)

August . . . Feast of St. Rose de Lima Members of La Rose Flower Society parade the streets in costume; Last Wednesday in August Market Vendor's Festival

October . . Feast of St. Margaret Alacoque – another local flower society parades in the streets in costume

November . . . St. Cecilia's Day is a musician's festival day

December . . . . National Day, celebrating the islands patron saint; Christmas; Boxing Day

Useful Websites

The tourist board's official website, **www.stlucia.org**, offers an event calendar, information on island history and culture, descriptions of local attractions, available activities, lists of hotels and restaurants, and a few links. Another informative site is **www.stluciatravel.com/lc**, the hotel association web page. The home page of this site is overwhelming. Look at the underlined choices across the top or bottom of the page, click on 'Things to Do" and a page with cute icons directs you to useful and specific data and web links. This site also offers good detailed maps (on the right column), although the map section takes a long time to load.

The Pier

The pier at **Pointe Seraphine** is to the left when entering the harbor area from the ocean. Facilities here were designed with cruisers in mind. There's a tourist information center, a money exchange and an outlet of the Philatelic Bureau all on the premises. Castries, the largest town on St. Lucia, is a short taxi ride from Pointe Seraphine.

The **Elizabeth II Pier** and three docking berths are situated near the business district of Castries, used for receiving cruise ships when two or more enter the port. Facilities are not specifically designed for cruise ship passengers, but the pier is only a short walk to the center of town.

The area code for St. Lucia is 758, and is a long distance phone call from the United States.

Pier Phones

The commercial piers are a short walk from a **Cable and Wireless** office that sells phone cards and provides public telephones at its office. The company offers a special number to use for calls to the US. Dial 1-800-255-5872 (CALL USA) to make collect calls, use a credit card, or US calling card. Voice instructions guide you through the procedure.

Excellent phone facilities are available at Pointe Seraphine, including telephones at either end of the shopping mall. Certain phones are designated for **AT&T** direct dial access or for credit cards. You can access AT&T from public phones by dialing ☎ (800) 872-2881. The tourist desk at Pointe Stephanie sells phone cards in E.C. denominations to use with the specially marked "Card Phones."

In Town

Currency

The currency here is the **Eastern Caribbean dollar**, or EC, tied to the US dollar at about EC $2.65 to US $1. Banking hours are 8 am to 3 pm on weekdays and until 5 pm on Fridays. Most banks are closed on weekends and holidays. A money exchange booth is available at Pointe Seraphine. Major credit cards and traveler's checks are accepted by merchants and tour operators.

> ➠ TIP: Carry small bill denominations to avoid receiving large amounts of EC in change.

Postage

The post office is on Bridge Street in Castries, just two blocks from the commercial piers. It's open 8:30 am to 4 pm weekdays. The Philatelic Bureau occupies a room to the right of the entrance and has another outlet at the Pointe Seraphine complex. St. Lucia's are great collectibles. The cost to airmail a postcard is approximately US 50¢. (Remember, US postage is not accepted.)

Museums & Historical Sites

The city of **Castries**, named after the Minister of The French Navy and the Colony, Marechal De Castries, was ravaged by four enormous fires. The buildings here are more modern than those in other Caribbean capitals. The cathedral, the Victorian library and the old French-designed buildings around Columbus Square are the best remaining historical buildings in town.

The **Cathedral of Immaculate Conception** is the most interesting building in downtown Castries. Built in 1894, the interior is covered in wood and has intricate and beautiful paintings on display. The effect is quite unusual. Visitors are permitted to enter the cathedral, but shorts are not considered acceptable attire. Just outside is **Columbus Square,** where the oldest and largest tree on the island, a saman tree, spreads its branches.

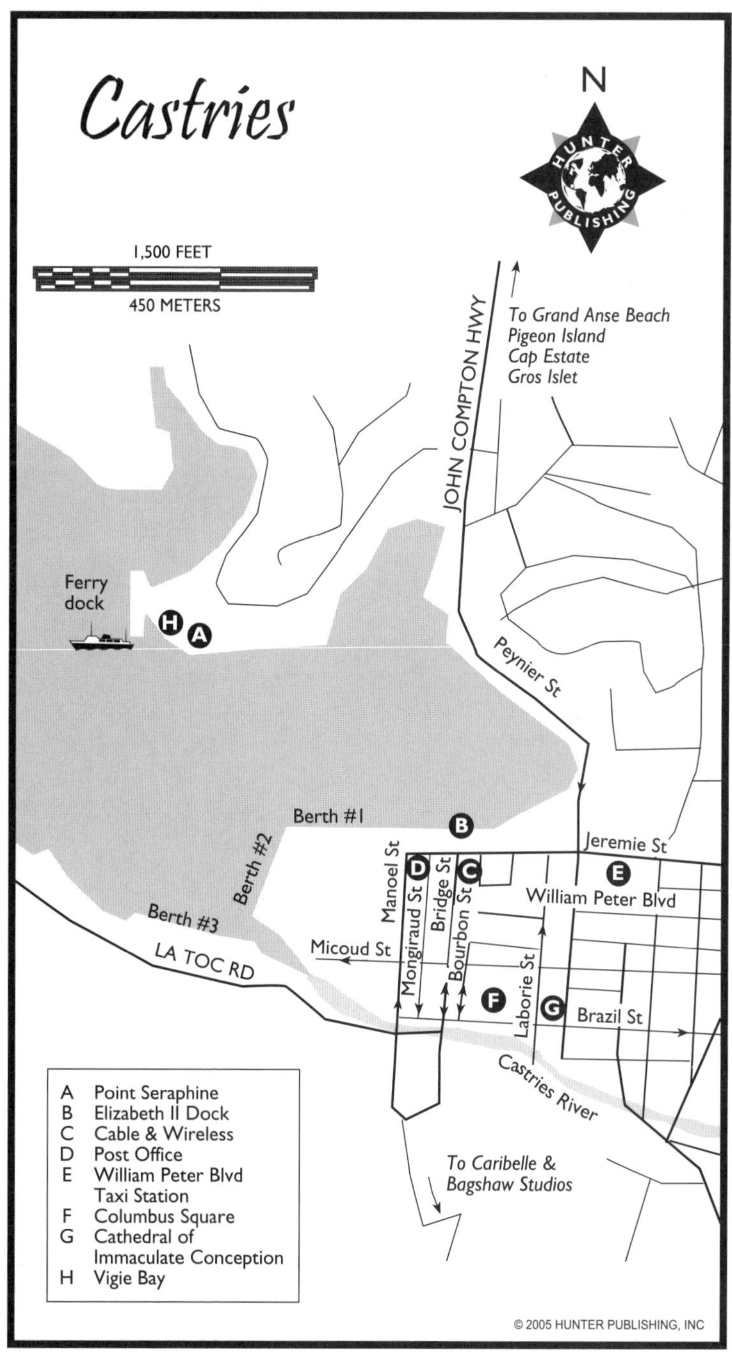
Castries
N
HUNTER PUBLISHING
1,500 FEET
450 METERS
JOHN COMPTON HWY
To Grand Anse Beach
Pigeon Island
Cap Estate
Gros Islet
Ferry dock
Peynier St
Berth #1
Berth #2
Berth #3
LA TOC RD
Manoel St
Mongiraud St
Bridge St
Bourbon St
Jeremie St
William Peter Blvd
Micoud St
Laborie St
Brazil St
Castries River
To Caribelle & Bagshaw Studios
A Point Seraphine
B Elizabeth II Dock
C Cable & Wireless
D Post Office
E William Peter Blvd Taxi Station
F Columbus Square
G Cathedral of Immaculate Conception
H Vigie Bay
© 2005 HUNTER PUBLISHING, INC

Morne Fortune, meaning "Hill of Good Luck," is a large, hilly area that once housed the main military fortification for the important Castries Harbour. Old British barracks and a few older French ruins are scattered over the Morne between modern luxury homes and hotels. Taxi drivers are happy to point out the historically important features of the Morne as you drive through the area.

Pigeon Island National Park is the most historically significant site on St. Lucia. Located to the north of Castries above Gros Islet, the park is now connected to the mainland by a manmade causeway. Due to its height and prominent location, Pigeon Island made an excellent lookout for pirates lying in wait for Spanish galleons heavily weighted with gold. Martinique was clearly visible to the north, so the site made a perfect location for an English military fort to defend against the French.

Today, Pigeon Island National Park is open daily. With the assistance of a map (available at the entry gate) you can wander through a maze of stone and brick ruins, the remnants of Admiral Rodney's naval station. In addition, an air-conditioned museum re-creates the famous and crucial battle of 1782 between the English and the French navies. The French had superior numbers with 150 ships to Rodney's 100 ships, but the French made a strategic naval error, which gave the victory to Admiral Rodney. A beautiful beach is set near a small restaurant and a splendid park here filled with tropical trees and flowers makes a delightful spot to picnic. (See *Self-Guided Tours,* page 240.)

Shopping

Pointe Seraphine Mall

Shopping for duty-free goods at Pointe Seraphine is a cool and comfortable experience. To insure duty-free prices, carry a passport and boarding pass while shopping. When you complete a purchase the shopkeeper supplies two copies of the sales invoice. The white copy is your receipt and the pink copy must be handed to the Customs official when departing the island. Liquor and tobacco products are required to be delivered directly to the ship, but other items can be taken with you at the time of purchase.

Bagshaw's Studio carries silk-screened designs that are unique to St. Lucia (the designs are not exported). The brightly colored hand-printed cloth is made into wall hangings, shirts, dresses and tropical clothing. The impressive Bagshaw Studio Factory, located on the Morne, is also open to the public (see *Shopping*, below).

Colombian Emeralds, part of the world-famous chain of jewelry stores in major cruise ship ports, guarantees the same price on its jewelry from island to island. Passengers who missed a great buy in St. Thomas or St. Maarten may be able to find the same item here.

Pickwick & Co. is another outlet to shop for imported china and crystal with names like Wimbledon, Pringle, Portmeirion, Wedgewood and Edinburgh Crystal to entice the buyer.

Images contains an excellent selection of international perfumes and cosmetics from Elizabeth Arden, Lancôme and Revlon, as well as a wide selection of Rayban sunglasses.

Jewelers Warehouse offers 50% discount off list prices for diamonds, emeralds, rubies, sapphires, tanzanite and watches. You get a certified appraisal with each purchase and access to a US-based service department.

Clear Blue sells original artwork, prints, painted pottery by St. Lucian artist Michelle Elliot, European silver jewelry, plus French and Creole fabrics.

Cocoa Joe's Beach Shack offers more beach stuff than any store on the island.

Kokotok sells children's clothing as well as adult fashions, T-shirts, sandals, beach bags and souvenirs. This store is the exclusive distributor for Jill Walker (a famous artist from Barbados) prints and placemats.

Sea Island Cotton can be purchased from three shops – **Raffles, Oasis** and **Peer.** If you want to wear silky-soft clothes that keep you cool, St. Lucia is the perfect place to shop. (Take a city tour that stops at Caribelle Batik factory for a full range of wonderful clothing, wall hangings and accessories.)

Other shops at Pointe Seraphine Mall sell books, rum, leather, kids clothing, jewelry, watches and electronics at duty-free prices.

Out On The Island

A visit to St. Lucia gives you the rare opportunity to visit several working factories where quality merchandise is manufactured and sold on-site. By viewing the process used to create unique designs, you can appreciate special purchases even more. It is easy to arrange for a shopping adventure. Start just outside Pointe Seraphine Mall and ask your cab driver to take you to the following shops:

Bagshaw's Studios & Factory is on the Morne, just two miles outside of Castries, overlooking the ocean. This factory manufactures vibrantly colored silkscreen designs by local artists Sydney Bagshaw and Virginia Henry. All the garments are made in St. Lucia from the finest materials.

☆ The **Caribelle Batik Factory** is on the Morne occupying the old Howelton House, which enjoys some of the best views on the island. This is one of two Caribelle factories in the Caribbean (the other is on St. Kitts and offers different clothing designs). Marvel at the skill displayed by the Caribelle workers as they apply searing hot wax to ultra-fine cotton. Each color in a batik requires hot waxing, dying and drying before the next color can be applied. A wall hanging containing many layers of color will, therefore, cost more than a fabric receiving one or two colors.

T-shirts, shirts, dresses, wall hangings, skirts, shorts and accessories for men and women are for sale in the large showroom. Wander onto the veranda behind the building, where you can buy a cool drink and see the dyeing rooms and colorful fabrics drying in the sun. This is an excellent spot to photograph phenomenal views of Castries Harbor. Caribelle batiks are sold in outlets around Castries and in major hotels, but a visit to the factory may be the highlight of a trip to St. Lucia.

☆ **Eudovic's Art Studio** is found on the Morne. This is the best woodworking studio in the Caribbean. Meeting the owner, Vincent Joseph Eudovic, is part of the total experience. He will proudly show you his work and enchant you with his winning personality. Small, very affordable pieces are available in the main showroom and the wall plaques depicting the tree of life (see page 231) are a genuine bargain. The artists use dead wood gathered in the rain forest from cobary, mahogany, red cedar and lourier cannea trees. The most spectacular sculptures are Eudovic's large freeform pieces on display in his second showroom – ask for a viewing. They capture the strength and character of the wood itself and the use of positive and negative space is reminiscent of the famous works by Henry Moore.

The pieces at Eudovic's are created by native artists without formal art training, but no finer craftsmanship and imagination can be found in art museums. The prices reflect many hours of work, and true art collectors will recognize them as bargains. A refreshment stand on-site serves West Indian cuisine.

Choiseul Craft Center is just outside the village of Choiseul, between Soufrière and Vieux Fort. If you are touring the south, arrange to stop at the Choiseul Craft Center, where volunteers come from around the world to teach various skills to children and locals. The goal of the center is to encourage islanders to start businesses for themselves, sell their creations to local store owners and to help improve the local economy through free enterprise. The skills of basket weaving, pottery and wood crafting are being preserved through the efforts of this center and the works are sold in a shop on the site.

Transportation & Excursions

Taxis

You'll dock at either the Elizabeth II Pier and commercial berths on the edge of downtown Castries, or Pointe Seraphine across the harbor. Both locations will have a string of taxis waiting. Rates are regulated by a taxi association and are priced for the whole taxi, for one to four persons. Rates may be given in EC dollars or US dollars, so be sure to question the driver for the correct fare before getting in. Taxis are available for island tours or trips to the beach, and round-trip fares can be negotiated.

Taxi Chart

All prices are given in US dollars.

Destination *from downtown Castries*	**Cost** *one to four people*
Anse Chastanet (take round-trip water taxi)	$59
Cap Estate Golf Club	$25
Halcyon Beach Hotel	$108
Marigot Bay	$25
New Vigie Beach Hotel	$8
Pigeon Island	$25
Rodney Bay Marina	$16
Royal St. Lucian Hotel	$16
Soufrière/Sulphur Springs (round-trip)	$140
St. James Club Morgan Bay	$10
Castries short tour, 1-4 people	$60
Full-day Island Tours, 1-4 people	$180

Rental Cars

Driving is on the left and the roads are constantly being repaired, which makes things difficult for foreigners. In addition, St. Lucia is large and hilly, with many winding roads. However, if you are willing to drive slowly and cautiously, honk around the blind curves and remember to stay to the left, rent a car for the day and you'll enjoy an exhilarating day of exploring.

> ➠ Many local bus and taxi drivers drive extremely fast, which might make driving stressful.

Cars can be rented at the pier area or at Vigie Airport for $50-$65 per day. You must acquire a temporary driver's license for $20, and the minimum age for rentals is 25. A collision damage waiver is available and your credit card can cover the $500 deposit for rental cars. Personal accident insurance is recommended.

Car Rental Agencies

The area code for St. Lucia is 758, a long-distance phone call from the United States.

Avis . . . . ☎ 452-2202; (800) 331-1084
avisslu@candw.lc; www.avis.com

Budget St. Lucia . . . . ☎ 452-8160
www.budgetstlucia.com

Courtesy Car Rental Ltd. . . . . ☎ 450-8140
e-mail courtesycar@candw.lc

Hertz . . . . ☎ 452-0679; (800) 227-7368
(at cruise ship dock); hertz@candw.lc

Self-Guided Tours

Pigeon Island

Pigeon Island National Park lies north of Castries and Rodney Bay. It comprises 40 acres of protected land dotted with ruins, forts and hidden caves, which may still contain pirate treasure. Before the island became a defensive military complex, the area was used as a hideout for the notorious French privateer, Wooden Leg. The park contains some of the oldest historical ruins on the entire island and you can spend hours wandering along the walkways. Despite its name, Pigeon Island has been connected to the mainland by a man-made peninsula.

A half-hour cab ride to the park will cost $25. Open hours are 9 am to 5 pm daily. An entrance fee of US $5 helps to maintain the park and a self-guided map is available for EC $1. The walk to the top of the observation peak takes approximately one hour if you're in good shape. Don't miss the air-conditioned museum here. After a few hours exploring the ruins, take advantage of a lovely little beach near the park's eatery, **Captain's Cellar Restaurant,** an authentic 18th-century tavern open daily 10 am to 11 pm. If you are more interested in snorkeling and swimming, try **Reduit Beach** just outside Pigeon Island.

Marigot Bay

A 30-minute drive south of Castries through the Cul-de-Sac Valley – lined with mile after mile of green banana plants – is the sheltered **Marigot Bay**. The winding road takes you into a private harbor area protected by steep mountains and lush foliage lining the cove. This was the location for the film, *Dr. Doolittle*. Today it is used by The Moorings, a major sailing operations center. The bay is the best hurricane shelter on the island and is always filled with small sailboats and dinghies. A taxi ride to Marigot will cost $25.

A short drive down the coast to Marigot can also include a stop at Eudovic's Art Studio (see *Shopping*, page 238). If you're driving, watch for the signs heading south out of Castries by way of Morne Fortune, down the hill through Cul-de-Sac to the entrance of Marigot Bay. Get a map at the car rental agency and drive carefully.

Organized Tours & Activities

Sunlink International provides complete island tours at reasonable prices. Various itineraries allow you to see the very best St. Lucia has to offer within a half-day or full-day time schedule. Make your reservations with Sunlink to ensure a spot; ☎ (758) 452-8232, fax (758) 452-0459, slurep@candw.lc. A credit card will guarantee the booking. Tours 1, 2 and 3 below are offered by Sunlink. They also offer private limousine service for up to four people for $125/hour or $375/day.

- Visit **Soufrière** by land or by sea for a full day of exploring. The trip by land takes you on a wild ride over the hills and valleys. Scheduled stops at the Sulphur Springs (the drive-in volcano), the Diamond Waterfall, and Diamond Baths natural spring and gardens are worth the winding bus ride. The return trip is by boat with a stop at Marigot Bay for a refreshing drink and a view of St. Lucia's Caribbean coastline.

  The alternative trip to Soufrière is a cruise down the coastline on a powerful speedboat, followed by a tour of the sites by bus. The scheduled stops are basically the same – Sulphur Springs, Diamond Waterfall and Baths – but the tour also includes a visit to the Soufrière Estate, a former sugar estate open to the public. If time allows, the return boat trip to Castries will also incorporate a ride around Marigot Bay and an opportunity to snorkel in the warm Caribbean Sea.

  Lunch at a local restaurant, all entrance fees, the boat trip with drinks and an informative tour guide are all included on both tours for $75/adult, $35/child. Excursions leave by 8 am and return between 4:30 and 5 pm, Tuesday and Saturday.

- A half-day excursion to the historical ruins of **Pigeon Island** is available on Wednesday for $35 per person. It begins at 1:30 pm and takes you past the picturesque Cap Estate out to the causeway leading to Pigeon Island. This two-hour guided trip takes you back in time to the exciting days of Admiral Rodney's naval station that once secured the island. Groups return to Castries at 5 pm, so you have half the day to explore the historical ruins on the 40-acre national park or to swim and snorkel off the park's beach.

- Take a day sail on a 140-foot replica of a 19th-century sailing ship. The brig ***Unicorn*** leaves from Vigie Bay, next to Pointe Seraphine, and sails along the west coast to Soufrière. Once in Soufrière, you take a guided tour of the Sulphur Springs, Diamond Falls and the Botanical Gardens. The return voyage to Castries includes complimentary drinks, a buffet lunch and a visit to Marigot Bay. The excursion leaves at 9:30 am and returns at 4:30 pm, and costs $90/adult, $43/child. Trips are available Tuesday through Friday. Make reservations through Sunlink or with *Unicorn* directly, ☎ (758) 452-6811.

Helicopter Rides

One of the most exhilarating ways to see St. Lucia is by air, on a flight with **St. Lucia's Helicopters**, ☎ (758) 453-6950. Both Sunlink and Spice Travel (see below) offer a choice of two tours for cruise passengers leaving from Pointe Seraphine.

⚓ The **South Island Flightseeing Tour** is approximately 20 minutes long, with flights along the west coast to Marigot Bay and Soufrière. It begins by flying over Castries Harbor, then to the bay at Marigot. You will see Soufrière's Pitons emerging out of the water to 2,700 feet above sea level – most impressive from the air. Don't forget to bring your camera to capture these dramatic creations of nature on film. The return trip brings you inland over the islands volcano and bubbling sulphur springs. The flight back to Castries also allows you to view the jagged peaks and lush tropical rain forest that dominate the island's terrain. The entire trip is well worth the time and effort. US $120 per person.

Recommended Tour Company

Another great company to work with is **Spice Travel**, which has a long list of excursions, offering helicopter tours for $120, a catamaran snorkeling trip to Soufrière for $85, a tour to Pigeon Island for $35, a Frigate Island and garden tour for $65, and an Errard Plantation tour for $80. They will customize trips if you call ahead. Contact Spice Travel at ☎ (758) 452-0865/0866, e-mail tthomm@candw.lc. Jump on-line to view their excursions at www.casalucia.com (click on Spice Travel).

Beaches

Beachside resorts are scattered all along the coast, so the sand is often packed with hotel guests, tourists, locals and sports enthusiasts. The beach at **Grand Anse** is where you'll find the Royal St. Lucian Hotel. This is one of the most popular beaches, with something for everyone. A volleyball net and watersports are available; the long stretch of beach for sunbathers and beachcombers may remind some of Miami Beach. A 20-minute taxi ride for $12 (one to four people) from Castries or Pointe Seraphine takes you to the entrance of the Royal St. Lucian Hotel and a walk through the property leads straight to the beach. The hotel has gift shops, restaurants and a beachside barbecue hut.

BEACH CHART	Facilities	Windsurfing	Snorkeling	Scuba Diving	Wave Runners	Swimming	Parasailing	Sailing	Water Skiing	Nude/Topless
Grand Anse	☆	☆			☆	☆	☆	☆		
Morgan Bay	☆	☆	☆			☆		☆		
Vigie Beach	☆		☆			☆				
Halcyon Beach	☆	☆			☆	☆		☆		

The **St. James Club Morgan Bay Resort** offers a stretch of private beach for its hotel guests. If you want to spend the day here, we highly recommend that you ask at the front desk if you can use the facilities. If you're willing to have lunch at the hotel and use the beachside bar, you'll be welcome at the resort and beach. Watersports, such as windsurfing, sailing, water skiing and snorkeling, are also available for a charge to non-hotel guests. The resort is only a 15-minute taxi ride from the pier ($10).

Vigie Beach, near the airport and Pointe Seraphine, is a five-minute taxi ride from the dock ($8). This is a long stretch of gray sand with no watersports or congestion from beachside resorts. The water is quite calm for swimming. It's not the most popular beach on the island, offering a quiet location for those who prefer peace and tranquility. **D's Restaurant** here serves the best island cuisine, and the waterfront location makes this a great place for lunch.

A smaller but beautiful beach is at the **Sandals Halcyon Beach Hotel**. Only 10 minutes from Castries, Halcyon Beach is a white sandy stretch offering watersports and beachside facilities. A taxi there will cost $10. Many of the inland hotels around Castries send their guests to Halcyon Beach, so it can be crowded with sunworshippers.

Island Activities

On Land

Golf

To the north of Castries is a nine-hole newly designed par 71 golf course at the **Cap Estate Golf Club**, situated among luxurious estates. The course is open to the public and is run by the St. Lucia Golf and Country Club. Greens fees are $70 for nine holes and $95 for 18 holes; club rentals are $20. The course is a 20-minute taxi ride from Castries ($25). You can make reservations by phone or on their website prior to arrival. Free transportation from the cruise dock can be arranged for three or more golfers. ☎ (758) 450-8523; www.stluciagolf.com.

Sandals Saint Lucia Golf Resort has a nine-hole course open to the public on a day pass that includes food, drinks, watersports, scuba diving, tennis and golf for a cost of $132. You can buy the pass at the hospitality desk at Pointe Stephanie cruise dock or at the resort's front desk. Without the pass, greens fees for non-guests are $75 for the first nine holes and $35 for an additional nine (includes lunch and drinks only). Caddy fees ($17 for 18 holes, $12 for nine holes), tips, cart rental ($20 for nine holes, $30 for 18 holes) are additional, even with a day pass. The $75 special package includes clubs, golf balls, caddy and cart rental. Come here if your partner prefers to lay on the beach or play tennis while you golf. ☎ (758) 452-3081; e-mail sandalslu@candw.lc.

Tennis

The **St. James Morgan Bay Resort** offers four courts with fees ranging from $10 to $20 an hour and a tennis pro available for lessons. Contact the resort for reservations at ☎ (758) 450-2511.

The **St. Lucia Racquet Club** is the premier location for tennis, with its professional services, tutoring and nine floodlit courts. ☎ (758) 450-0551 for reservations.

The **Sandals St. Lucia Golf Resort** includes tennis as part of their all-inclusive one-day pass for cruise passengers (see *Golf*, above). ☎ (758) 452-3081; e-mail sandalslu@candw.lc.

The **St. Lucian Hotel**, ☎ 453-8351, has two courts and reasonable rates.

Horseback Riding

You can tour the north portion of St. Lucia on horseback. **Trim's National Riding** group offers daily beach rides along the beaches and scenic inland rides around the Cap Estate and Pigeon Island. A one-hour ride costs $40, the two-hour rides cost $50 per person and must be reserved prior to arrival on the island; for groups of eight or more, a beach barbecue can also be arranged at $70 (including the ride) per person on Wednesday and Friday. For reservations and more information, contact director Rene Trim. ☎ (758) 450-8273; e-mail trims ridingstables@candw.lc.

The **International Riding Stables** are just one mile inside the old Beausejour Estate at Gros Islet in the north of the island. They provide a wide range of healthy, gentle Creole and pedigree horses to suit the taste of the most discriminating rider. Guests have a choice of three exciting tours. The regular one-hour beach ride costs $40, a two-hour ride costs $50, and the four-hour (10 am to 2 pm) BBQ ride costs $70. Complimentary transportation is included with advance arrangements. ☎ (758) 452-8139; e-mail stefanof@candw.lc; www.stluciatravel.com.lc/internat.htm.

Mountain Biking

Island Bike Hikes runs a half-day rain forest tour at US $49 per person. This excursion provides a unique look at St. Lucia's rural and rugged heart. Riders learn about fruits, trees and see the island's most beautiful waterfall. Unlike cycling on the busy roads in the island's north, riders are unlikely to experience traffic here. What they will enjoy is miles of unspoiled scenery. Some cruise ships offer a similar tour through the shore excursion desk, insuring that passengers get back on time. If your ship does not, join a group by calling ☎ (758) 458-0908; e-mail mtnbikeslu@candw.lc. Visit www.cyclestlucia.com to make on-line reservations (be sure to explain in the Comments section that you need to join a cruise ship group tour).

Jungle Reef Adventures provides a full-day of jungle biking. Guided rides on high-quality Cannonade bikes travel through 12 miles of jungle, include lunch and snorkeling at Anse Chastenet, and a water taxi ride from the cruise ship dock for $79 per person. (See *Diving, Jungle Reef Adventure*, below, for contact information.)

In The Ocean

Windsurfing

Windsurfing rentals cost $20-$25 per hour and are available at the **St. Lucian Hotel, Halcyon Beach Hotel** and the **St. James Club Morgan Bay Resort**. All the hotel locations along the Caribbean side of the island have excellent conditions for beginners and the waters near the rocky coastline are perfect for advanced windsurfers.

Scuba Diving

One of the most dramatic coral reefs in St. Lucia is in Anse Chastanet Bay. A dive here will reveal bright orange and yellow coral gardens, six-foot-wide sea fans and a multitude of tropical fish, and may well be the highlight of your time on St. Lucia.

Many watersports enthusiasts make St. Lucia their vacation destination. (Image courtesy Middleton & Gendron.)

Scuba St. Lucia has changed its name to **Jungle Reef Adventures** to reflect the expanded activities now available. They still offer great diving, but also offer mountain biking and guided kayak tours in all-inclusive packages. Their mountain bike ride or kayak adventure includes snorkeling and lunch at Anse Chastenet and a round-trip water taxi from the cruise ship dock. Both adventures cost $79. Snorkeling alone with lunch and water taxi costs $59. The scuba operation takes you to various locations around Soufrière as well as to the nearby bay that will amaze and impress even the most experienced divers.

St. Lucia has much to offer below the surface. Certified divers and snorkelers should make an effort to explore these coral wonderlands. Scuba St. Lucia offers a special two-tank dive package for cruisers Tuesday through Saturday. The cost is $99 per person, including all equipment, and the package includes a boat ride to Anse Chastanet at 9:30 am; tanks for a beach dive and a boat dive; lunch in the hotel's restaurant; and a boat trip returning to Castries by 4:30 pm. The $5 marine park fee is included in the dive rate fee.

Passengers interested in only snorkeling are offered the same boat trip to and from Anse Chastanet, lunch and all-day snorkeling rental for $59 per person. For first-time divers, an Introduction to Scuba course is available at $95 per person, including the boat trip, diving and lunch. Scuba St. Lucia tries its best to accommodate cruise ship passengers and to make their time on the island the best experience possible. Reservations must be made in advance to coordinate boat pick up and space availability. If you want to dive at Anse Chastanet, contact the resort, ☎ (758) 459-7000, 459-7755, (888) GO LUCIA, fax 459-7128 and ask for the Scuba St. Lucia dive group. E-mail them at scuba@candw.lc.

Among the best dive locations is **Key Hole Pinnacles,** named for the keyhole shape cut into the rock that marks its location. Four underwater pinnacles rise from the bottom of the sea to 10 feet below the surface. Here, divers can spend all of their air time circling the rock formations that teem with underwater creatures, corals and colorful fish. Another unique dive site is named **Superman's Flight**, because a scene from a *Superman* movie was filmed here. The gentle ocean current allows the divers to drift over the lower half of the pitons, volcanic mountains that slope hundreds of feet into the ocean. The effect is like flying over a spectacular coral world.

The **Anse Chastanet Reef** is another dramatic spot for diving, offering sites for every skill level. The reef begins directly off the beach and descends to 140 feet. The shallow plateau makes an excellent area for snorkelers as well as for first-time divers. The reef wall, which has its best sites at 50-60 feet, is alive with trunkfish, spotted drums, angel fish and the occasional luminescent squid. Divers should watch for, but should not touch, the bright orange fireworms crawling along the coral and the shy but curious moray eels.

Buddies, at the Vigie Bay Marina near Pointe Seraphine, takes divers to Anse Chastanet and Anse Cochon for excellent coral-head diving and spectacular wall dives. A two-tank dive package for $60 per person and includes all equipment and tanks. Dive trips leave at

12:30 pm and return at 4:30 pm, Monday thru Saturday. Buddies is near the cruise ship ports in Castries and offers scuba courses for all levels. For more information, contact them at ☎ (758) 452-5288.

Sandals St. Lucia Golf Resort offers scuba for certified divers as part of their one-day pass for $135 per person (see *Golf*, above). Divers need to be on the property by 9 am to participate in the pre-dive orientation. Dives are scheduled Monday through Saturday. ☎ (758) 452-3081; e-mail sandalslu@candw.lc.

Frog's Diving offers snorkeling trips to Anse Cochon in Soufrière for $55 per person. Their one-tank dive costs $60, and the two-tank dive costs $90 (both prices include equipment). The taxi fare to Harmony Suites in Rodney Bay is $20. However, Frog's will provide free transportation for five or more divers. ☎ (758) 450-8831, www.frogsdiving.com.

Dive Fair Helen is the official dive operation for the St. James Club Morgan Bay Resort. The group offers a snorkeling trip for $50 for adults and $25 for children under 12, including lunch and water taxi. A two-tank dive costs $84 (including tanks and weights). BCD vest and regulator can be rented for $10 each. River kayaking for up to two hours includes lunch, beverages, equipment and transportation (be sure to bring bug repellent and sunscreen). ☎ (758) 451-7716 or 450-1640, fax (758) 451-9311, e-mail housons@candw.lc; www.divefairhelen.com.

One-Day Itinerary

If you're interested in seeing the best of St. Lucia, travel from the Castries cruise ports down the coast to **Soufrière** and the only drive-in volcano in the Caribbean. The Sulphur Springs, Diamond Waterfall, Botanical Gardens and the Anse Chastanet Resort are sites every traveler should see. Plan your excursion ahead of time to ensure a successful day.

The dive operator at the Anse Chastanet Resort, **Jungle Reef Adventures**, offers daily boat trips from Castries Harbour customs dock or Vigie Bay, near Pointe Seraphine, down the west coast to Anse Chastanet. You must first contact Scuba St. Lucia to arrange for space on the boat, which leaves daily at 9:15 am from the Customs dock and 9:30 am from Vigie Marina, returning at 4:30 pm. Let them know you would like to spend one to two hours snorkeling on the reef off the resort's beach and an hour for lunch in the hotel's restaurant. Boat reservations can be made by calling the resort and speaking with Scuba St. Lucia directly, ☎ (758) 454-7000. **Spice Travel** offers a similar tour to Anse Chastenet. ☎ (758) 452-0865/0866, e-mail tthomm@candw.lc or visit www.casalucia.com and click on "Spice Travel."

Before arriving at the Anse Chastanet Resort, ask the hotel to have a taxi waiting so that you can begin your sightseeing immediately. The resort will accommodate cruisers for lunch or for snorkeling at the reef. Costs for the tour, boat trip, lunch and snorkeling are listed below.

The boat trip costs $59 per person and the charge includes lunch and snorkeling equipment. A taxi tour costs approximately $60 for one-four people and takes 1½-2 hours. Entrance fees to the Sulphur Springs, Diamond Waterfall and Botanical Gardens will cost a total of US $3-$4. (Tipping is extra for guides.) The entire day run approximately $90 per person.

What to Bring

For the trip to Soufrière, bring along sunscreen, a hat, a lightweight jacket (for a possible rain shower), a camera and a bathing suit for snorkeling. You do not need your own snorkel equipment. Lockers are available for your valuables and clothes, but bring a towel for lying on the beach and drying off. Lunch at the Anse Chastanet Resort is included.

Directions

Refer to the island map, opposite.

An Island Tour

Jungle Reef Adventures will meet you at Castries Harbour Customs dock at 9:15 am or Froggy Jack's Restaurant in Vigie Bay. The shuttle boat leaves at 9:30 am, arriving at Anse Chastanet by 10:15 am. The trip down the west coast will pass dramatic cliffs and the hurricane-safe port of Marigot Bay. You get a great view of the twin pitons emerging from the water in front of Soufrière.

When you're dropped at the Anse Chastanet Resort, leave right away with the taxi driver and tell him you wish to visit the Diamond Waterfall, Botanical Gardens, Sulphur Springs and the Soufrière Estate.

It's a 10-minute drive to the **Diamond Botanical Gardens, Waterfall and Mineral Baths**. You can request a guide at the entrance of the private estate to take you through the gardens, point out the var-

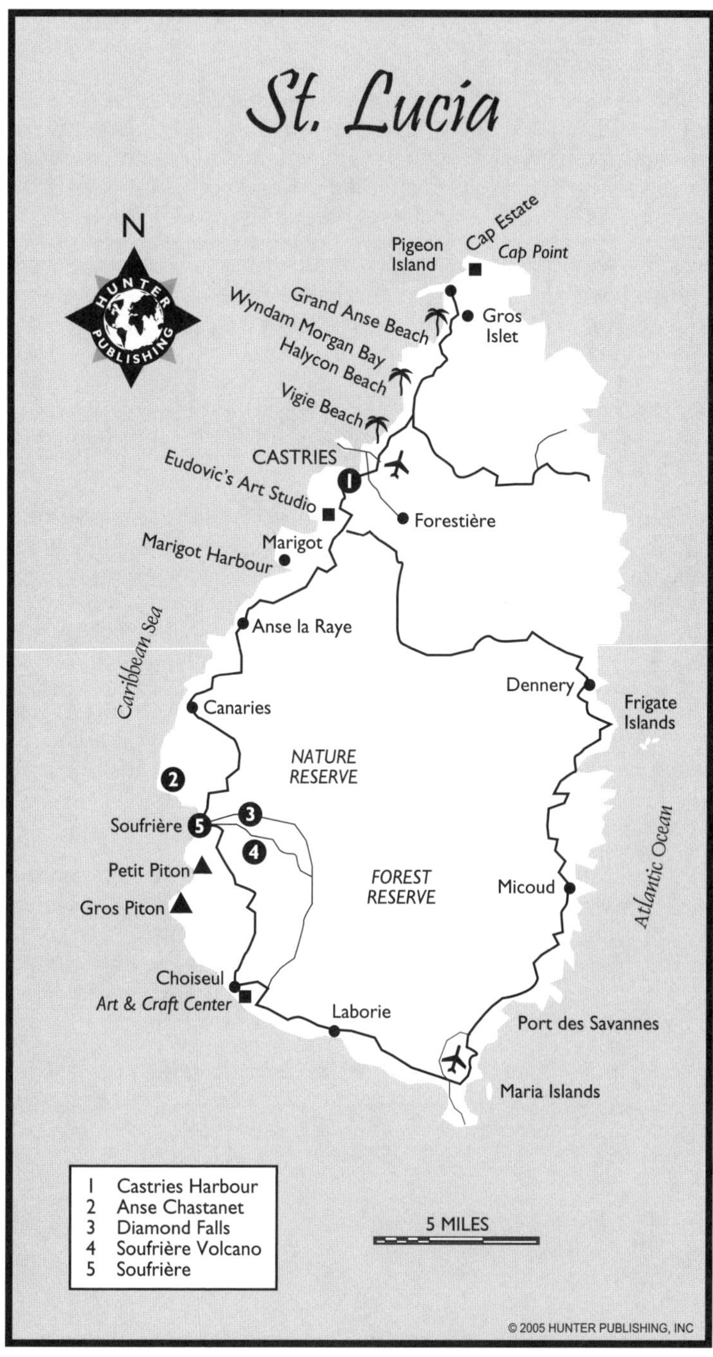
St. Lucia
N
HUNTER PUBLISHING
Pigeon Island
Cap Estate
Cap Point
Grand Anse Beach
Gros Islet
Wyndam Morgan Bay
Halycon Beach
Vigie Beach
CASTRIES
Eudovic's Art Studio
Forestière
Marigot
Marigot Harbour
Caribbean Sea
Anse la Raye
Canaries
Dennery
Frigate Islands
NATURE RESERVE
Soufrière
Petit Piton
Gros Piton
FOREST RESERVE
Micoud
Atlantic Ocean
Choiseul
Art & Craft Center
Laborie
Port des Savannes
Maria Islands
1 Castries Harbour
2 Anse Chastanet
3 Diamond Falls
4 Soufrière Volcano
5 Soufrière
5 MILES
© 2005 HUNTER PUBLISHING, INC

ious island plants and escort you to the waterfall. (A tip is expected if you are pleased with the guide.)

Originally built in 1785, the estate features special mineral baths that are believed to help skin inflammations and other ailments. The baths have been carefully restored and you can take a dip for a nominal charge. The beautifully manicured gardens contain a wide assortment of colorful flowers and trees unique to the Caribbean.

Diamond Waterfall is a popular photo attraction with its water streaming over the orange volcanic rocks. The coloring is created as part of a chemical reaction between the hot water and the iron composites in the volcanic rock.

> NOTE: The waterfall is unsafe for bathing because of harmful bacteria caused by small snails living in the water.

Back in the cab, another 10-minute drive will take you to the **Sulphur Springs**, St. Lucia's unique drive-in volcano. The bubbling sulphur springs are alive with steam and black molten lava. A guide will take you on a half-hour walking tour, explaining the creation of the springs, and allow you to see the remains of the once-active volcano at close range. (Again, tip if you are happy with your guide.)

A 15-minute ride will take you to the final stop, the **Soufrière Estate**, which was originally part of a 2,000-acre estate granted to the Devaux family by King Louis XIV in 1713. It is open to the public for tours of the mini-zoo and the machinery that once harvested copra and cocoa fields.

Between 12:40 and 1 pm, you should return to the **Anse Chastanet Resort** for lunch in the exquisite beachside restaurant. After lunch, take an hour or two to snorkel over the colorful reef that lies just 20 feet off the left side of the beach (as you face the water). Snorkel equipment is included in the fee and there are lockers (ask for a lock at the dive shop), showers and restrooms for changing.

At 3:15 pm the boat departs from the resort to return to **Castries,** arriving by 4:30 pm. Ask to dropped off directly at Pointe Seraphine cruise ship dock. The total trip should take just over seven hours.

Barbados

Little England

Island Description

The first Europeans to land on Barbados were **Portuguese** sailors, who stopped here in 1536 to secure provisions on their route to Brazil. The sailors dubbed the island "Los Barbados" (meaning the Bearded Ones) because the fig trees have hanging aerial roots that resemble a man's beard.

Arawak Indians were still living on the island when the Portuguese landed, but by the time Captain Henry Powell came here in 1625 the island was uninhabited. Powell stumbled onto the island due to navigational errors and promptly claimed it for the **British**. In 1627 Powell returned with 80 settlers and a number of slaves, landing at Holetown, named after a community in England. Bridgetown, the capital of Barbados, was founded in 1628 and named after an old Indian bridge.

Early settlers planted cotton, tobacco, yams and cassava but, after 10 years of difficulties, Sir James Drax introduced the alternate crop of **sugarcane**. There was high demand for sugar in Europe and the crop thrived. The original system of using indentured servants to man the vast plantations proved inadequate and plantation owners soon imported slaves from Africa to fill the shortage. Most of the great wealth amassed by the harsh system remained on the island and funded its infrastructure.

A unique factor in the history of Barbados is that the British remained in continuous control for over 300 years. The islanders established their own Parliament in 1652 and earned the nickname Little England, since the laws, traditions and even the appearance of the cities in Barbados mirrored the mother country. Today, the Barbados Parliament has the distinction of being the third-oldest continuous government in the British Commonwealth.

Barbados is slightly outside the arc of islands that make up the Windward Island chain, and is shaped like a pork chop. The majority of the population lives in and around the capital of **Bridgetown**, while the rest of the island is sparsely populated and agricultural in nature. The land consists of a very old coral and limestone geological base, which sometimes exceeds 300 feet in depth. The coral helps to filter natural rainfall into a system of underground streams and caves, making the water pure and clean.

Barbados is still agricultural, producing sugarcane and other cash crops. Surprisingly, the most serious threat to this industry has come from the **green vervet monkey**, which was imported from Africa as a pet during colonial times. Monkeys enjoy eating mangoes, papayas, guavas and bananas but, to test for ripeness, a monkey takes small bites out of many fruits, spoiling them all in the process. Government studies indicate the monkey population, which has increased tremendously over the last three decades, may be responsible for crop losses as high as 40%. Although the government pays a bounty for dead monkeys, the Barbados Primate Research Center pays more per monkey, $50 if captured alive and unharmed in cage traps supplied by the center. The research center operates the **Barbados Wildlife Reserve**, where wild monkeys and people roam freely together and stare at one another with equal curiosity. The monkeys mingle with the other fauna in the sanctuary hares, tortoises, deer and river otters. The animals live in a well-provisioned natural environment and crop damage has already decreased due to the center's efforts.

Although agriculture is important, **tourism** has become the largest industry on Barbados. In 1986 the government began a program to educate its population about the importance of tourism, beginning in the schools and ultimately involving every walk of life. With its slogan that "tourism is everybody's business," the program's success is evident in improved tourist attractions and the friendly attitude of islanders, who are eager to help make the tourists stay on Barbados memorable.

Island People

With cultural roots grounded in 300 years of British heritage, the Bajan (pronounced BAY-shun) people are more British in tradition than other Caribbean islands. British names appear on landmarks, local parish sectors and churches, while their Houses of Parliament and Trafalgar Square are modeled on London's. Echoes of the era when slaves worked the plantations are evident throughout the island. The slave trade was abolished by Britain in 1807, due to increasing world condemnation of the cruel system. Full emancipation of the slaves on Barbados did not take place until 1838. Many slaves remained on plantations and experienced little change in their lives, while other slaves left their work and created a new middle class on the island. Samuel Jackman Prescod became the first non-white member of the House of Assembly in 1843, although universal suffrage was not granted until 1950, after 117 years of struggle and social turmoil.

Chattel Houses

As you tour the island, notice the small wooden houses sitting above the flood plain on concrete blocks. These structures are called **chattel houses**, derived from an old term meaning "movable personal property." In the early days, changing a job meant moving the entire house, which needed to be small enough to transport by mule cart. The wooden chattel house could be expanded by adding on sections (each movable separately) or by adding a veranda. As the owner prospered, the house could be made to look very grand by adding new sections, elegant carved detailing and bright paint. Few examples of chattel houses have survived, but tourism has revived an interest in the architecture of the working man's house. As a result, some chattel houses have been preserved and converted into boutiques or shops. (See *Chattel House Village*, page 262.)

Island Proverbs

Bajans speak English with a very understandable accent, but over the years they have developed their own slang.

Cheese on! . . . . Right on!
Fingersmith . . . . Pickpocket
Being in goat heaven . . . . Being in hog heaven
Rest off . . . . Take a coffee break
A lick-mout' . . . . A gossip
Jam . . . . Eat like a pig
A yard fowl . . . . A yes man

Holidays

Museums, post offices and banks close on national holidays, but are open during festivals. The shops and tourist attractions should be open unless we say otherwise in the description. Festival periods are often the most fun time to visit the island.

Annual Holidays & Events

For more details and precise dates, contact the island tourist board (see *Appendix*).

January . . . . . . New Year's Day; Errol Barrow Day (honors the country's first leader after emancipation)

February . . . . Holetown Festival (week-long medieval celebration for the arrival of the first settlers)

April. . . . . Good Friday; Easter Monday (Oistin's Fish Festival on Easter weekend pays tribute to the island's fishing industry with two days of boating events)

May . . . . May Day; Whit Monday

July . . . . Crop Over Festival (celebrates the completion of the sugarcane harvest with calypso, dancing, drama and contests)

August. . . . . Kadooment Day – climax of Crop Over, a national holiday with costumed bands and fireworks

October. . . . . United Nations' Day

November . . . Independence Day; National Independence Festival of the Creative Arts, with a month of art events; final exhibitions are on Independence Day

December . . . . Christmas; Boxing Day

Useful Websites

The tourism authority's website is wonderful. Visit **www.barbados.org** and you can spend hours exploring all your options on this large island. Be sure to visit the "nature" section, which provides a list of all the exceptional natural attractions.

The Pier

Barbados has one of the finest docking facilities in the islands. **Deep Water Harbour** is a short distance from the capital city of Bridgetown. The concrete pier has room for several ships at one time, allowing you to walk straight from the ship to the new terminal. This remarkable facility boasts over 20 shops that offer a range of items, including jewelry and watches, fine china and crystal, electronic goods and perfumes at duty-free prices. A modern telecommunications center provides numerous services, post office, banking, facsimile services, direct-dial phones, rental of cellular phones and even typing services.

Pier Phones

The new Barbados telecommunications center offers plenty of clearly marked phones with USA Direct and credit card options available. Dial **Cable & Wireless,** ☎ (800) 744-2000, and follow the instructions (in English) for completing your call using a credit card. To use your **AT&T** credit card, ☎ (800) 872-2881 on public phones only. Machines vending island phone cards have clear instructions. Phone cards are available for purchase in the center. Keep in mind that a call to the US will cost a minimum of US $5 just to make the connection, so be sure to purchase a card with sufficient credit.

The area code for Barbados is 246, an overseas phone call from the United States.

Shopping At The Pier

Shop in air-conditioned comfort as you purchase tax-free merchandise in the new cruise ship terminal. Exclusive stores like **Columbian Emeralds** were quick to join local names like **The Royal Shop, Cave Shepherd** and **Best of Barbados,** offering duty-free shopping convenience to cruise ship passengers. Barbados is one of the first islands to recognize the importance of encouraging crafts as a means of providing full employment for its citizens. **Pelican Village**, a complex designed to house 37 local craft shops, is a five-minute walk from the pier. (See *Shopping*, page 261.) To reach the village, leave the harbor area through the main gates, continue along Princess Alice Highway toward Bridgetown, then look for Pelican Village on the left side of the road. Remember, duty-free means there is no tax added to imported items, but locally made items can be more interesting and less expensive.

In Town

Currency

The **Bajan dollar** (BDS) is the official currency of Barbados and it comes in the same denominations as used the US dollar. However, most stores here price their merchandise in both Bajan and US dollars. The exchange rate is approximately BDS $2 for US $1, but the value of the Bajan dollar fluctuates, so check with the Tourist Information Desk at the pier for the current rate. Both EC and US currency are accepted in Barbados, but try to avoid receiving Bajan currency in change. Credit cards should be used whenever possible, and check that the credit card slip is clearly marked to indicate BDS or US dollars.

Banks are open from 8 am to 3 pm weekdays and until 5 pm on Friday. The **Caribbean Commercial Bank** on Broad Street in downtown is open until noon on Saturdays and the **Royal Bank of Canada** has machines to access Visa and Plus System ATM cards for cash advances in Bajan dollars. Banking facilities are located in the cruise ship terminal.

Postage

A stamp window at the cruise pier facility opens from 8 am to 3 pm. The airmail rate to send a postcard is about US 60¢. (Remember, US postage is not accepted.)

Museums & Historical Sites

Barbados has a wealth of historical, cultural and ecological sites. The Barbados National Trust offers a voucher system called the **Heritage Passport**, which allows access to 15 sites at almost half the cost normally charged for the same attractions. The passport runs US $35 and can be ordered in advance by calling the Board of Tourism, ☎ (800) 221-9831. A **Mini Passport** good for five sites is only $18, and children are free when accompanying an adult passport holder. The Barbados National Trust has a booth at the terminal building.

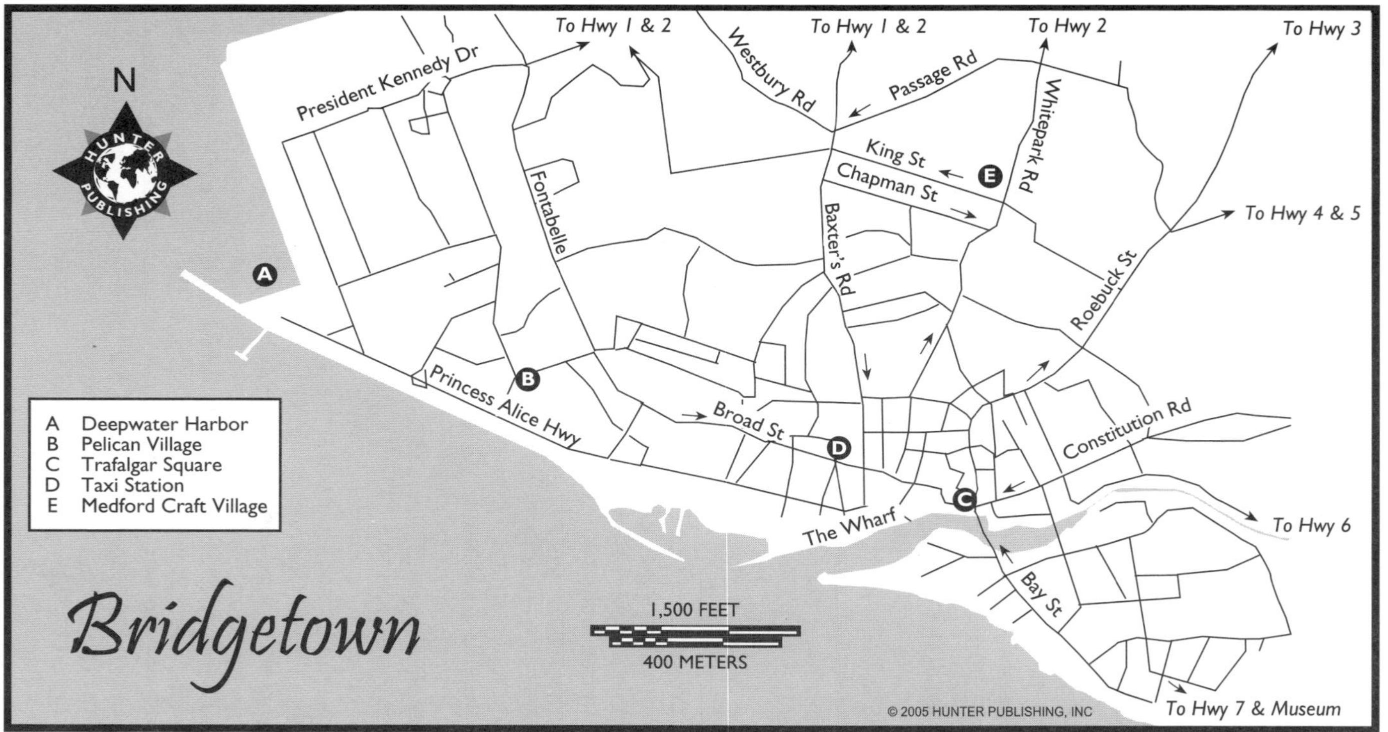
Bridgetown
A Deepwater Harbor
B Pelican Village
C Trafalgar Square
D Taxi Station
E Medford Craft Village
N
HUNTER PUBLISHING
To Hwy 1 & 2
To Hwy 1 & 2
To Hwy 2
To Hwy 3
To Hwy 4 & 5
To Hwy 6
To Hwy 7 & Museum
President Kennedy Dr
Westbury Rd
Passage Rd
Whitepark Rd
King St
Chapman St
Fontabelle
Baxter's Rd
Roebuck St
Princess Alice Hwy
Broad St
Constitution Rd
The Wharf
Bay St
A
B
C
D
E
1,500 FEET
400 METERS
© 2005 HUNTER PUBLISHING, INC

The **Parliament Buildings** are on Bridge Street in the center of Bridgetown. The buildings were constructed in 1871, nearly 240 years after Parliament was established. Entry may be restricted on weekdays, when government business is taking place.

British Admiral Lord Horatio Nelson was especially important in protecting the island of Barbados from foreign invasion. While Nelson was in the process of assembling his fleet in the Barbados harbor for the Battle of Trafalgar, the French and Spanish combined their fleets to execute a secret attack on Barbados. When they caught sight of Lord Nelson's formidable fleet, they knew they were outgunned and fled. Nelson's imposing presence saved Barbados from attack and a statue commemorating the courageous British Admiral was built in Bridgetown's version of **Trafalgar Square**.

The **Jewish Synagogue and Cemetery**, Coleridge Street and Magazine Lane, is the oldest synagogue in the western hemisphere, built in 1654. The Jewish community's introduction of sugarcane had a great influence on the island economy. The adjoining cemetery has tombstones dating back to 1630 and is open to the public Monday through Friday from 9 am to 4 pm.

The **Garrison Historic Area** contains many colonial buildings of architectural and historic value, including the Bush House, where George Washington visited his ailing half-brother in 1751. Barbados was the only place Washington ever visited outside the continental United States. The **Barbados Museum** in the Garrison Historic Area is housed in the 19th-century Military Garrison, a former prison. The museum has a circular walking pattern, starting with a natural history section and ending with several island art galleries. A superb collection of plantation house furniture is particularly interesting and represents the lifestyle common to wealthier families on islands throughout the Caribbean. The exhibits are arranged to represent complete rooms that might have existed in a colonial mansion. Settlers were eager to establish a European environment to make their secluded life in the islands more bearable. Victorian-style furniture was shipped from England at great expense, then meticulously copied by craftsmen using highly polished mahogany and lavish imported fabrics. Today, plantation furniture can be more prized by collectors than the original antiques that were copied. The Domestic and Decorative Arts display includes intricate examples of shell-craft called Sailor's Valentines. Sailors would buy or commission shell paintings, flowers fabricated from shells, and decorated boxes or mirrors from local artisans. They gave them as gifts to their wives and sweethearts. The most intriguing section is the Children's Gallery, designed to familiarize children with Barbados' heritage, especially the influence of slavery. Included is a full-scale model of the slaves living quarters, making the meager conditions in which slaves lived come to life. Other exhibits in the museum include contemporary art, military history, old maps and prints, period paintings and an example of a prisoner's cell. Do not miss the museum shop and library, where unique island merchandise and collectible stamps are offered for sale. The museum is open Monday through Saturday from 9 am to 5 pm (except holidays) and on Sunday from 2 pm to 6 pm. Admission is US $5, half-price for children up to 16 years of age. We recommend a visit to this interesting museum.

Shopping

You don't have to go downtown to get duty-free prices, but no matter where you shop, carry your passport and boarding pass to qualify for the discount. Up to 40% can be saved with proper ID and using credit cards or traveler's checks to pay for purchases. Place the duplicate copy of the sales receipt in the Customs box at the cruise terminal before boarding the ship.

Shopkeepers in Barbados have also established outlets in many of the major hotels near or on the route to tourist attractions.

Bridgetown

☆ **Pelican Village** is on Princess Alice Highway, a five-minute walk from the pier. The complex is the best of its kind, and other islands would do well to encourage local artisans to form similar enterprises. The 37 shops offer expert woodcarvings, coral jewelry, baskets, pottery, original fine art, dolls, clothing and unique souvenirs all handcrafted on Barbados. Shopping at Pelican Village supports the local economy and provides exceptional gifts for family and friends at reasonable prices. After shopping here, hail a cab outside the village, or continue walking into Bridgetown. A café offers snacks, drinks and lunches.

The Royal Shop is a leading watch and jewelry dealer, offering some of the world's most coveted names in watches, exquisite diamond tennis bracelets and elegant Italian necklaces. The shops carry figurines from Tuscany, Florence that are crafted by the master Guiseppe Armani, and is the exclusive carrier of the world-famous Hummel pieces.

Best of Barbados has locations in the cruise terminal and De Costa's Mall. It's one of the shops that features the artwork and crafts of Jill

Walker. This savvy lady may be responsible for the craft revival on Barbados, which is spreading through the Caribbean. Original fine art, prints, posters, trays, coasters and other merchandise are decorated with Jill's Caribbean scenes. Other shops that carry Jill's merchandise are found in prime tourist attractions – the Flower Forest, Sam Lord's Castle and Andromeda Gardens.

Harrison's resembles a fine department store in the US, offering all the major names in crystal, perfume and ceramics. Fine leather products are also available, including Gucci, Land and Gold Pfeil, which are exclusive to Harrison's on Barbados. There are two locations downtown and outlets in hotels around the island with the same prices.

Cave Shepherd is another major department store in Barbados, competing with Harrison's for the duty-free business. Cave Shepherd has virtually every kind of product from housewares to crystal, shoes to sporting goods, books to dress fabrics – all at duty-free prices. The store is large and roomy and bargains are easy to find in every department.

Out On The Island

The **Chattel House Village** is a collection of restored chattel houses that has been converted into charming shops. It's located in St. Lawrence Gap, en route to Sam Lord's Castle, and is worth a stop for the handicrafts and to see the picturesque cottages. Restored chattel houses are also open to the public in two other locations – the **Chattel House Shopping Village** in Holetown, and the **Tyrol Cot Heritage Village** in St. Michael (about 15 minutes from the cruise ship terminal). Tyrol Cot is a National Trust site ($5.75 admission) that combines a restored mansion with authentic chattel houses occupied by craft vendors working on site (see *One-Day Itinerary*).

Daphne's Shell Shop, ☎ 423-6180, is at the graceful old plantation Great House off Congo Road in St. Philip, also on the way to Sam Lord's Castle. It features shell artwork, baskets, mirrors, picture frames and flower-like creations. This shop was started in 1980 by Daphne Hunte, who has since been joined by her daughters in creating shellcraft.

The **Shell Gallery** is at the Carlton House in the parish of St. James, the home of the owner/designer Maureen Edghill. The gallery is famous for elegant shell mirrors and a spectacular display of shells from countries all over the world. In 1984 the Barbados Museum commissioned Maureen to make a Sailor's Valentine for Queen Elizabeth II. The gallery is open 9 am to 4 pm, Monday through Friday, and on Saturday from 9 am to 2 pm. ☎ (246) 422-2593 or 422-2635.

Medford Mahogany Craft Village is just outside Bridgetown at Barbaree's Hill, near Baxters Road in the parish of St. Michael. It is the residence of Dr. R. Medford, and mahogany woodcrafters work here, creating pieces of art in all sizes from massive tree roots. There's also a selection of other handmade crafts, including pottery, batik, basketry, coral and T-shirts for sale. ☎ (246) 427-3179.

Fairfield Pottery & Gallery in St. Michael's Parish is a pottery complex operated by the Bell family. They use local red clay for their pieces. The special works of Chalky Mount and Castle Potteries are also available at the gallery. Located at Fairfield Cross Roads, ☎ (246) 424-3800.

Foursquare Rum Factory and Heritage Park combines a tour of a modern computerized rum distillery with an art foundry, craft shops, food and drink stalls, and beautiful gardens. The park is near Daphne's Sea Shell Studio off Six Cross Roads. Open daily, 9 am to 5 pm; ☎ (246) 420-1977.

Transportation & Excursions

Taxis

Taxis are abundant and easily identified by the sign on their roof and the "Z" on their license plates. They are not metered, but follow an established rate system set by the taxi association. Establish the rate before entering the taxi. Fares are based on one to five persons. A taxi rate board is posted outside the cruise terminal listing the current rates for the whole taxi. This can be used when bargaining for fares (be aware that drivers quote their rate in Bajan dollars). Rates for a trips to town are not flexible, but the price for excursions out on the island can be negotiated.

There are many taxis available, so if one driver does not bargain or follow the regulated fares, try another one who is friendly and courteous to tourists. Taxis offer a regulated island tour at $16 per hour for one to four people.

Taxi Chart

All prices are quoted in US dollars.

Destination *from Deep Water Harbour*	**Cost** *one to four people*
Barbados Wildlife Reserve	$20
Carlisle Bay	$12
City center	$3
Crane Beach	$17
Flower Forest	$15
Harrison's Cave	$15
Hilton Hotel	$6
Paradise Beach	$6
Sandy Lane	$11
Sam Lord's Castle	$18
St. Lawrence	$9

Tipping is not required when driving from one location to another within Bridgetown. However, if a driver arranges a round-trip rate to a beach or outer island site, a 10% tip is customary. For round-trip fares, pay the driver at the end of the trip to ensure he returns.

> TIP: Never have a taxi driver wait when traveling to a beach. The driver will charge a separate rate (US $4 per hour) while he waits. Instead, arrange to have him come back for the return trip, or take another taxi back.

Local Buses

Barbados has two types of local transportation. One is the government-regulated **Transport Board bus system**. The other consists of minibuses driven by private operators. The Transport Board uses vehicles painted yellow with a heavy blue trim, the colors of the national flag. The privately operated minibuses are clearly marked with a "ZR" on their license plates and have signs in their front window and on the side of their vans designating their destination. The Transport Board buses also display the name of their destination on a sign above their front windshields.

The cost is BDS $1.50 or US 75¢ for either bus to any part of the island. The minibuses can be flagged down on the main roads or at the main terminal on River Road in Bridgetown. The large Transport

Board buses can be waved down at any Bus Stop sign marked "To City" or "Out of City." You must wave to have the bus stop or it will drive on by.

Buses may be inexpensive and easy to track down, but they make many stops along the roads and travel slowly. If time is not a consideration, try them out.

Rental Cars

Driving is on the left, with English-style roundabouts (rotaries) and many unmarked roads. Get a map from the tourist bureau or from the rental agency. Rental cars are available; reserve ahead.

Agencies can have a car waiting at the pier terminal when you arrive if contacted beforehand. You must get a temporary driver's license for $5. These are available at the police station in downtown Bridgetown or from selected stations arranged through the rental agency.

Prices for four-door cars range from $50 to $60 per day and the popular minimoke (an open-air jeep) is $60-$85 per day. Collision insurance is offered for $11.50. A credit card is usually required to cover the damage deposit and the minimum age to rent a car is 23.

Bridgetown is congested, but once you get out on the island, the open roads are easy to maneuver. Although many do not have proper direction markers, adventurers can usually find their way.

Car Rental Agencies

The area code for Barbados is 246, an overseas phone call from the United States.

Jones Garage . . . . ☎ 426-4589/5030; www.rentalcarbarbados.com jonescars@sunbeach.net

National Car Rentals. . . . ☎ 422-3000 or (800) 227-7368; www.cwts-bds.com

Top Car Rentals . . . . ☎ 435-0378; www.barbadoscarrentals.com get 10% off by reserving at topcar@caribsurf.com

Courtesy Rent-A-Car (free pickup/delivery) . . ☎ 431-4160 www.courtesyrentacar.com

Self-Guided Tours

Barbados Wildlife Reserve

Animal lovers should definitely visit the **Barbados Wildlife Reserve**, open daily from 10 am to 5 pm. The shady pathways are full of animals, some close to extinction and others living a protected life in this environment. Walk quietly so as not to scare away creatures, or sit on a bench and see what wanders your way. Remember, you are the visitor in their habitat.

Everything from brocket deer, regal peacocks, armadillos, wallabies, porcupines, hares, red foot tortoises and iguanas will cross the pathways and run to safety under the large mahogany trees. Caymans (South American alligators) and pelicans coexist peacefully here. Nearby you may find a family of playful river otters. The saltwater aquarium has a wide variety of tropical fish and the walk-in aviary houses exotic birds like macaws, cockatoos, cockatiels, pheasants, toucans, parakeets and the near-extinct St. Vincent parrot. The only animals securely contained away from visitors are a pair of reticulated pythons.

A special laboratory and quarantine area breeds and researches the population of green vervet monkeys in the reserve. The mischievous monkeys derive their name from the color of their coat, which is brownish grey with flecks of yellow and olive green. In sunlight, it appears entirely green. These curious and humorous creatures are the highlight of the park and are most active in the afternoon from 2 to 3 pm, when the park rangers bring out bunches of bananas at feeding time. The monkeys might come right up to you, but they are still considered wild and may bite. Be cautious. The monkeys make great subjects for pictures, but watch out: shiny objects attract them and they have been known to steal glasses right off a visitor's head!

The park has paths designed for the handicapped and small children. A friendly staff is available to answer wildlife questions. An entrance fee of US $12 for adults and US $6 for kids helps to maintain the natural environment and funds the $50 reward to capture live monkeys. This price includes entrance to the nearby Grenade Hall Forest & Signal Station, which has been restored. The forest has nature trails and picnic tables.

A drive to the reserve takes between 45 minutes and an hour. Combined with an island tour, a stop here makes for a terrific day.

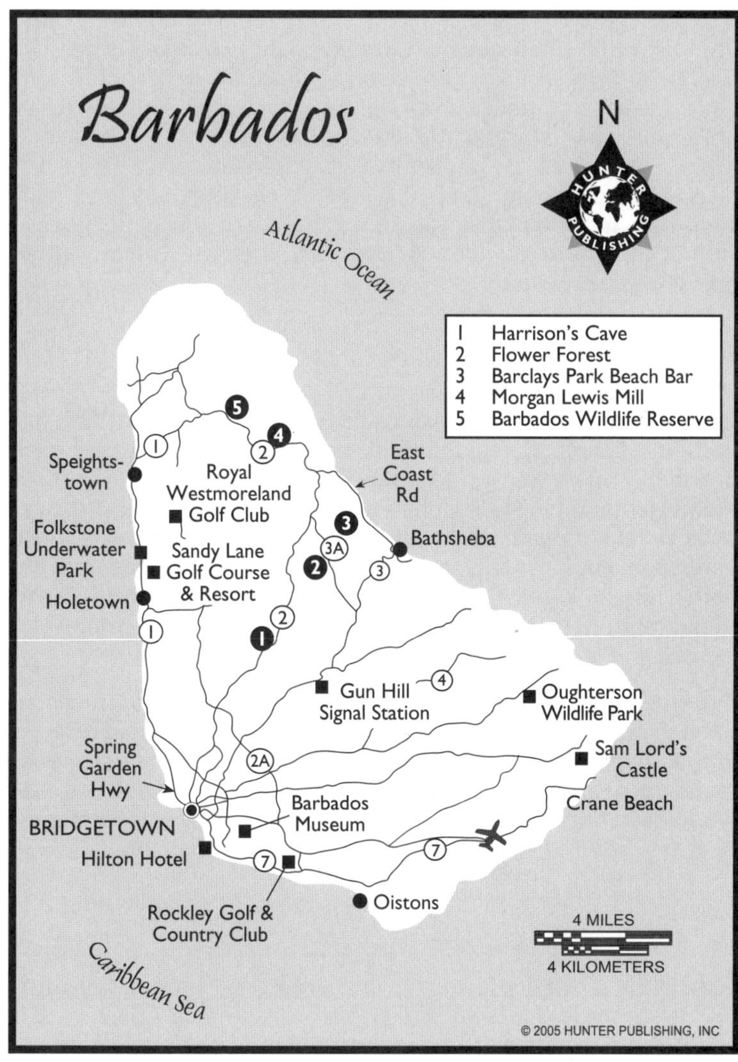

Harrison's Cave

A trip to Barbados would not be complete without a visit to Harrison's Cave, where a motorized tram transports you underground for a guided view of caverns, bubbling streams and waterfalls cascading into natural pools. The mile-long cave tour allows you to see stalagmites and to touch stalactites hanging from the crystallized ceiling of the caves. Artificial lighting allows photographs to be taken with a flash or with a video camera. Cave tours are available through tour operators or by reserving in person at the front desk of Harrison's Cave. The park is open seven days a week, and offers eight to 16 half-hour tours daily, starting at 9 am. The last tour of the day leaves at 4 pm. Entrance is US $16/adult, $7/children; seniors with valid ID receive 20% discount. There's a food stand, restrooms and a gift shop here too. You can make reservations at www.harrisonscave.com. A 35-minute cab ride will take you to the cave, a unique attraction not to be missed!

Flower Forest

Colonial plantations on Barbados boast some of the most lush gardens and flowering vegetation in the Caribbean. One of the most beautifully manicured garden estates is the Flower Forest at the Richmond Plantation in St. Joseph's Parish. The 50-acre estate displays a wide variety of plants and trees from the natural hothouses of the Caribbean. You can easily spend 45 minutes wandering the trails and pathways. All plants and trees have been clearly identified with botanical and common names in English. A map in English and explanation of plants are available at the entrance.

The entrance fee is US $7/adults, $3.50/children. The gardens are open daily from 9 am to 5 pm. A snack bar, restrooms and a Best of Barbados gift shop featuring Jill Walker prints, watercolors, gifts and crafts are at the main entrance building. Look for Walker's special works depicting scenes in the Flower Forest. It takes only 35 minutes by taxi to reach this most beautiful garden on the island.

Gun Hill

Gun Hill Signal Station is a meticulously restored historical site just 15 minutes from Bridgetown. The station was originally built in 1818 and its excellent location provides sweeping views of Barbados' rolling sugarcane fields. Restored in 1982, it is currently open to visitors Monday through Saturday, except public holidays, from 9 am to 5 pm. A US $5 entrance fee is charged to help fund further restoration and to maintain the surrounding gardens. Be sure to visit the famous British Military Lion, carved from coral limestone on the site by British soldiers in the 19th century. The lion sits below the station on the hillside and makes a great photo.

Orchid World

This exciting new attraction is located on Highway 3B between Gun Hill Station and St. John's Church. A former six-acre chicken and pig farm surrounded by sugarcane, Orchid World is now home to over 20,000 orchids. A well-landscaped path meanders past a waterfall, through a coral grotto and, eventually, through five orchid houses. Many orchids are displayed growing naturally along the path's edge or attached to trees. There's also a snack bar, wedding chapel, gazebo and a **Best of Barbados** gift shop. Open daily from 9 am to 5 pm; admission is US $7 for adults and $3.50 for children.

Sunbury Plantation

Sunbury Plantation House is the only Great House on the island with all of its rooms available for viewing. It's over 300 years old and steeped in history, featuring mahogany antiques, old prints and a collection of horse-drawn carriages. Sunbury is located in St. Philip's Parish, along Highway 5 (watch for the sign just before Six Cross Roads), and many tour operators stop here on their way to Sam Lord's Castle. A guided tour, conducted daily from 9 am to 4:30 pm, costs US $7.50 for adults, $3.75 for children.

Organized Tours & Activities

Specialty Tours

Boyce's Tours offers a specialty excursion for photographers at $40 per person. You'll get some super shots on this engaging four-hour trip that takes in glistening white sand and turquoise waters on the island's west coast. You leave the port and head toward **Shermans**, just beyond the busy port of Speightstown. Continuing through the semi-arid parish of St. Lucy brings you to **Animal Flower Cave**, near the northernmost point of Barbados. The cave and its surroundings offer excellent photographic opportunities. You have to be quick to capture the huge 50-foot waterspouts created as waves pound the craggy cliffs.

A relatively short drive away is **Pico Tenerife**, a chalky pyramid-like peak standing sentinel over the island's lone pebble beach. Traveling inland through the woods of St. Peter, you arrive at **Cherry Tree Hill**, 800 feet above sea level, with a fantastic picture of the Scotland District. Travel down the twisting road that leads to **Morgan Lewis Sugar Mill**, a large windmill undergoing complete restoration, next to a quiet palm-fringed brown beach.

The tour heads for the hills to watch potters at **Chalky Mount** crafting clay into jugs and vases on an enchanting site overlooking the local highlands. You'll return to ship via the luxuriant parish of St. Thomas, with its abundant fruit trees and plants.

Call **Boyce's Tours** at ☎ (246) 425-5366 and ask for "Photographer's Dream Tour B," or e-mail your reservation to tours@boycestours.com. Visit www.toursbarbados.com and click on "Boyce Tours" to read about other tour options.

Cruises

Tall Ship Cruises offers three cruises. The first is the famous ***Jolly Roger* cruise**, which includes pirates walking the plank, a rope swing and lethal rum punches. The four-hour *Jolly Roger* cruise heads up the west coast for watersports, snorkeling, beachcombing, or simply jumping off the ship's deck into the warm Caribbean Sea. For lunch, there's barbecued chicken, steak, or pan-fried flying fish and drinks. After everyone has eaten, the party really begins. Calypso music and international hits start everyone dancing. The cruise is quite popular, so reservations are needed, ☎ (246) 436-6424. The ***Jolly Roger*** pirate cruise is available on Tuesday, Thursday and Saturday at a cost of US $65 per adult and $32.50 for children under 12.

The second option is the **Harbour Master Lunch Cruise** offered on Wednesday at $65 per person. The MV *Harbour Master* is a 100-foot motor launch, 40 feet wide and four decks high, with lots of fun and games, food and drink all included. Below deck is a state-of-the-art retractable semi-submersible, so you can view the fascinating world of underwater life (an extra US $10 per person). The boat travels the west coast to a secluded bay with opportunities for swimming off the sandy beaches and snorkeling in the clear waters. Aboard, you can relax with a refreshing cocktail, or slide down into the water via a "wild slide."

The third cruise adventure is the ***Tiami* Catamaran Lunch Cruise**. From the moment you step aboard *Tiami* the crew pampers and indulges you. Daily cruises leave at 10 am and return at 3 pm, with three stops for swimming and snorkeling – a shallow shipwreck, a reef, and a swim with turtles. The price ($70/adult, $35/child) includes round-trip transportation, all drinks, and an excellent buffet lunch at anchor in a secluded bay. Floating mattresses and snorkel equipment are provided, but bring a towel, sun block and a smile. The friendly crew will ensure you have a fabulous day. The website for all three cruises profiled above is www.tallshipscruises.com.

Submarine Adventure

***Atlantis* Submarine** enables everyone to safely travel to a depth of 150 feet through the mysterious undersea world surrounding Barbados. Spend an hour viewing vibrant orange fire corals or watching iridescent parrotfish, elegant angelfish, or even a shark, all within the safety and comfort of an air-conditioned submarine.

Most cruise ships offer one or two tour times for the submarine trip through the shore excursion office. You can book a time through the ship or take one of the other seven scheduled dives by reserving directly through the submarine's main office on Lower Broad Street (away from the terminal toward downtown Trafalgar Square, a 15-minute walk from the ship or a five-minute taxi ride).

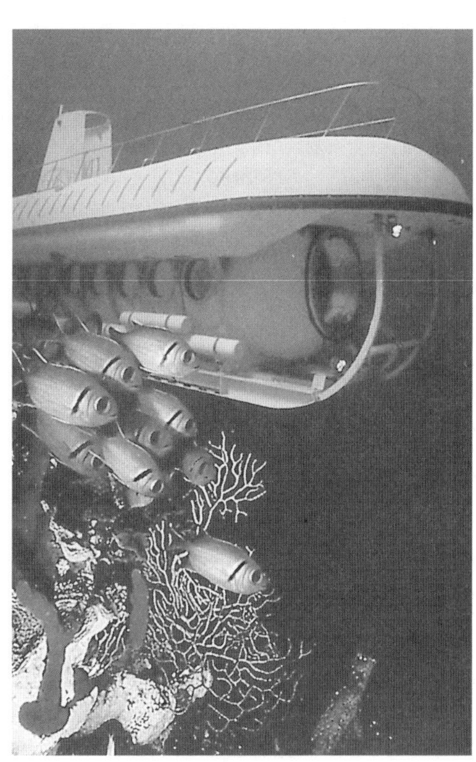

The Atlantis *sub.*
(Image courtesy Atlantis.)

Plan to arrive 15 minutes before the scheduled two-hour tour to receive a brief orientation. The cost for the dive is $82.50 adult, $52.50 for children aged 13-18, and $40 for children aged four-12. Visit them at www.atlantisadventures.com. A submarine dive with Atlantis is definitely worth the time and effort.

Helicopter Rides

Fasten your seat belts for a ride over the rolling hills and beach-lined coast with **Bajan Helicopters**. A sightseeing guide/pilot points out island attractions as he flies over sugarcane fields, beaches and tropical gardens. The 10 flights scheduled daily are either 20 minutes for $75, or 30 minutes for $135 per person. Reservations can be made by calling ☎ (246) 431-0069, Monday through Saturday, 10 am to 5 pm. Only four passengers are allowed per flight, so book early.

Sailing & Snorkeling

Atlantis Submarines, www.atlantisadventures.com, now offers a full list of tours for cruise ship passengers, including snorkeling at Carlisle Bay, an eco-hike, a sea turtle snorkeling tour and the Rhino Rider water safari (three hours on two-person inflatable boats). All excursions are available only through cruise ship shore excursion departments, so check on prices and scheduling with your ship.

Beaches

Crane Beach is a 30-minute drive from Deep Water Harbour, and it is the most beautiful cove on the entire island. The Crane Beach Hotel sits high above this white beach cove with pounding Atlantic waves on the eastern coastline. It charges an entrance fee of $2 to non-hotel guests, but you can redeem that at the hotel bar in the form of a free drink. A set of stairs leads from the hotel down to the beach for fun in the sand and surf. There are no watersports. People come here to relax on the beach or frolic in the blue-green waters. The hotel has a fine restaurant for lunch.

The **Hilton Hotel beach** is near the pier area, a 15-minute cab ride through Bridgetown. The Hilton was torn down recently, to make way for a new resort that is currently under construction, but the beach is still a desirable place to visit. There are watersports available, as well as food stands and restrooms. Check with the watersports group about their Watersports Bonanza package that includes four to five hours use of water skis, knee boards, boogie boards, Hobie Cats, windsurfers, Wave Runners and a snorkeling gear – all for $42. The beach is not as crowded as some others and is wide enough to provide a little bit of privacy for beachcombers, too.

BEACH CHART	Facilities	Windsurfing	Snorkeling	Scuba Diving	Wave Runners	Swimming	Parasailing	Sailing	Water Skiing	Nude/Topless
Crane Beach	☆					☆				
Hilton Beach Hotel	☆	☆	☆	☆	☆	☆		☆	☆	
Sandy Lane Beach	☆	☆	☆		☆	☆	☆	☆	☆	
Sam Lord's Castle	☆					☆				

Folkstone Underwater Park is a snorkeler's paradise with a protected inshore reef and underwater trail designed for snorkelers. It's just 20 minutes from Deep Water Harbour by taxi. The aquarium and museum here has displays of coral, sponges and photographs of marine life native to Barbados. Admission to the museum is 50¢. It is open from 10 am to 5 pm, Sunday through Friday. The park rents snorkeling gear for approximately $15 per set, per hour. You will find food vendors and restroom facilities here as well.

A few yards down the coast from the underwater park is the famous **Sandy Lane Hotel**, ☎ (246) 432-1311, which was recently rebuilt from the ground up. The hotel is now a high-end resort with amenities to match, including a championship golf course. The beach is public and offers a wide variety of watersports equipment, including Wave Runners, snorkeling gear, sailboats and windsurfers. Glass-bottom boat rides around the bay are offered for $6-$10 per hour. There are no food vendors on the beach and the hotel restaurant can be quite expensive; consider taking a picnic lunch . The beach can be crowded due to its close proximity to other hotels.

Sam Lord's Castle, set on the Atlantic side of the island, is the perfect place to spend an entire day. A 45-minute drive through sugarcane fields and open countryside will bring you to the entrance of Marriott's Sam Lord's Castle. The grounds contain much more than an old plantation-turned-resort. There is a monkey, parrot and shark exhibit to intrigue daily visitors. A gift shop, frozen yogurt stand, restored castle, colorful gardens and a beautiful stretch of beach are among the many features you'll see for a US $6 entrance fee. The beachside food stand has excellent Bajan dishes as well as tasty sandwiches. Bring a camera to capture one of the most picturesque resorts on the island and spend the entire day enjoying a piece of

Bajan paradise. If you are taking a taxi to the hotel, have him return for you at a pre-arranged time. (Drivers always charge a waiting fee if not instructed to return later.)

Sunbury Plantation House is located near Sam Lord's Castle. You may wish to stop here and take a tour if you're headed that direction (see *Self-Guided Tours*, page 269).

Island Activities

On Land

Golf

The most prestigious golf course on the island is at Sandy Lane, on the west coast. The **Sandy Lane Golf Club** offers an 18-hole course for its hotel guests, but cruise passengers can reserve tee times by calling prior to arrival on Barbados. Greens fees are $60 (nine holes) and $100 (18 holes). Club rentals are $15 (nine holes) and $30 (18 holes). The course is currently being expanded to 44 holes by architect Tom Fazio. ☎ (246) 432-2829/2831.

Another challenging course is the **Rockley Golf and Country Club**. The nine-hole course is southeast of Bridgetown and is open between 7 am and 3 pm on weekdays. (Open on weekends only by pre-arrangement.) The greens fees are $63 (nine holes) or $92 (18 holes). Clubs and cart rentals are $29. Contact Rockley Golf Club for tee times, ☎ (246) 435-7873; tee-off@rockleygolfclub.com; www.rockleygolfclub.com. The club is a 15-minute taxi ride ($12) from the pier.

The world-class **Royal Westmoreland Golf Course**, in St. James Parish north of Holetown, was designed by Robert Trent Jones, Jr. This is a superb 18-hole (par 72) championship course, where every hole has a view of the shimmering ocean. Greens fees for visitors are $200 Dec-April and $125 May-November. ☎ (246) 422 4653, www.royalwestmoreland.com.

The Barbados Golf Club, on the east coast near Sam Lord's Castle, was designed by Ron Kirby. The 18-hole (par 72) championship course is in a beautiful location that overlooks the ocean. Greens fees are $119 Dec 15-April 15; $79 April 16-Dec 14; cart rental is $20; club rental is $20. ☎ (246) 42T-TIME or (246) 428-8463, e-mail bgc@caribsurf.com; www.barbadosgolfclub.com.

Tennis

Almost every resort on the island has courts, but one of the most exotic spots is the **Crane Beach Hotel** (☎ 423-6220). You can play a set of tennis, then spend the rest of the day relaxing on the enchanting beach. Or play for a small court fee at the **Rockley Golf and Country Club** (☎ 435-7873), **Sandy Lane Hotel** (☎ 423-1311), and **Sam Lord's Castle** (☎ 423-7350). Fees run $15-$20, including racket rental.

Horseback Riding

Barbados has long stretches of beach perfect for horseback riding.

The **Beau Geste Farm** offers a ride in the Bajan countryside. Groups head out at 9:30 am and 3 pm on a tranquil ride through sugarcane fields and past historic sites. The one-hour ride through the parish of St. George costs $20 per person. A two-hour ride takes you through the grounds of the **Francia Plantation House** for $35 per person. You are allotted 30 minutes for exploring the restored plantation house and gardens, then you resume the horseback ride through the countryside. Long pants are recommended for riding. A 15-minute cab ride to the riding stables will cost approximately $15. Reservations are required. Call Allison Cox at the Beau Geste Farm, ☎ 429-0139.

The **Highland Adventure Center** offers horseback riding, ATV tours and hiking tours to cruise ship passengers through shore excursion departments. Check your ship for rates and times.

Other horse riding facilities are **Brighton Riding Stables** (☎ 425-9381) located near Mount Gay Visitor's center, the **Caribbean Int'l Riding Centre** (☎ 422-7433), near the Barbados Wildlife Reserve and Flower Forest, and **Ye Olde Congo Road Stables** (☎ 423-6180), near Sam Lord's Castle. All rides take you through beautiful terrain, and sometimes along the beach.

Bicycling

The relatively flat countryside makes bicycling a pleasure. Pedal past sugarcane fields and old ruins. Take the beach route, stopping at rum factories, or picnic and swim in the warm waters. Bicycles can be rented at the cruise ship terminal, or directly with **Flex Bicycle Rentals**, ☎ (246) 419-BIKE (2453); flexbikes@barbados.org.

Hiking

The Barbados National Trust schedules guided hikes at the **Nature and Heritage Trail** in Speightstown. There are two guided trails from which to choose on Wednesday, Thursday and Saturday from 9 am to 2:30 pm. Each costs US $7.50 for adults and half-price for children. Every Sunday at 6 am and 3:30 pm, the Barbados National Trust leads free hikes starting from different locations. ☎ (246) 426-2421 to reserve the guided trail hikes and/or get details about the meeting points for the free Sunday hikes.

In The Ocean

The **Hilton beach** (not the hotel), **Sandy Lane, Paradise Beach** and **Carlisle Bay**, all 10-15 minutes from Deep Water Harbour, offer a full variety of watersports, which we have profiled below. All rates are quoted in US dollars but, when bargaining with watersports vendors, confirm whether the price is quoted in US or Bajan dollars. In addition, the **Coral Reef Club** in St. James (see *Scuba Diving*) offers a full range of watersports activities, including a high-tech scuba boat. They can arrange transportation from the dock.

Windsurfing

Windsurfer rentals are available for $20-30 per hour. Each of the hotels listed above is on the west coast, which offers calm to choppy water conditions for beginners and intermediates.

Wave Runners

Wave Runners are available through the watersports operators or from locals on the beach. The rates are $50 for 30 minutes and $250 for a half-day. Better rates can be negotiated for two or more persons.

Water Skiing

Speed boats offer water skiing at $20-30 for 15 minutes of skiing. They are only available when there are several people to fill the boat.

Parasailing

Flights are available from free-floating platforms situated off the beaches at $40 for 15 minutes and $60 for 30 minutes. The boats are safe and instruction is provided before lift-off. You can also book with **Skyrides Parasail**, ☎ (246) 435-0570.

Sailing

Hobie Cats are offered at $30-$80, depending on time allotment and if a "chauffeur" is required. Sunfish boats are available for one or two people at $30-35 per hour. Lessons are also offered and after a few minutes it is easy sailing.

Ocean Kayaking

High Tide Watersports at the Coral Reef Club in St. James offers kayak rentals for $12 per hour. ☎ (800) 513-5763 or (246) 432-0931).

Scuba Diving

Barbados boasts an abundance of shipwrecks in 20 to 100 feet of water. There are 15 wrecks right off the coast of Bridgetown, all easily reached by boat. Island dive operators work with the beachside resorts, and they also take advance bookings directly.

> NOTE: There's a 15% VAT tax on all scuba diving charges.

Explore Sub Barbados has customized dive boats, underwater camera equipment and quality dive gear rental. They maintain a booth in the cruise ship terminal for bookings. The group is a PADI training center and employs only experienced and qualified dive masters. Explore Sub offers three daily dives as follows:

- Deep Water Dive. Goes to various spots depending on weather and ocean conditions. Leaves at 9:30 am daily. This dive allows for 45 minutes of bottom time. The highlight is a supervised encounter with Southern stingrays and moray eels. Leaves at 12:30 pm on Monday, Wednesday and Friday.

⚓ A trip to Carlisle Bay, where you can explore three shipwrecks. The dive allows for one hour of bottom time in shallow water. Leaves at 2:30 pm daily.

Two-tank dives cost US $83 and single-tank dives cost US $45 (includes tanks and weights). Rental of BCD, regulator, mask and fins costs $15 extra. Snorkeling costs $24 per person, including equipment. There is no extra charge for transportation from the cruise terminal. Explore Sub tries to accommodate even last-minute cruise ship arrivals, but space is limited and it's best to book ahead. ☎ (246) 435-6542, www.skyviews.com/x-sub, e-mail x-sub@caribsurf.com.

Underwater Barbados runs its operation from Carlisle Bay and is willing to pick up dive participants at the Barbados Tourism Authority in the cruise terminal at no extra charge. They offer two dives , the first leaving the terminal at 8:30 am and the second at 2 pm. A two-tank dive costs US $88 and a one-tank dive costs $44, including tanks and weights. Rental gear is $6 for regulator and $6 for BCD vest. ☎ (246) 426-0655; www.underwaterbarbados.com.

High Tide Watersports at the Coral Reef Club in St. James has a new high-tech boat with a walk-through transom for easy entries and exits, a freshwater shower, comfortable wrap-around seating, dry storage, camera table and refreshments. A one-tank dive costs US $45 and a two-tank dive cost $80, with tanks and weights included (add $15 to $20 for full equipment rental). The operation offers "buddy diving," free transportation, underwater camera rentals, sales and other equipment rentals. Snorkeling equipment rents for $6 per hour.

The **Coral Reef Club's** on-site fun center offers a full range of watersports, including water skiing ($25/hour), windsurfing ($23/hour or $50/day), banana or tube rides ($11.50), chauffeured Hobie Cat sailing ($80/hour), Sunfish rental ($34/hour) and ocean kayaks ($12/hour). All prices include the 15% VAT. ☎ (800) 513-5763 or (246) 432-0931; www.divehightide.com; e-mail hightide@sunsetbeach.net.

One-on-One Scuba offers specialized diving for all skill levels. If you've ever felt frustrated diving with a large group – where the leader swims too fast, or other divers interfere with a perfect photo – this dive operation is for you. Hire a dive instructor as your "dive buddy," and he'll seek out the sea creatures, allowing you time to photograph them and tailoring the dive to your experience level.

Regular diving $65/one-tank $110/two-tank and $150/three-tank dives. Semi-private dives $85/one-tank, $150/two-tank, and $220/three-tank dive.

Group dive prices are: single-tank, US $65; two-tank, $110; three-tank, $150. Semi-private dives are available at the following rates: single-tank, $85; two-tank, $150; three-tank, $220. Special interest dives include deep diving, wrecks, multi-level dives, nature, drift, photography and more. www.one-on-one-scuba.com; e-mail sayers@sunbeach.net; ☎ (246) 438-0691 (home) or (246) 435-9811.

One-Day Itinerary

Hiring a taxi is the best option if you want to spend a whole day seeing all the natural wonders. The roads are not difficult to maneuver, but they are not clearly marked and you may run into delays as you try to orient yourself. Since you will be spending the whole day with your driver, interview several candidates. Be clear about the itinerary you want to follow and tell your driver that the total trip should be no longer than seven hours, including waiting time.

The cost for the taxi can be negotiated, and should run in the region of $75-$95 for four to six persons. (Government regulated fares are $16 per hour driving time, plus $4 per hour waiting time.) The more people in the group, the cheaper the total fare per person, but remember to bargain for the whole taxi in US dollars.

The sites, driving time from one location to the next and the entrance fees in US dollars per person are listed below. The total entrance fees come to $39 per person.

Harrison's Caves . . . . 35 mins., $10
Flower Forest . . . . 15 mins., $7
Morgan Lewis Mill . . . . 15 mins., $2
Barbados Wildlife Reserve . . . . 15 mins., $12
Tyrol Cot Heritage Village . . . . 45 mins., $6
Return to Harbor . . . . 15 mins., $2

What to Bring

A camera is a necessity to capture the beauty of the island. If there are clouds, bring a lightweight jacket and a hat. The showers on Barbados are brief and should not prevent you from enjoying the attractions. If you'd like to picnic, bring a box lunch from the ship (make a request the day before). Snack stands are available at each attraction except the Morgan Lewis Mill.

Directions

Refer to the island map on page 267.

An Island Tour

Call in advance to reserve a tour time at **Harrison's Cave**, ☎ (246) 438-6640/6641/6643/6644/6645. Begin your excursion no later than 8 am and try to get on the 8:45 tour, their first of the day. You will spend 35 minutes driving across the countryside to the cave; you have a better chance to get on the first tour without reservations if you arrive early. You can always wander in the gift shop before the 30-minute tour starts. If you are unable to go on the first tour of the day but can reserve a later tour, skip to number 2 on the itinerary (the Flower Forest) and return here later. The last tour leaves at 4 pm.

The **Flower Forest of Barbados** is an immaculately manicured garden plantation only a 15-minute drive from Harrison's Cave. The pathways are clearly marked with the names of each plant, tree and colorful flower grown on the grounds. Spend up to an hour wandering through the estate and be sure to visit the gift shop for island-made crafts and watercolors by Jill Walker (see Best of Barbados store on page 261).

In 1995 the Barbados National Trust and the Chiltern Partnership made the decision to completely restore the **Morgan Lewis Mill** to working condition. They began by bringing millwrights from the United Kingdom to work on a new main driveshaft, bearings, new arms for the sails, a new tailtree and a new roundhouse to protect the working parts from the elements. A blacksmith from the United Kingdom fashioned replacement parts for those beyond salvage. The restoration is nearly complete, and when the sails are attached, the mill will be in working condition. Spend 20-30 minutes viewing the progress at the mill, then a 15-minute ride takes you to the next (and best) stop of the day.

For animal lovers or those tired of visiting ordinary zoos, the **Barbados Wildlife Reserve** is certainly the best attraction on the island. The optimum time to visit is between 2 pm and 3 pm, when the green vervet monkeys are fed by park rangers. The monkeys scramble through the bushes and descend from every tree to greedily attack bunches of bananas. They seem fearless, eating just a few feet away from curious humans, but keep in mind that these animals are still wild. For your own protection, do not get too close to them or make sudden movements that might frighten them.

Spend up to two hours enjoying the unique park and taking pictures. When wandering through the park, look up, down and carefully inside the bushes for all sorts of animals. The reserve creates a natural environment where the animals are free to roam uncaged, so you become the visitor in the animal world. The Barbados Wildlife Reserve is the best example of a managed natural animal habitat in the entire Caribbean. The admission price now allows visitors to enter nearby **Grenade Hall Forest and Signal Station**. Nature trails and picnic tables make this forest a great place to enjoy your box lunch.

The return trip to Deep Water Harbour takes 45 minutes to an hour (plus time spent at the last stop, below), so plan your time accordingly.

Stop at **Tyrol Cot Heritage Village** on the route back to the ship. Tyrol Cot was the home of Sir Grantley Adams, the first premier of Barbados. Constructed in 1854, the mansion is a gem of Palladian architecture tempered by tropical features. It was restored by the Barbados National Trust and is now furnished with original antiques and memorabilia owned by Grantley Adams.

While here, you can also explore a collection of attractive chattel houses in the surrounding **Heritage Village**. The houses are occupied by traditional craftsmen and artists working on site. Consider buying their leather goods, ceramics, pottery, clothing, pieces of art and local confections as gifts for friends at home. The traditional **Rum Shop** here serves sandwiches, fish cakes, and, of course, world famous Cockspur Rum. At this point you are only 15 minutes from the cruise ship dock.

Grenada

The Spice Isle

Island Description

Green rolling hills and snug harbors prompted homesick **Spanish** sailors to name the island Granada when they first landed on its shores in the southern part of the Caribbean. It was the British who converted the name to Grenada. When the **British** attempted to settle Grenada in 1609, they were chased off by savage Carib Indians. In 1650 a **French** expedition bought extensive stretches of land from the Caribs for a few beads and knives and settled near the current town of St. George's. The site proved to be a poor choice because the buildings became mired in a swamp during the rainy season. Also, the Caribs became hostile within the year. The ensuing military campaign against them ended in 1651 when the last 40 Indians chose to jump from a cliff at the northern end of the island rather than live under French rule.

The French and the British fought for control of the island until 1783, when it was finally ceded to the British. Under English rule, Grenada established a parliamentary government and became an independent British commonwealth in 1974 under the leadership of Sir Eric Gairy. Gairy's main political opponent, Maurice Bishop, seized control of the government while Gairy was overseas in 1979. Maurice Bishop became a dictator and invited the Cubans and Soviets onto the island to build military facilities and a new airport. Private property was seized, including a luxury hotel that Bishop commandeered for his residence and governmental headquarters. In 1983 a radical faction within Bishop's own government placed him under house arrest and took control, executing several of Bishop's aides. Due to a perceived threat to US medical students and the urgent pleas of other governments in the Eastern Caribbean States, the US military became involved. Combined forces from America, Barbados and the Eastern Caribbean States launched a rescue mission in 1983 to restore peace and democracy to Grenada. The successful plan met with overwhelming support from the local Grenadian population and in 1984 the first free elections were held since 1979.

Americans find it fascinating to drive past the now famous medical school on Grand Anse Beach near the Renaissance Grenada Hotel. The school is thriving, with 550 American students currently attending classes, and has plans to expand enrollment to 750 students. Pictures and documents in the local museum record the events leading up to the intervention, when barbed wire was strung across the beach. The empty shell of the bombed-out residence that was occupied by Maurice Bishop stands in ruins on the hill overlooking the harbor as an eerie testimonial to Grenada's troubled past.

Grenada is oval in shape, with tall mountains and dense rain forest in the northern portion and a little tail at the southern end where the **Pt. Salines International Airport** is located. Grenada's extinct volcano, **Grand Etang**, formed an interesting round "bottomless" lake where the National Park Visitors Center has been established.

The island's rich volcanic soil is perfect for agriculture, yielding more spices per acre of land than anywhere else in the world. Grenada's number one industry is **nutmeg production** and throughout the island you can sample and purchase delectable smelling spices. The capital of St. George's conveys an atmosphere akin to the French Riviera, with red-tile-roof buildings climbing the hills and cathedral spires that reach to the blue sky. Massive grey stone fort walls emerge above narrow, winding lanes to provide a sense of romance and drama. The streets are so narrow that police must direct traffic. Watch for the elevated traffic station where officers blow their whistles and wave directions at drivers with their white-gloved hands.

Island People

French and English cultures meld together on Grenada with towns and landmarks bearing titles from both languages. Grenadians are proud of the spices grown in abundance throughout the countryside and a visit to the Nutmeg Processing Plant or a spice plantation is an extraordinary experience. Machinery is not widely used, so ingenious traditional methods of cultivation and processing the valuable spices can still be seen. Honest labor produces a surprising variety of spices – cinnamon, bay leaves, cloves, allspice, cocoa and tarragon – but nutmeg is the principal spice grown, processed and exported from Grenada.

The Whole Nut of the Nutmeg

Locals have learned over the years to use every part of the nutmeg. The outer fruit, which resembles a peach, is made into jam and liqueur, and the orange membrane surrounding the nut is used as a separate spice called **mace**. The interior nutmeat of the fruit is ground to produce nutmeg, while the shells are used like gravel to line walkways and driveways. In addition, alcohol derived from sugarcane is mixed with nutmeg and other spices to create exotic perfumes, lotions and body oils in a local factory.

Grenada has become a popular retirement destination for Europeans, Canadians and Americans. The rugged Caribbean coastline is lined with exclusive retirement homes and residents can be seen hiking, running or walking every other Saturday. The Hash House Harriers began as a group wanting to get back in shape and evolved into a club with a newsletter and growing membership. The Harrier's fun-loving attitude exemplifies the attraction of the island, a place where hiking, swimming, boating and diving can be enjoyed all year.

Island Proverbs

If these few samples of island proverbs pique your interest, look for books in the islands that specialize in island folklore, proverbs and language.

If de goat wanna roll, it can roll up de hill.

If someone is bent on doing something, no obstacle will hold him back.

Yuh don't got to eat the whole pig to know yah eatin' pork.

A sample is all you need to know the value of the product.

Holidays

Ships docking on a Sunday or holiday may find just a few shops open for shopping and souvenirs, although vendors and taxi drivers are always on hand.

Annual Holidays & Events

For more details and precise dates, contact the island tourist board (see *Appendix*).

January . . . . New Year's Day
February . . . . Independence Day; Carriaco Carnival (disguise shows, parades, dancing)
April . . . . Good Friday; Easter
May . . . . Labor Day; Whit Monday
June. . . . . Corpus Christi (religious procession); Fisherman's Birthday Celebration to bless boats
October. . . . . Thanksgiving Day
December . . . . Christmas; Boxing Day

Useful Websites

Grenada Tourism's official website is **www.grenada.org**. It offers general information about the island, history, topography, and links to pages describing hikes and tours. You'll find names of tour operators and car rental agencies by clicking on "Transportation," but there are no e-mail or website links.

Another useful site is **www.grenadaexplorer.com**, which links to tour operator web pages, as well as local businesses. A tour agency site, **www.travelgrenada.com**, offers free maps and a street guide. The site also has everything from car rentals and sightseeing tours to travel tips and recipes. They will also help you book excursions.

The Pier

Ships dock at (or tender boats into) St. George's cozy harbor, the picturesque town climbing the hills surrounding the horseshoe-shaped harbor. At the pier you'll see a gift shop with local crafts, T-shirts and jewelry, along with a tourist information center. The main Grenada Tourism Office is across from the Pedestrian Plaza on the Carenage (pronounced CAR-nah-geesh), but plans are underway to expand the current docking facility and move the tourism headquarters. The Carenage is a short walk from the cruise ship terminal and offers a variety of shops, restaurants and historical sites.

St. George's Harbour.

Pier Phones

Island phone card machines and telephones that accept major credit cards are located at the cruise ship dock. Phone Cards can be purchased in EC currency denominations at the Tourist Information Center at the pier, or from the **Grentel** office on the Carenage near the Pedestrian Plaza. The Grentel office also has a calling station for tourists and the number to dial to access the **AT&T USA direct** calling service from Grenada is ☎ (800) 872-2881. **Cable & Wireless** offers a special phone number to use for calling the States. Dial 1-800-255-5872 (CALL USA) to make collect calls, use a credit card, or US calling card. Voice instructions guide you through the procedure. The area code for Grenada is 473, a long-distance call from the US.

Javahool Internet Café, on the Carenage, offers Internet services.

Arts & Crafts

The walk from the ship to the Carenage is lined with vendors selling spice baskets and a variety of handicrafts. Spice baskets are the most reasonably priced gifts to take home to friends, often decorated with shells or hand-stitched designs. Buy yours from locals (six baskets run about US $10) to encourage a local cottage industry. The Carenage is home to cheery island shops offering a variety of local crafts, perfumes, batiks and art perfect for island souvenirs.

In Town

Currency

The local currency is the **East Caribbean dollar** (EC), which is tied to the US dollar at approximately EC $2.65 to US $1. Shops and restaurants accept US currency, but do not give the best rate of exchange. Several banks are a short walk from the Carenage for those who wish to cash traveler's checks or exchange currency. To find the nearest bank, turn right on Young Street and walk to Church Street or Cross Street. Banking hours are Monday through Thursday, 8 am to 2 pm, and Friday from 8 am to 1 pm, then again from 2:30 pm to 5 pm.

Postage

The General Post Office in St. George's is open Monday through Thursday from 8 am to 3:30 pm and until 4:30 pm on Friday. The cost to airmail a postcard is about US 35¢. (Remember, US postage is not accepted.) The post office is located on the opposite end of the Carenage, near the National Library. A section of the post office is set aside for the Philatelic Bureau, which offers an incredible variety of specialty stamps. Collectors can also order special issues from Travel Grenada at www.travelgrenada.com/stamps.htm.

Historical Walking Tour

The horseshoe-shaped inner harbor of the Carenage is an easy walk from the historical sites in the town of St. George's. The distance of this walking tour is about one mile, with a moderately steep slope and some stairs. The entire walk should take about 1½ hours.

From the cruise ship pier, walk to the middle of the horseshoe that forms the Carenage. Always filled with boats, the harbor contains many rows of sailing sloops for hire. The walking tour begins at the center of the Pedestrian Plaza near the statue of **The Christ of the Deep**. The statue was presented to Grenada by Costa Cruise Lines in appreciation for the heroic rescue of passengers and crew in 1961, when the *Bianca C* burned and sank in the outer harbor of St. George's. When the harbor alarm sounded, every boat available in the vicinity, from fishing vessels to small dinghies, rushed to the rescue.

Continue to walk along the Carenage, passing local businesses, restaurants and gift shops. The tour returns to this area later for an opportunity to eat and shop. When passing Young Street, notice the cannons that were removed from the forts and are currently used as bollards to tie up ships. The tile-roofed warehouses at the end of the Carenage are 18th- and 19th-century brick structures. The red fish-scale tiles were brought to Grenada on European trade ships, which used the tiles as ballast.

At the corner of Matthew Street is the **National Library,** housed in a former brick warehouse. The library was established in 1846 and has occupied this location since 1892. Open Monday-Friday, 9:30 am-4:30 pm; Saturday, 10 am-1 pm.

Turn right on Matthew Street and walk uphill to the top of the short street. At the corner of Matthew and Young streets is the **National Museum**, in a building originally erected in 1704 by the French as an army barracks. Later, the building was used by the British as a women's prison, then transformed into the Antilles Hotel. Notice the rare metal balcony on the exterior, one of four remaining in St. George's from the French occupation period. The museum charges admission of US $2 and is open Monday through Friday from 9 am to 4:30 pm and Saturday 10 am to 1:30 pm. It contains a fine collection of Indian artifacts, military pieces, Josephine Bonaparte's marble bathtub, island documents, African and slave relics, the actual cells which were used to house women prisoners and an exhibit showing pictures of the revolution and rescue mission of 1983. The museum's extraordinary collection may tempt you to linger and talk with one of the friendly staff. A variety of books and pamphlets on Grenada's history and culture is available. Upon leaving the museum, turn left onto Young Street.

Next door is **Tikal**, a boutique which is worth perusing (see *Shopping*, page 292). Walk to Church Street (there are several other shops on the way) and turn left again for the climb to **Fort George**. At the top of the street, take the steps to the left leading to a viewing platform a wonderful place to photograph the red tile roofs of the town and picturesque harbor.

Fort George was originally built by the French in 1705 and named Fort Royal. Later additions were constructed by the British to expand the fort and the area is used today as barracks for the local Grenadian police. You can walk through a tunnel and climb to another viewing spot to the right, but a full tour of the fort is not currently available.

Leaving the fort, walk back down Church Street. Notice St. Andrews Presbyterian Kirk on the left, popularly known as the **Scots Kirk**. The church was built in 1831 with the assistance of the Freemasons.

Continue on Church Street for another block and you'll reach **St. George's Anglican Church**, a beautiful stone and pink stucco building and another good viewing place. The church was built by the British in 1825 and contains an array of historical plaques and statues.

Walk up the hill on Hospital Hill Road and notice the residences with exterior porches. At one time, the specially designed entrances, called *porte-cochères*, were used to keep visitors dry when exiting their carriages during the rainy season. When passing Market Hill, you can see the brick **Houses of Parliament**, the center of Grenada's government, on the left.

Straight ahead on the right is the Roman Catholic **Cathedral of the Immaculate Conception**. The tower was constructed in 1818 and the cathedral was built in 1884 on the site of an older church dating back to 1804. Grenada was tossed back and forth between French and English rule, and the French Catholics were forced by the Anglicans to move their church to the remote site on top of the hill. The two religious factions endured years of animosity and sometimes physical violence during these political upheavals. However, religious tolerance and cooperation have flourished over the past hundred years.

Turn left on St. John Street and walk to Grenville Street, which leads to **Market Square**, the gathering place for locals selling produce and spices. The square is also the popular location for parades, political speeches and religious activities.

Leaving Market Square, walk down either Hillsborough Street or Granby Street to Melville and turn left. Across the way is the **Esplanade**, the commercial waterfront for the outer harbor in St. George's.

Turn left on Cross Street and stop at the **Yellow Poui Art Gallery** upstairs (see *Shopping*, page 292 284). Turn right on Young Street and walk downhill, then turn left to walk back along the Carenage.

A wonderful place to stop for refreshments is **The Nutmeg**, about half a block from Young Street on the left side of the harbor. Locals, yachtsmen and tourists all enjoy the congenial atmosphere here. It serves excellent food, has good service and offers harbor views. The walking tour ends at the Carenage, where shops sell island souvenirs.

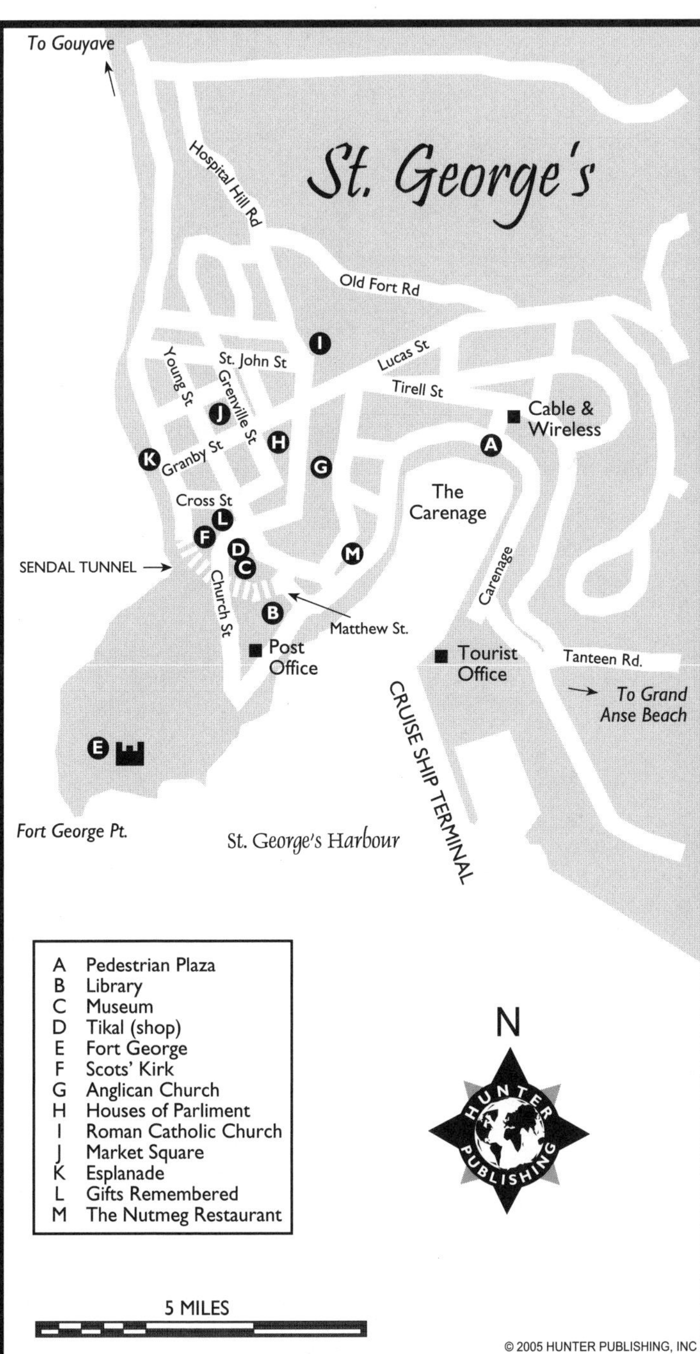
To Gouyave
St. George's
Hospital Hill Rd
Old Fort Rd
Lucas St
St. John St
Young St
Grenville St
Tirell St
Cable & Wireless
Granby St
Cross St
The Carenage
SENDAL TUNNEL
Church St
Matthew St.
Carenage
Post Office
Tourist Office
Tanteen Rd.
To Grand Anse Beach
CRUISE SHIP TERMINAL
Fort George Pt.
St. George's Harbour
A Pedestrian Plaza
B Library
C Museum
D Tikal (shop)
E Fort George
F Scots' Kirk
G Anglican Church
H Houses of Parliment
I Roman Catholic Church
J Market Square
K Esplanade
L Gifts Remembered
M The Nutmeg Restaurant
N
HUNTER PUBLISHING
5 MILES
© 2005 HUNTER PUBLISHING, INC

Shopping

On The Carenage

Shops are generally open weekdays, 8 am-noon and 1-4 pm; 8 am to noon on Saturdays; and closed on Sundays unless indicated.

Huggins Havana House is a duty-free, air-conditioned shop featuring china, crystal, porcelain figures and jewelry. **Glitten's Duty-Free** and **Duty Free Caribbean** are also located on the Carenage and offer similar fare.

Sea Change Book & Gift Shop is below The Nutmeg restaurant and carries a wide selection of American and British books, island books, children's books and international newspapers.

Bye Bye Grenada and **Ganzee** are two upscale T-shirt shops that can be found on other Caribbean islands too. Their products are high quality, and the designs are innovative.

Figleaf on the Carenage is an arts and crafts store, offering locally made products as well as crafty items imported from other Caribbean islands.

St. George's

☆ **Tikal,** next to the National Museum, is our pick for the most interesting shop in town. The owners have gathered a wide selection of quality products from Grenada and Latin America, including dolls, batiks, paintings, sculpture, jewelry, woven baskets and clothing.

Art Fabric Batik Studio is across the street from Tikal on Young Street (look for the blue door). This is a working batik studio similar to Caribelle Batiks on St. Kitts and St. Lucia. You can tour the studio to see how batiks are made, then shop for one-of-a-kind pieces of art, clothing and accessories.

Yellow Poui Art Galleries has two locations, one next to Barclays Bank at Church St. and Halifax St., and the other above the Gifts Remembered shop on Cross Street. These galleries contain a large selection of Caribbean prints, maps, engravings, watercolors, line drawings and sculptures by local artists.

Grand Anse Shopping Center is across from the Grand Anse Beach outside St. George's. It features, among others, the following shops.

The Gift Shop sells the widest variety of imported watches, Land leather bags, crystal, china and name-brand figurines. Carry your passport and ship ID to guarantee duty-free prices. **Pocoloco Boutique** carries Caribbean-made casual wear, shoes, accessories, beachwear and crafts. **Imagine** offers Caribbean handicrafts, dolls, straw ware, clothing, stamps for the collector and local batiks.

Transportation & Excursions

Taxis

Taxis are always available along the Carenage for trips around the island. The majority of cars used as taxis are minivans with clearly marked taxi signs or with the letter "H" on the windshield or the roof. Taxis are not metered, but use regulated taxi fares dictated by the government; a rate schedule is posted at the pier. Fares are often quoted in EC and priced for the whole taxi, carrying one to five persons. Negotiate your price (in US dollars) before entering. Feel free to barter on fares for excursions out on the island, but understand that Grenada's taxi drivers are friendly, honest, hardworking and follow the government regulated guidelines. Tipping is not required for short trips around St. George's, but drivers who take you on outer-island excursions usually deserve a 10% tip.

Taxi Chart

Fares are one way, unless indicated, in US dollars.

Destination	**Cost**
from cruise ship pier, St. George's	*one to four people*
Bay Gardens	$12
Gouyave Spice Factory (round trip)	$40
Grand Anse Beach	$12
- by water taxi	$2
Grand Etang (round trip)	$35
Grenada Golf Course	$12
La Sagesse (as Organized Tour, lunch included)	$30
Morne Rouge Bay/Pointe Saline	$20
- by water taxi	$5
Hourly Tour Rate	$20

GRENADA

Taxi Tours

The following excursions are available from the cruise ship dock; all incorporate a tour of the city. The price is for the whole taxi, one-four passengers. Additional passengers are charged at a rate of $10 per person, and the charge is split evenly between all people in the taxi.

- **Grand Etang, National Park, Grenville Nutmeg Plant** – three-four hours, $100
- **Gouyave Nutmeg Plant, Douglaston Estate** – three hours, $75
- **Hampstead, La Sagesse Beach, Natural Works** – three-four hours, $100
- **Arawak Islands, Bay Gardens, Laura Herb & Spice Garden** – two hours, $50
- **Concord Waterfalls** – 2-2½ hours, $60
- **Scenic island tour**, including spice and nature – five-six hours, $150

Rental Cars

Driving is on the left and only for the very adventurous at heart. Roads are steep, with sharp turns, and are not in very good condition. If you are brave enough to try driving, remember to stay left after dodging a pothole! Rental cars are available for $45-$65 per day and collision insurance is optional. A temporary driver's license is required at a cost of $12 and can be obtained from the traffic department next to the Fire Station on the Carenage, or from the larger rental firms. The minimum age to rent a car is 23 and a credit card is recommended for covering the damage deposit required by most agencies.

Car Rental Agencies

The area code for Grenada is 473. a long-distance call from the US.

Avis (Spice Island Rentals) . . . . ☎ 440-3936/2624; or (800) 331-1084; www.avis.com

Dollar Rent-a-Car . . . . ☎ 444-4786

David's Car Rentals (pier delivery). . . . ☎ 444-3399/2323;

www.davidscar.com; e-mail cdavid@caribsurf.com

McIntyre Car Rentals (pier delivery). . . . . . . ☎ 444-5263; www.grenadaexplorer.com/mcintyre/; e-mail macford@caribsurf.com

Budget Rental Car (pier delivery) . . . . ☎ 444-2277; e-mail sunsetmo@caribsurf.com

Sundance Scooter ($25 per day) . . . . ☎ 444-3627; e-mail scooterent@caribsurf.com

Self-Guided Tours

Bay Gardens

Located just outside St. George's, this is a botanist's paradise. Keith St. Bernard is the proprietor of the gardens and has personally planted and overseen the placement of all the exotic plant life and colorful flowers on the estate. A guide will take you on an informational walk through the winding pathways, pointing out plants and trees unique to the Caribbean. Keith has created new varieties of plants by cross-breeeding plants to form hybrids. The estate is currently building a pathway access for wheelchairs and adding labels for the trees and plants along the walkways. The garden is always developing, and you will be amazed at the exceptional plant specimens. A taxi to the

A scenic view at Bay Gardens.

gardens takes 15 minutes and the round-trip costs $30. A $2 admission fee helps maintain the pathways and promotes the ongoing presentation of new plants and trees. This is one of the best botanical gardens in the Caribbean.

Morne Gazo Nature Trail is a self-guided rain forest trail just 15 minutes outside of St. George's, between Bay Gardens and Laura's Spice Gardens, off the main road to St. David's. Watch for the sign for Morne Gazo Nature Trails. (If you reach the Texaco Station, you've gone too far.) The trail is open daily (except holidays), and the forestry department has provided trail signs and gives free flyers with information about the rain forest ecosystem. The walking trails are simple to follow, with handrails on the steeper slopes and shade from the forest canopy. Walk to the morne's summit on a nutmeg-shell path, where a platform affords the best views back to St. George's, across the forested hills, and down to La Sagesse. Be sure to bring your camera. The entrance fee is US $2.

La Sagesse Nature Center

La Sagesse Nature Center, 20 minutes from St. George's, is nestled between two protective peninsulas in St. David's Parish. La Sagesse, which means "the wise woman" in French, is a quiet seaside plantation estate containing a mangrove estuary, three beautiful beaches, coral reefs and acres of thorn scrub cactus woodlands. A restaurant on the property serves a delicious seafood and continental cuisine ideal for an afternoon lunch.

You can either take a taxi straight to La Sagesse, or join an island tour with Arnold's Tours, which includes a stop here. (See *Organized Tours*, below.) Between 10 am and 2 pm, La Sagesse offers a guided nature walk which includes lunch and transportation to the property for $30 per person. Reservations can be made by contacting the owners prior to arrival on Grenada. Phone Mike Meranski, ☎ (473) 444-6458, (lsnature@caribsurf.com) to arrange a day at one of Grenada's best hidden secrets. Visit their website for more details, www.lasageese.com.

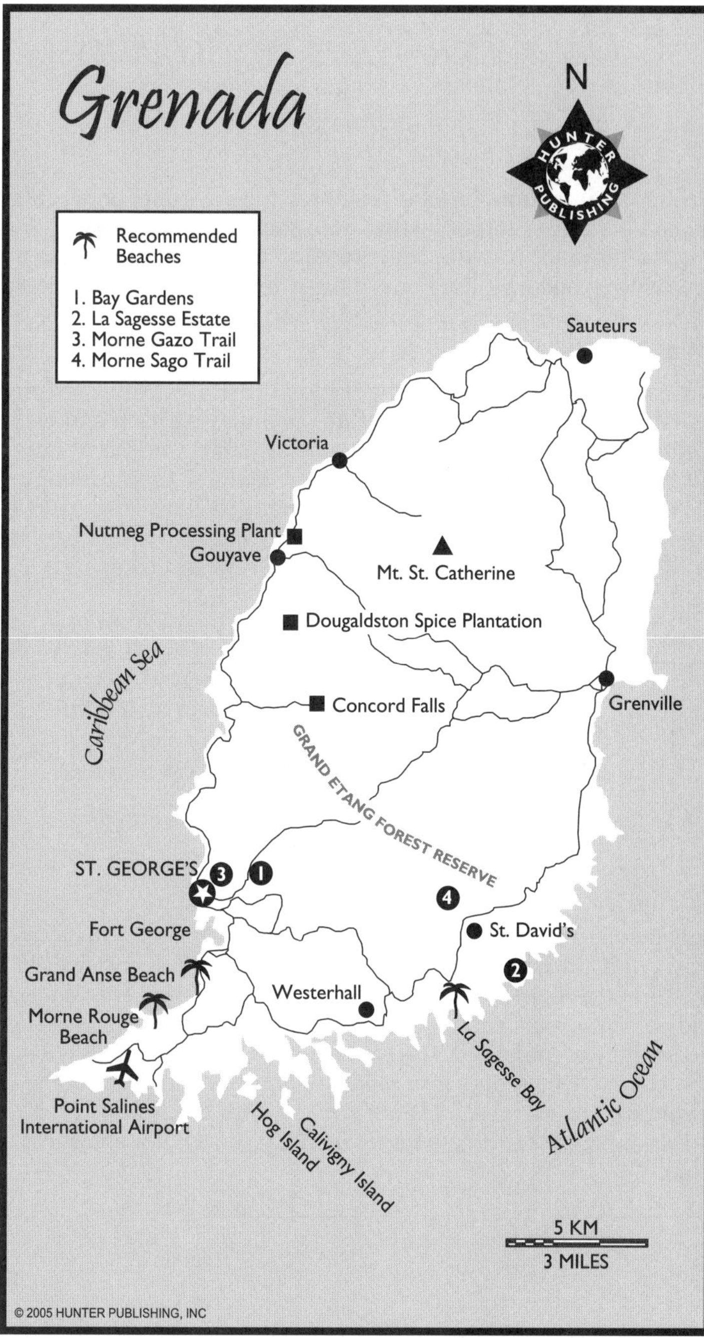
Grenada
N
HUNTER PUBLISHING
Recommended Beaches
1. Bay Gardens
2. La Sagesse Estate
3. Morne Gazo Trail
4. Morne Sago Trail
Sauteurs
Victoria
Nutmeg Processing Plant
Gouyave
Mt. St. Catherine
Dougaldston Spice Plantation
Caribbean Sea
Grenville
Concord Falls
GRAND ETANG FOREST RESERVE
ST. GEORGE'S
Fort George
St. David's
Grand Anse Beach
Westerhall
Morne Rouge Beach
La Sagesse Bay
Point Salines International Airport
Hog Island
Calivigny Island
Atlantic Ocean
5 KM
3 MILES
© 2005 HUNTER PUBLISHING, INC

Organized Tours & Activities

Day Tours

Grenada Sunsation Tours offers three full-day tours on a rotating schedule Monday through Friday, costing US $55 per person. There are five different part-day tours ranging from US $28-35 (also on a revolving schedule). The tours take groups to the most popular attractions on Grenada and often add something unique (like visiting private homes).

Our favorite part-day tour is the "Hidden Treasures" tour, which visits Bay Gardens, Laura Spice Estate, La Sagesse Beach and Nature Center and Fort Judy. (This tour is similar to our One-Day Itinerary.) Visit the Sunsation Tours website at www.grenadasunsation.com for a full description of excursions, and book on-line to get a 10% discount. Design your own private tour with a guide for $15 per hour. ☎ (473) 444-1594/2243; e-mail qkspice@caribsurf.com.

> ➠ TIP: **Travel Grenada** books trips with local tour operators. They also book rental cars, provide maps and personalized service, including free pick-up and delivery from the cruise dock. Visit their informative website, www.travelgrenada.com, to purchase maps and shopping guides, reserve rental cars and book tours online.

Jeep Tours

Adventure Jeep Tours offers full-day (9:30 am to 5:30 pm) jeep tours with lunch at a plantation and swimming. They cost US $65 for adults and $40 for children age six-12. The terrain covered is navigable with four-wheel-drive vehicles only. Swimming is in a secluded area with waterfalls and is an experience that few encounter. Be sure the tour schedule and your ship's sailing times work together, or arrange a private tour to fit your schedule. ☎ (473) 444-5337; e-mail adventure@caribsurf.com for reservations; www.grenadajeeptours.com.

Hikes

For the adventurous hiker, **Pete's Mystic Tours** offers a guided and informational hiking tour ideal for a cruisers short time in port. The island excursion brings you to the Concord Valley to see the cascading waterfalls, where you can take a guided 90-minute hike, explore a spice plantation, or simply enjoy the river. The next scheduled stop is the Nutmeg Processing Plant in Gouyave, then on through the Central Mountain Range.

Mystic Tours follow the seldom-used roads winding through plantations, the tropical rain forest and picturesque volcanic valleys. The return trip to St. George's takes you to the Grand Etang Lake and National Park Visitors Center, home of the Mona monkey exhibit. The tour takes five-six hours for $35 per person. For more information and reservations, contact Dennis Henry, ☎ (473) 440-1671; www.mystictours.com; pmistictors@caribsurf.com.

Mystic Tours also offers bike tours, with lunch, for $60 per person, a half-day island tour for $25 per person, and a shorter hike for $20 per person. Some cruise ship companies sell Mystic Tours so check with your shore excursion office.

Spice Island Trekking schedules hikes to Seven Sisters (9:30 am to 5 pm) for US $45 per person, and another trip goes to Concord Falls, Levera, Bathway beaches and Grenville rum factory (9 am to 5 pm) for US $50 per person. The waterfalls trip takes four-five hours (only two hours of easy hiking, with the rest of the time is spent driving) for US $35 per person (9 am to 2:30 pm). Snacks and refreshments are included. (Remember to add a 5% tax to all tour prices.) They also offer bicycle tours ranging from US $25 to $65. For tour descriptions, visit www.spiceislandtrekking.com; ☎ (473) 444-0385; e-mail spicetreks@caribsurf.com.

Mountain Biking

Trailblazer Tours offers full-day mountain biking tours. They travel on off-road trails through shallow streams, stop to swim/snorkel at a beach, and enjoy scenic picture stops. They guarantee that no ride is on busy main roads, and the tour can be enjoyed by people on all skill levels. The price of US $60 per person includes transportation, lunch, bikes with front suspension shocks, and safety helmets. ☎ (473) 444-5337 or e-mail trailblazers@grenadajeeptours.com for schedules and reservations.

Beaches

The most popular beach, **Grand Anse**, is always alive with activity. It's south of St. George's, a five-minute taxi ride from the pier. Hotels lining the beach here offer a multitude of watersports and an assortment of beachside restaurants offer lunch. The hotel pool areas have restroom facilities. Grand Anse is a two-mile stretch of sand with room for everyone to find a private spot. It's also swarming with locals trying to sell everything from spice baskets to a cool drink. If you aren't interested, a firm "no" should be sufficient.

Morne Rouge is a smaller cove just 10 minutes from St. George's, over the hill from Grand Anse. The beach is home to the *Rhum Runner* party cruise and has a variety of watersports available when the booze cruise comes ashore. A small beachside restaurant offers lunch. If you want privacy, head farther down the sandy stretch of sand. Do not bring valuables with you.

La Sagesse estate is a hidden piece of paradise just 20 minutes from St. George's. The beach cove here is perfect for privacy, peace and tranquility. There are actually three beaches on the property, two of which are within a short hiking distance from the guest house and restaurant. This is the place to escape from the real world and enjoy the natural wonders of the plantation. The Nature Center, dedicated to increasing environmental awareness, provides an overview of the natural environment surrounding the property. A guided tour of the area is also possible (see *Self-Guided Tours*, page 295) and lunch at the restaurant is worth the taxi ride out to the estate. Spend the whole day exploring, or make it part of an island tour.

Island Activities

On Land

Golf

The **Grenada Golf Club**, just above Grand Anse, offers a nine-hole golf course with lush greens and beautiful surroundings. Greens fees are $15 for nine holes and $22 for 18 holes. Club rentals are $8 for the nine holes. This golf course has the lowest prices of any golf courses in the Caribbean. Full clubhouse facilities, golf instruction and refreshments are available. ☎ (809) 444-4128 to reserve tee times.

Tennis

The **Grenada Grand Beach Resort** on the beach of Grand Anse has courts available by the hour. After your game, enjoy all the amenities on the beach. The resort is a five-minute cab ride from the pier. Contact the resort, ☎ (473) 444-4371/4372, paradise@grandbeach.net, for current rates and court reservations, which run approximately $15 per hour.

In The Ocean

Watersports

Working out of the Grenada Grand Beach Hotel on Grand Anse Beach, **Aquanauts** offers a variety of watersports rentals: Hobie Cat ($25 per hour); ocean kayaks ($10 per hour); snorkel gear ($10 per hour); waterskis and wakeboards ($20 per round); Jet Ski ($25, 15 minutes); and windsurf boards ($20 per hour). Aquanauts also offers scuba diving (see below), as well as deep-sea fishing, whale-watching, eco-kayak tours, sail and snorkel trips. ☎ (473) 444-1126; fax 444-1127).

Scuba Diving & Snorkeling

> NOTE: Beautiful coral reefs await scuba divers, but remember that you should not touch or remove sea life.

Sanvics Watersports offers snorkeling equipment at $10 per set for a half-day, requiring a refundable deposit. Scuba diving for certified divers, including equipment, costs US $35 for a single dive and $55 for a dive to the sunken cruise ship *Bianca C*. A two-tank dive costs $65 per person and explores the coral reefs surrounding the St. George's area. Call ☎ (473) 444-4371, ask for the watersports operator)

Dive Grenada operates out of the Allamanda Beach Resort on Grand Anse Beach, and offers free pick-up service. Snorkeling trips are US $20, a one-tank dive costs $35, a two-tank dive costs $65, and a deep dive to the *Bianca C* shipwreck costs $40 (plus 5% tax on all). You can rent full equipment for $10, and get a 10% discount by booking over the Internet. ☎ (473) 444-1092; www.divegrenada.com; e-mail diveg'da@caribsurf.com.

Spice Divers Aquanauts and **Ecodive** have combined operations to offer diving from three locations – True Blue Bay Resort (a $15 taxi ride), Spice Island Beach and Blue Horizons. These dive operators are committed to exploring the underwater world in an eco-sensitive manner. They have custom-built dive boats with shade covers, a full ladder and rinse buckets for cameras. A one-tank dive costs $42, the two-tank dive costs $68, and equipment rental is $5 per piece or $16 for a full setup. They now offer a Kids Bubblemaker program for children eight-10 years old that costs $53 per child. (Add 5% tax to all sales charges.) ☎ (473) 444-1126; fax 444-1127; www.aquanaut-grenada.com.

Sailing & Motor Cruises

First Impressions, Ltd. offers ocean excursions with drinks and sandwiches included in the price. ☎ (473) 440-3678 or 407-1147 (cell); www.catamaranchartering.com; e-mail starwindsailing@caribsurf.com.

- ⚓ The **Sandy Island** excursion is a relaxing cruise on a catamaran that goes along the scenic western coastline (with a chance to encounter whales and dolphins along the way), passing quaint villages en route to the island. The secluded white-sand beach and countless palm trees makes this a perfect place to snorkel and soak up sun. The cost is US $90/adult, $45/child age five-11 (minimum six people) and approximate time is seven hours.
- ⚓ Set sail on a power catamaran to a **Southeast Secluded Beach.** There is the option to go skinny-dipping, and this exotic beach is perfect for sunbathing. The cost is US $45/adult, $22.50/child age five-11 and the trip takes about four hours.
- ⚓ The four-hour **Whale/Dolphin Watching Cruise** (also aboard a catamaran) is popular. It costs US $60/adult, $30/child age five-11.

Half-day sailing adventures or motorboat snorkeling tours, including refreshments and light sandwiches, range from $50-$60 for adults and $25-$30 for children age five-11. Children 12 and over pay adult rate and children under age five are free.

Spice Island Trekking offers a boat trip to **Sandy Island** for US $55 (plus 5% tax). The 15-minute boat ride leaves leaves at 9:30 am and returns at 5 pm. Enjoy the fantastic reef, gentle waters, and abundant shade. ☎ (473) 444-0385, www.spiceislandtrekking.com; e-mail spicetreks@caribsurf.com.

Blue Marlin Charters schedules private fishing trips to catch blue marlin, sailfish, yellowfin tuna, swordfish and wahoo. They arrange custom trips too. ☎ (473) 440-5046, fax 440-2863, or e-mail bluemarlin@grenadaexplorer.com to get a price quote or reservation.

Footloose Yacht Charters offers two day-sailing excursions. The price of each trip includes a BBQ lunch of swordfish or chicken, plus fruit salads, an open bar of rum punch, beer, and soft drinks, plus the use of snorkeling equipment.

- ⚓ A trip to **Calivigny Island** costs US $75 per person, leaving at 9 am and returning by 4 pm. You'll probably experience a variety of water conditions and some superb sailing. Upon arrival at the island, a large shade awning is erected, and you can enjoy swimming, snorkeling, or relaxing before lunch.
- ⚓ The **West Coast** trip costs US $75 per person, leaving at 10 am and returning by 4 pm. The yacht sails to Point Salines and out into the Atlantic before heading north to Victoria, where turtles and dolphins often appear. This gentle sail is appropriate for less adventurous sailors, stopping at a secluded beach, where you can relax under a shade awning, swim, snorkel and eat lunch.

Half-day sailing adventures with Footloose Charters cost $45 per person, and a full-day charter costs $550 for up to six people.

Expect an exhilarating sail and a relaxing day aboard a real yacht. The yacht ***Footloose*** leaves from the jetty in the St. George's lagoon, a short walk from the cruise ship dock. A half-day sail costs $45 per person, or you can charter the entire boat for $550 per day. ☎ (473) 440-7949, fax (473) 440-6680; e-mail footloos@caribsurf.com.

One-Day Itinerary

Grenada offers the opportunity to escape the hustle and bustle of everyday life, to simply enjoy the beauty of nature. This *One-Day Itinerary* is designed for exploring the island's natural side.

Call one of the tour operators (see our *Organized Tours* section, above) and arrange for a customized trip. Or you can arrange to travel by taxi, readily available along the Carenage. You can either bargain with drivers to take you on the following itinerary, or take a separate taxi to each location. The standard tour rate is US $20 per hour for one to four passengers. The following rates/times are estimates for a point-to-point one-way taxi ride for a total $100 in taxi fares, plus $5 per person in entry fees:

Bay Gardens ($2 entry fee). . . . . 10 mins., $15
Morne Gazo Nature Trails ($2 entry fee) . . . 15 mins., $15
La Sagesse Estate . . . . 25 mins., $20
Return to Cruise Ship Dock . . . . 25 mins., $20

What to Bring

Comfortable walking shoes, a bathing suit, a towel and sunscreen are essential items for La Sagesse Nature Center and the beaches. A camera with a flash is also vital for capturing views of the beautiful flowers at the Bay Gardens. It rarely rains on Grenada, but you might wish to bring along a light jacket and hat just in case.

Directions

Refer to the island map on page 297.

An Island Tour

The journey begins at 9 am with a taxi ride to **Bay Gardens**. Owner Keith St. Bernard or one of his gardeners will guide you through this magnificent floral paradise. Spend up to an hour wandering through the shaded pathways and see how many different plants and flowers you can recognize. Ask your guide to point out the many spices growing in their natural state, like nutmeg, cinnamon, pepper and others.

Morne Gazo Nature Trails is a National Forest with marked self-guided walking trails and information about the rain forest ecosystem. Walk to the summit on a nutmeg-shell path, where a platform affords the best views back to St. George's, across the forested hills, and down to La Sagesse.

Have the taxi drive along the coastline, through a large banana plantation, out to the nearly hidden **La Sagesse** estate. Ask your driver to return at 2:30 pm, or plan to catch a different cab for the return trip to St. George's.

If you arrive between 10 am and 2 pm, you can take a guided nature hike around the property to learn about the environmental systems that make up the beach, coastline, mangrove and coral reefs. La Sagesse has three beach areas to explore and the hiking trails and banana plantation also make interesting side trips. Spend the next four hours enjoying La Sagesse and have lunch at the restaurant, which serves delightful seafood or continental cuisine. The atmosphere is very relaxed.

Get a taxi back into downtown **St. George's** at 2:30 pm. You can spend a half-hour or so at the National Museum and shops just off the Carenage, or you may wish to follow the *Historical Walking Tour* (see page 288) or just wander around the colorful port. Enjoy an afternoon drink at The Nutmeg restaurant and visit the shops along the Carenage until your cruise ship departs.

This day on Grenada should last between six and seven hours. Be sure to buy some spice baskets from the local street vendors for friends and family at home.

Appendix

Tourism Offices

Those who'd like some additional island information should contact the following tourism offices:

Puerto Rico . . . . ☎ (800) 866-7827
www.prtourism.com

St. Thomas . . . . ☎ (800) 372-8784
www.usvi.net

Sint Maarten . . . . ☎ (800) 786-2278
www.st-maarten.com

St. Martin . . . . ☎ (312) 751-7800 or (310) 271-6665
www.frenchcaribbean.com

Antigua . . . . ☎ (888) 268-4227 or (212) 541-4117
www.antigua-barbuda.org

St. Kitts & Nevis. . . . . ☎ (800) 582-6208
www.stkitts-nevis.com

Guadeloupe . . . . ☎ (732) 302-1223
www.frenchcaribbean.com

Dominica. . . . . ☎ (212) 949-1711
www.dominica.dm

Martinique . . . . ☎ (212) 838-7800 or (800) 391-4909
www.martinique.org

St. Lucia. . . . . ☎ (212) 867-2950 or (800) 456-3984
www.stlucia.org

Barbados . . . . ☎ (800) 221-9831 or (212) 986-6516
www.barbados.org

Grenada . . . . ☎ (800) 927-9554
www.grenada.org

Useful Websites

There are hundreds of useful resources on the Internet. Two great sources are **www.caribbeans.com** and **www.interknowledge.com**, both of which offer information about all Caribbean islands. Also try:

www.caribeline.com – Provides general Caribbean information and great on-line maps of each island (hard copies can be ordered).

www.diveguide.com and **www.scubayellowpages.com** – Each provide lists of dive operators by island, diver's insurance resources, and general dive tips.

www.travelfacts.com – Includes descriptions of island attractions.

www.customs.ustreas.gov – This valuable US government site provides current customs information and restrictions. You can download brochures, access frequently asked questions and read travel alerts. Use the "Travel Information" link.

http://travel.state.gov/passport_services.html – The official US Government passport website. Everything you need to know about applications, requirements and forms.

http://travel.state.gov/ – US Department of State Bureau of Consular Affairs. All kinds of travel information, including advisories, overseas adoption, passports, visas and more.

www.turq.com – Specializes in Caribbean information, with links to island tourism boards, cruise ship websites, weather, a photo album and books on the Caribbean. The "Things to Do & See" section provides links to golf courses, dive operators, sailing charters and other activities by island.

www.smallshop.com/caribbeanwebsites.htm – Offers links to island businesses as well news bulletins.

www.candw.gd – The Cable and Wireless website. Provides local phone directories of islands serviced by their network. Click on "Links," then click on your island of choice.

www.cruisemon.com – Online guide to ships cruising the Caribbean, offering vessel statistics, scheduled stops, price guidelines and valuable recommendations. They make money by booking cruises, but offer this information free of charge.

Cruise Company Sites

Carnival Cruise Lines. . . . . www.carnival.com
Celebrity Cruises. . . . . www.celebritycruises.com
Crystal Cruises . . . . www.crystalcruises.com
Disney Cruise Lines. . . . . . . www.disney.com/disneycruise
Holland America Line. . . . . www.hollandamerica.com
Norwegian Cruise Lines . . . . www.ncl.com
Princess Cruises . . . . www.pocruises.com
Royal Caribbean Cruises . . . . . . www.royalcaribbean.com
SilverSea Cruises . . . . www.silversea.com
Star Clippers. . . . . www.starclippers.com
Windjammer Barefoot Cruises . . . www.windjammer.com
Windstar Cruises . . . . www.windstarcruises.com

Index